3/23

Fr

P O I

C000139938

Las Vegas

by Mary Herczog

Macmillan • USA

ABOUT THE AUTHOR

Mary Herczog lives in Los Angeles and works in the film industry. She is the author of *Frommer's New Orleans,* and contributed to *Frommer's Los Angeles.* She still isn't sure when to hold and when to hit in blackjack.

ACKNOWLEDGMENTS

Very special thanks to Rick Garman.

Thanks to Dan Glover, Robin Ochiba-Campbell, Carolyn McCue, An Dragavon, John Griego, Cheryl Ladd-Campbell, Thomas Lynch, Steve Hochman (for Saltines and Jell-O), Leslie Ransdall, Mr. Wayne Newton, *Scope* magazine, and especially to everyone at Frommer's for their much appreciated patience this past year.

MACMILLAN TRAVEL

A Simon & Schuster Macmillan Company
1633 Broadway
New York, NY 10019

Find us online at **www.frommers.com**

ISBN 0-02-862699-0
ISSN 1090-5472

Editor: Dan Glover
Production Editor: Donna Wright
Photo Editor: Richard Fox
Design by Michele Laseau
Digital Cartography by Ortelius Design and Gail Accardi
Page Creation by John Bitter, Toi Davis, and Linda Quigley

SPECIAL SALES

Bulk purchases (10+ copies) of Frommer's and selected Macmillan travel guides are available to corporations, organizations, mail-order catalogs, institutions, and charities at special discounts, and can be customized to suit individual needs. For more information write to Special Sales, Macmillan General Reference, 1633 Broadway, New York, NY 10019.

Manufactured in the United States of America

Contents

List of Maps vi

1   Introducing Las Vegas 1

1 Frommer's Favorite Las Vegas Experiences 1
★ *Favorite Vegas Movies from the Mayor of
   Las Vegas* 2

2   Planning a Trip to Las Vegas 4

1 Visitor Information 4
2 When to Go 4
★ *Las Vegas Calendar of Events* 6
★ *Major Convention Dates for 1999* 8
3 Tips for Travelers with Special Needs 9
4 Getting There 9

3   Getting to Know Las Vegas 13

1 Orientation 13
2 Getting Around 16
★ *Fast Facts: Las Vegas* 17

4   Accommodations 21

1 Best Bets 21
★ *Reservations Services* 22
2 South Strip 24
★ *Family-Friendly Hotels* 29
3 Mid-Strip 33
4 North Strip 42
5 East of the Strip 48
6 Downtown 54

5	**Dining 60**

1 Best Bets   60

2 South Strip   63

3 Mid-Strip   69

4 North Strip   76

5 East of the Strip   81

★ *Have You Heard the One About the Belly Dancer?*   84

★ *Family-Friendly Restaurants*   86

6 West Las Vegas   90

7 Downtown   92

8 Buffets & Sunday Brunches   95

6	**What to See & Do in Las Vegas 101**

1 Las Vegas Attractions   101

2 Getting Married   108

3 Especially for Kids   110

4 Playing Golf & Tennis   114

5 An Excursion to Hoover Dam & Lake Mead   116

7	**About Casino Gambling 122**

1 The Games   123

★ *Baccarat Rules*   124

★ *Roulette Bets and Odds*   132

★ *Slot Clubs*   134

2 The Casinos   136

8	**Shopping 146**

1 The Malls   146

2 Factory Outlets   148

3 Hotel Shopping Arcades   149

4 Vintage Clothing   153

5 Reading Material: Used Books, Comics & a Notable Newsstand   154

6 Antiques   155

9	**Las Vegas After Dark 157**

1 What's Playing Where 158

2 The Major Production Shows 159

★ *Family-Friendly Shows* 161

★ *12 Inaccuracies in the Movie* Showgirls 166

★ *Wayne Newton's Top-10 Favorite Lounge Songs* 169

3 Piano Bars 170

4 Other Bars 171

5 Dance Clubs 174

6 Strip Clubs 176

★ *Two Strippers Give 9 Strip-Bar Etiquette Tips* 177

Index 178

General Index 178

Accommodations Index 183

Restaurant Index 184

Buffet Index 184

List of Maps

Las Vegas & Environs   5

Las Vegas at a Glance   15

South Strip
   Accommodations   25

Mid-Strip
   Accommodations   35

North Strip
   Accommodations   43

Accommodations East of
   the Strip   49

Accommodations
   Downtown   55

South Strip Dining   65

Mid-Strip Dining   71

North Strip
   Dining   77

Dining East of the
   Strip   83

Dining Downtown   93

Las Vegas
   Attractions   103

Lake Mead &
   Vicinity   117

An Invitation to the Reader

In researching this book, we discovered many wonderful places—hotels, restaurants, shops, and more. We're sure you'll find others. Please tell us about them, so we can share the information with your fellow travelers in upcoming editions. If you were disappointed with a recommendation, we'd love to know that, too. Please write to:

Frommer's Portable Las Vegas '99
Macmillan Travel
1633 Broadway
New York, NY 10019

An Additional Note

Please be advised that travel information is subject to change at any time—and this is especially true of prices. We therefore suggest that you write or call ahead for confirmation when making your travel plans. The authors, editors, and publisher cannot be held responsible for the experiences of readers while traveling. Your safety is important to us, however, so we encourage you to stay alert and be aware of your surroundings. Keep a close eye on cameras, purses, and wallets, all favorite targets of thieves and pickpockets.

What the Symbols Mean
✪ Frommer's Favorites

Our favorite places and experiences—outstanding for quality, value, or both.

The following abbreviations are used for credit cards:

AE	American Express	ER	enRoute
CB	Carte Blanche	JCB	Japan Credit Bank
DC	Diners Club	MC	MasterCard
DISC	Discover	V	Visa

Find Frommer's Online

Arthur Frommer's Outspoken Encyclopedia of Travel (www.frommers.com) offers more than 6,000 pages of up-to-the-minute travel information—including the latest bargains and candid, personal articles updated daily by Arthur Frommer himself. No other Web site offers such comprehensive and timely coverage of the world of travel.

Introducing Las Vegas

As often as you might have seen it on TV or in a movie, there is nothing that prepares you for that first sight of Las Vegas. The skyline is hyperreality, a mélange of the Statue of Liberty, a giant lion, a pyramid and a Sphinx, and preternaturally glittering buildings. At night, it's so bright, you can actually get disoriented—and also get a sensory overload that can reduce you to hapless tears or fits of giggles. And that's without setting foot inside a casino, where the shouts from the craps tables, crash of coins from the slots, and general roar combine into either the greatest adrenaline rush of your life or the eleventh pit of hell.

Las Vegas is a true original; there is nothing like it in America or arguably the world. In other cities, hotels are built near the major attractions. Here, the hotels *are* the major attractions. Las Vegas can be whatever the visitor wants, and for a few days, the visitor can be whatever he or she wants. Just be prepared to leave all touchstones with reality behind. Just for this time, you will rise at noon and gorge on endless amounts of rich food at 3am. You will watch your money grow or (more probably) shrink. You will watch a volcano explode and pirates fight the British. And after awhile, it will all seem pretty normal. This is not a cultural vacation, okay? Save the thoughts of museums and historical sights for the real New York, Egypt, and Rome. Vegas is about fun. Go have some. Go have too much. It won't be hard.

The result of all this is that once you go to Vegas, you will want to come back again, if only to make sure that you didn't dream it all. Love it, loathe it, or both, no one has ambivalent feelings about Vegas.

1 Frommer's Favorite Las Vegas Experiences

- **A Stroll on the Strip After Dark.** You haven't really seen Las Vegas until you've seen it at night. This neon wonderland is the world's greatest sound and light show. Begin at Luxor and work your way down past the incredible new New York New York. If your strength holds out, you will end at Circus Circus, where live

Favorite Vegas Movies from the Mayor of Las Vegas
Jan Laverty is the mayor of Las Vegas.

- *Oceans 11*
- *Viva Las Vegas*

10 Other Vegas Movies the Mayor Didn't Pick & Possible Reasons Why

- *Leaving Las Vegas.* Alcoholics and hookers are not good role models.
- *One from the Heart.* Shot on a sound stage rather than in Las Vegas.
- *Vegas Vacation.* Griswald family not typical Vegas tourists.
- *Casino.* Puts the squeeze on heads rather than on wallets.
- *They Came to Rob Las Vegas.* The title says it all.
- *The Electric Horseman.* Robert Redford successfully steals valuable horse from casino.
- *Indecent Proposal.* Robert Redford successfully wins a million dollars from casino.
- *Fear and Loathing in Las Vegas.* Bad Craziness not the kind of image the Tourist Commission wishes to promote.
- *Showgirls.* Need we say more?
- *Honeymoon in Vegas.* Beats us. Who doesn't love Flying Elvii?

acrobat acts take place overhead while you gamble. Make plenty of stops en route to take in the ship battle at Treasure Island, see the Mirage volcano erupt, and enjoy the light, sound, and water show at Bally's.

- **Casino-Hopping on the Strip.** The interior of each lavish new hotel-casino is more outrageous and giggle-inducing than the last. Just when you think they can't possibly top themselves, they do. From Rome to ancient Egypt, from a rain forest to a pirate's lair, from King Arthur's castle to New York City, it is still all, totally, completely, and uniquely Las Vegas. See chapters 4 and 7 for our reviews.
- **The Penny Slots at the Gold Spike.** Where even the most budget-conscious traveler can gamble for hours. See chapter 7.

- **A Dinner Show at Caesars Magical Empire.** A solid dinner plus hours of entertainment, including your own personal magic show, make this one of the best values in Vegas, and a heck of a good time. See "Las Vegas Attractions" in chapter 6.
- **Buffets.** They may no longer be the very best of bargains, as the cheaper ones do not provide as good food as the more pricey ones, but there is something about the endless mounds of food that just screams "Vegas" to us. We've covered the best in chapter 5.
- **Cirque du Soleil.** You haven't really seen Cirque du Soleil until you've seen it at Treasure Island, with a showroom equipped with state-of-the-art sound and lighting systems, and a seemingly infinite budget for sets, costumes, and high-tech special effects. It's an enchantment. See chapter 9.
- **An Evening in Glitter Gulch.** Set aside an evening to tour Downtown hotels and take in the overhead light show of the Fremont Street Experience. Unlike the lengthy and exhausting Strip, Downtown allows you to hit 17 casinos in about 5 minutes. See chapters 4 and 6.
- **The Liberace Museum.** It's not the Smithsonian, but then again, the Smithsonian doesn't have rhinestones like these. Nowhere else but here. See "Las Vegas Attractions " in chapter 6.
- **The Forum Shops at Caesars Palace.** This is an only-in-Vegas shopping experience—an arcade replicating an ancient Roman streetscape, with classical piazzas and opulent fountains. Don't miss the scary audio-animatronic statues as they come to glorious, cheesy life. See "Hotel Shopping Arcades" in chapter 8.

2

Planning a Trip to Las Vegas

*B*efore any trip, you need to do a bit of advance planning. When should I go? Should I take a package deal or make my own hotel and airline reservations? Will there be a major convention in town during my visit? We'll answer these and other questions for you in this chapter, but you might want to read through chapter 6 if you tire of gambling.

1 Visitor Information

For advance information call or write the **Las Vegas Convention and Visitors Authority,** 3150 Paradise Rd., Las Vegas, NV 89109 (☎ 800/332-5333 or 702/892-0711; www.lasvegas24hours.com). They can send you a comprehensive packet of brochures, a map, a show guide, an events calendar, and an attractions list; help you find a hotel that meets your specifications (and even make reservations); and tell you if a major convention is scheduled during the time you would like to visit Las Vegas. Or stop by when you're in town. They're open Monday to Friday 8am to 6pm and Saturday and Sunday 8am to 5pm.

Another excellent information source is the **Las Vegas Chamber of Commerce,** 711 E. Desert Inn Rd., Las Vegas, NV 89109 (☎ 702/735-1616). Ask them to send you their *Visitor's Guide,* which contains extensive information about accommodations, attractions, excursions, children's activities, and more. They can answer all your Las Vegas questions, including those about weddings and divorces. They're open Monday to Friday 8am to 5pm.

And for information on all of Nevada, including Las Vegas, contact the **Nevada Commission on Tourism** (☎ 800/638-2328). They have a comprehensive information packet on Nevada.

2 When to Go

Since most of a Las Vegas vacation is usually spent indoors, you can have a good time here year-round. The most pleasant seasons are spring and fall, especially if you want to experience the great

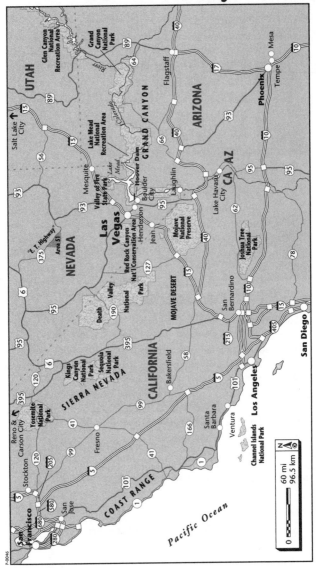

outdoors. Weekdays are slightly less crowded than weekends. Holidays are always a mob scene and come accompanied by high hotel prices. Hotel prices also skyrocket when big conventions and special events are taking place. The slowest times of year are June and July, the week before Christmas, and the week after New Year's. If a major convention is to be held during your trip, you might want to change your date.

One thing you'll hear again and again is that even though Las Vegas gets very hot, the dry desert heat is not unbearable. This is true. The humidity averages a low 22%, and even on very hot days there's apt to be a breeze. Also, except on the hottest summer days, there's relief at night when temperatures often drop as much as 20°. But it also gets really cold, especially in the winter, when at night it can drop to 30° and lower. The breeze can also become a cold, biting wind. If you aren't traveling in the height of summer, bring a wrap. Also, remember your sunscreen and hat—even if it's not all that hot, you can burn very easily and fast. (You should see all the lobster-red people in the casinos at night.)

LAS VEGAS CALENDAR OF EVENTS

You may be surprised that Las Vegas does not offer as many annual events as most tourist cities. The reason is Las Vegas's very raison d'être: the gaming industry. This town wants its visitors spending their money in the casinos, not off at Renaissance fairs and parades. When in town, check the local paper and call the **Las Vegas Convention and Visitors Authority** (☎ **800/332-5333** or 702/ 892-0711), **Las Vegas Events** (☎ **702/731-2115**), or the **Chamber of Commerce** (☎ **702/735-1616**) to find out about other events scheduled during your visit.

January
- **The PBA Classic.** The **Showboat Hotel,** 2800 Fremont St. (☎ **800/826-2800**), hosts this major bowling tournament every January.

March
- **The PBA Invitational.** Another major annual bowling tournament, also at the Showboat Hotel.

April
- **The World Series of Poker.** This famed 21-day event takes place at **Binion's Horseshoe Casino,** 128 Fremont St. (☎ **702/ 382-1600**), in late April and early May, with high-stakes gamblers

and show-biz personalities competing for six-figure purses. There are daily events with entry stakes ranging from $125 to $5,000. To enter the World Championship Event (purse $1 million), players must put up $10,000. It costs nothing to go watch the action.

- **TruGreen-ChemLawn Las Vegas Senior Classic.** This 4-day event in mid- to late April or early May takes place at the **Tournament Players Club (TPC),** The Canyons, 9851 Canyon Run Dr., in nearby Summerlin. For details and driving information, call ☎ **702/382-6616.**

June

- **Helldorado.** This Elks-sponsored Western heritage celebration takes place over a several-day period in mid-June. It includes bull riders, a trail ride, a barbecue, and four major Professional Rodeo Cowboys Association (PRCA) rodeos at the Thomas and Mack Center at UNLV. For information call the **Elks Lodge** (☎ **702/ 870-1221**) or check the local papers. For **tickets,** call ☎ **702/ 895-3900.**

September

- **Oktoberfest.** This boisterous autumn holiday is celebrated from mid-September through the end of October at the Mount Charleston Resort (☎ **800/955-1314** or 702/872-5408) with music, folk dancers, sing-alongs around a roaring fire, special decorations, and Bavarian cookouts.

October

- **PGA Tour Las Vegas Invitational.** This 5-day championship event, played on three local courses, is televised by ESPN. For details, call ☎ **702/382-6616.**

December

- **National Finals Rodeo.** This is the Super Bowl of rodeos, attended by close to 170,000 people each year. The top 15 male rodeo stars compete in six different events: calf roping, steer wrestling, bull riding, team roping, saddle bronc riding, and bareback riding. And the top 15 women compete in barrel racing. An all-around "Cowboy of the Year" is chosen. In connection with this event, hotels book country stars in their showrooms, and there's a cowboy shopping spree—the NFR Cowboy Christmas Gift Show, a trade show for Western gear—at Cashman Field.

The NFR runs for 10 days during the first 2 weeks of December at the 17,000-seat Thomas and Mack Center of UNLV. Order tickets as far in advance as possible (☎ **702/895-3900**).

Major Convention Dates for 1999

Listed below are Las Vegas's major annual conventions with projected attendance figures for 1999.

Consumer Electronics Show
1999: Jan 6–10   100,000

Western Shoe Associates
1999: Feb 9–12   25,000

Men's Apparel Guild in California (Magic)
1999: Mar 3–4   70,000

Associated Surplus Dealers
1999: Feb 21–25   50,000

Snowsports Industries of America
1999: Mar 9–13   28,000

Networld/Interop
1999: May 10–14   60,000

International Council of Shopping Centers
1999: May 23–27   35,000

Associated Surplus Dealers
1999: Aug 15–18   32,000

Softbank Comdex
1999: Nov 15–19   200,000

- **Las Vegas Bowl Week.** A championship football event in mid-December pits the winners of the Mid-American Conference against the winners of the Big West Conference. The action takes place at the 32,000-seat Sam Boyd Stadium. Call ☎ **702/ 895-3900** for ticket information.
- **Western Athletic Conference (WAC) Football Championship.** This collegiate championship event takes place the first week in December. Call ☎ **792/731-5595** for ticket information. Ticket prices range from $15 to $100.
- **New Year's Eve.** This is a biggie (reserve your hotel room early). Downtown, Fremont Street is closed to traffic between Third and Main streets, and there's a big block party with two dramatic countdowns to midnight (the first is at 9pm, midnight on the East Coast). Of course, there are fireworks.

3 Tips for Travelers with Special Needs

FOR PEOPLE WITH DISABILITIES Write or call **The Independent Living Program,** Nevada Association for the Handicapped, 6200 W. Oakey Blvd., Las Vegas, NV 89102 (☎ **702/ 870-7050**). They can recommend hotels and restaurants that meet your needs, help you find a personal attendant, advise you about transportation, and answer all questions.

In addition, the **Nevada Commission on Tourism** (☎ **800/ 638-2328**) offers a free accommodations guide to Las Vegas hotels that includes access information.

FOR SENIORS Always carry some form of photo ID that includes your birth date so you can take advantage of discounts wherever they're offered. And it never hurts to ask.

If you haven't already done so, consider joining the **American Association of Retired Persons** (☎ **800/424-3410** or 202/ 434-2277). Annual membership costs $8 per person or couple. You must be at least 50 to join. Membership entitles you to many discounts. Write to Purchase Privilege Program, AARP Fulfillment, 601 E St. NW, Washington, DC 20049, to receive their *Purchase Privilege* brochure, a free list of hotels, motels, and car-rental firms nationwide that offer discounts to AARP members.

FOR FAMILIES Las Vegas in the '90s is discussed in the "Especially for Kids" suggestions in chapter 6 and in the Best Bets in chapter 4.

Children under 12, and in many cases even older, stay free in their parents' rooms in most hotels. Look for establishments that have pools and other recreational facilities (see "Family-Friendly Hotels" in chapter 4).

FOR GAYS & LESBIANS The *Las Vegas Bugle,* a monthly magazine serving the gay community, provides information about bars, workshops, local politics, support groups, shops, events, and more. A subscription costs $20 for 12 issues. For details call ☎ **702/ 369-6260.** If you're on the Internet, check out **Gay Vegas** at www.gayvegas.com, which has helpful advice on lodging, restaurants, and nightlife.

4 Getting There

BY AIR
THE MAJOR AIRLINES

The following airlines have regularly scheduled flights into Las Vegas (some of these are regional carriers, so they may not all fly from your point of origin): **Air Canada** (☎ 800/776-3000), **Alaska Airlines** (☎ 800/426-0333), **America West** (☎ 800/235-9292), **American/American Eagle** (☎ 800/433-7300), **American Trans Air** (☎ 800/543-3708), **Canadian International** (☎ 800/426-7000), **Condor** (☎ 800/524-6975), **Continental** (☎ 800/525-0280), **Delta/Skywest** (☎ 800/221-1212), **Frontier** (☎ 800/432-1359), **Hawaiian** (☎ 800/367-5320), **Kiwi** (☎ 800/538-5494), **Midway** (☎ 888/226-4392), **Midwest Express** (☎ 800/452-2022), **Northwest** (☎ 800/225-2525), **Reno Air** (☎ 800/736-6247), **Southwest** (☎ 800/435-9792), **Sun Country** (☎ 800/359-6786), **TWA** (☎ 800/221-2000), **United** (☎ 800/241-6522), **US Airways** (☎ 800/428-4322), and **Western Pacific** (☎ 800/930-3030).

THE LAS VEGAS AIRPORT

Las Vegas is served by **McCarran International Airport,** 5757 Wayne Newton Blvd. (☎ **702/261-5743;** TDD **702/261-3111;** www.mccarran.com). It's just a few minutes' drive from the southern end of the Strip. This big, modern airport—with a brand-new, $500-million expansion—is rather unique in that it includes a casino area with more than 1,000 slot machines. Although these are reputed to offer lower paybacks than hotel casinos (the airport has a captive audience and doesn't need to lure repeat customers), it's hard to resist throwing in a few quarters while waiting for luggage to arrive. **Bell Trans** (☎ **702/739-7990** or fax 702/384-2283) runs 20-passenger minibuses daily between the airport and all major Las Vegas hotels and motels almost around the clock (4:30am to 2am). Several other companies run similar ventures—just stand outside on the curb and one will be flagged down for you. Buses from the airport leave about every 10 minutes. For departure from your hotel, call at least 2 hours in advance (though often you can just flag one down outside any major hotel). The cost is $3.50 per person each way to Strip and Convention Center area hotels, $4.75 to Downtown properties (any place north of the Sahara Hotel and west of I-15).

Even less expensive are **Citizen's Area Transit (CAT)** buses (☎ **702/CAT-RIDE**). The no. 108 bus departs from the airport and will take you to the Stratosphere where you can transfer to the 301, which stops close to most Strip and Convention Center area hotels. The no. 109 bus goes from the airport to the Downtown Transportation Center at Casino Center Blvd. and Stewart Ave. The fare is $1.50 for adults, 50¢ for seniors and children. *Note:* If you

Driving Distances to Las Vegas (in miles)			
Chicago	1,766	New York City	2,564
Dallas	1,230	Phoenix	286
Denver	759	Salt Lake City	421
Los Angeles	269	San Francisco	586

have heavy luggage, you should know that you might have a long walk from the bus stop to your door (even if it's right in front of your hotel).

RENTING A CAR   All of the major car-rental companies are represented in Las Vegas. We like **Allstate** (☎ **800/634-6186** or 702/736-6148), the least expensive of the airport-based car-rental agencies. Besides the usual mix, their fleet of more than 1,500 vehicles includes an inventory of 15 passenger vans, four-wheel drives, Jeeps, minivans, sports cars, and convertibles. We've found this local, family-owned company (the largest independent operator in Las Vegas) friendly and competent, with an invariably charming staff at the airport. They're open 24 hours. And they've agreed to offer our readers a **20% discount off regular rental rates** at any Allstate location (just show the agent your copy of this book). In addition to McCarran Airport, there are Allstate car desks at the Aladdin, Riviera, Stardust, and Jackie Gaughan's Plaza hotels, and the company offers free pickup anywhere in Las Vegas.

National companies with outlets in Las Vegas include **Alamo** (☎ 800/327-9633), **Avis** (☎ 800/367-2847), **Budget** (☎ 800/922-2899), **Dollar** (800/842-2054), **Enterprise** (☎ 800/325/8007), **Hertz** (☎ 800/654-3131), **National** (☎ 800/227-7368), and **Thrifty** (☎ 800/367-2277).

BY CAR

The main highway connecting Las Vegas with the rest of the country is I-15; it links Montana, Idaho, and Utah with Southern California. From the East Coast, take I-70 or I-80 west to Kingman, Arizona, and then U.S. 93 north to Downtown Las Vegas (Fremont Street). From the south, take I-10 west to Phoenix and then U.S. 93 north to Las Vegas. From San Francisco, take I-80 east to Reno and then U.S. 95 south to Las Vegas. If you're driving to Las Vegas, be sure to read the driving precautions under "By Car" in chapter 3's "Getting Around" section.

PACKAGE DEALS

When you make reservations on any airline, also inquire about money-saving packages that include hotel accommodations, car rentals, tours, and so forth with your airfare.

For instance, at press time, a **Delta Dream Vacation** package leaving from New York could cost as little as $350 per person based on double occupancy, including round-trip coach air transportation, two nights at your choice of several major casino hotels, a rental car for 24 hours, airport transfers, and bonus discounts and admissions. At press time Southwest Airlines was offering round-trip airfare from Los Angeles with two nights at several different hotels complete with ground transportation; per person based on double occupancy, for the Mirage it was $174, and for the Golden Nugget $119. (Of course, this was midweek.) Similar packages are available from such companies as **American Airlines Fly Away Vacations, America West Vacations,** and **US Airways Vacations.** Prices vary according to the season, seat availability, hotel choice, whether you travel midweek or on the weekend, and other factors.

Getting to Know Las Vegas

*L*ocated in the southernmost precincts of a wide, pancake-flat valley, Las Vegas is the biggest city in the state of Nevada. Treeless mountains form a scenic backdrop to hotels awash in neon glitter. For tourism purposes, the city is quite compact.

1 Orientation

VISITOR INFORMATION

All major Las Vegas hotels provide comprehensive tourist information at their reception and/or sightseeing and show desks. Other good information sources are: the **Las Vegas Convention and Visitors Authority,** 3150 Paradise Rd., Las Vegas, NV 89109 (☎ **800/ 332-5333** or 702/892-0711; www.lasvegas24hours.com; Monday to Friday 8am to 6pm, Saturday and Sunday 8am to 5pm); the **Las Vegas Chamber of Commerce,** 711 E. Desert Inn Rd., Las Vegas, NV 89109 (☎ **702/735-1616,** Monday to Friday 8am to 5pm), and, for information on all of Nevada, including Las Vegas, the **Nevada Commission on Tourism** (☎ **800/638-2328**).

FOR TROUBLED TRAVELERS

The **Traveler's Aid Society** is a social-service organization geared to helping travelers in difficult straits. Their services might include reuniting families separated while traveling, feeding people stranded without cash, or even emotional counseling. If you're in trouble, seek them out. In Las Vegas there is a Traveler's Aid office at McCarran International Airport (☎ **702/798-1742**). It's open daily from 8am to 5pm. Similar services are provided by **Help of Southern Nevada,** 953-35B E. Sahara Ave. (suite 208), at Maryland Parkway in the Commercial Center (☎ **702/369-4357**). Hours are Monday to Friday 8am to 4pm.

CITY LAYOUT

There are two main areas of Las Vegas, the **Strip** and **Downtown.** For many people, that's all there is to Las Vegas. But there is actually more to the town than that; maybe not as glitzy and glamorous—okay, definitely not—but you will find still more casino action on Paradise Road and in east Las Vegas, mainstream and alternative culture shopping on Maryland Parkway, and different restaurant choices all over the city. Confining yourself to the Strip and Downtown is fine for the first-time visitor, but repeat customers (and you will be) should get out there and explore. Las Vegas Boulevard South (the Strip) is Ground Zero for addresses; anything crossing it will start with 1 East and 1 West (and go up from there) at that point.

THE STRIP

The Strip is probably the most famous 3¹/₂-mile stretch of highway in the nation. Officially Las Vegas Boulevard South, it contains most of the top hotels in town and offers almost all of the major showroom entertainment. We divide the Strip into three sections: **South Strip** can be roughly defined as the portion of the Strip south of Harmon Avenue, including the MGM Grand, the Monte Carlo, New York New York, and the Luxor hotels. **Mid-Strip** is a long stretch of the street between Harmon Avenue and Spring Mountain Road, including Caesars, the Mirage and Treasure Island, Bally's, the Flamingo Hilton, and Harrah's. **North Strip** stretches north from Stardust Road all the way to the Stratosphere Tower and includes the Stardust, the Sahara, the Riviera, Desert Inn, and Circus Circus. It's on the Strip where first-time visitors will, and probably should, spend the bulk of their time. If mobility is a problem, then South and Mid-Strip locations are the best bets.

EAST OF THE STRIP/CONVENTION CENTER

This area has grown up around the Las Vegas Convention Center. Las Vegas is one of the nation's top convention cities, attracting more than 2.9 million conventioneers each year. The major hotel in this section is the Las Vegas Hilton, but in recent years Marriott has built Residence Inn and Courtyard properties here, and the Hard Rock Hotel has opened. You'll find many excellent smaller hotels and motels southward along Paradise Road. All offer close proximity to the Strip.

DOWNTOWN

Also known as "**Glitter Gulch**" (narrower streets make the neon seem brighter), Downtown Las Vegas, which is centered on Fremont Street between Main and 9th streets, was the first section of the city to develop hotels and casinos. With the exception of the Golden

Las Vegas at a Glance

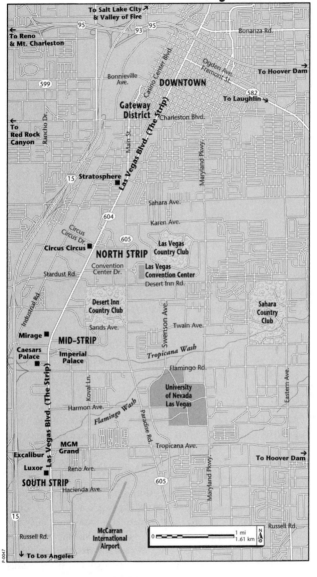

To Salt Lake City & Valley of Fire

To Reno & Mt. Charleston

Bonanza Rd.

95   93   95

599

Ogden Ave.
Fremont St.

To Hoover Dam →

Bonnieville Ave.

DOWNTOWN

582

To Laughlin →

Gateway District

Charleston Blvd.

To Red Rock Canyon

Rancho Dr.

Main St.

Las Vegas Blvd. (The Strip)

Maryland Pkwy.

15

Stratosphere ■

Sahara Ave.

604

Karen Ave.

Circus Circus Dr.

605

Las Vegas Country Club

Circus Circus ■

NORTH STRIP

Convention Center Dr.

Las Vegas Convention Center

Stardust Rd.

Desert Inn Rd.

Desert Inn Country Club

Sahara Country Club

Industrial Rd.

Sands Ave.

Swenson Ave.

Twain Ave.

Mirage ■

MID-STRIP

Tropicana Wash

Caesars Palace ■

Imperial Palace

Flamingo Rd.

Koval Ln.

Las Vegas Blvd. (The Strip)

Harmon Ave.

Flamingo Wash

University of Nevada Las Vegas

Paradise Rd.

Eastern Ave.

MGM Grand

Tropicana Ave.

Excalibur ■

Reno Ave.

Luxor ■

SOUTH STRIP

Hacienda Ave.

605

Maryland Pkwy.

To Hoover Dam →

15

Russell Rd.

Russell Rd.

McCarran International Airport

0   1 mi
1.61 km

N

↓ To Los Angeles

P-0047

Nugget, which looks like it belongs in Monte Carlo, this area has traditionally been more casual than the Strip. But with the advent of the **Fremont Street Experience** (see chapter 6 for details), Downtown is experiencing a revitalization. The area is clean, the crowds low-key and friendly, and the light show overhead as silly as anything on the Strip. Don't overlook it. Las Vegas Boulevard runs all the way into Fremont Street downtown (about a 5-minute drive from the Stratosphere if traffic is good).

BETWEEN THE STRIP & DOWNTOWN

The area between the Strip and Downtown is a seedy stretch dotted with tacky wedding chapels, bail-bond operations, pawnshops, and cheap motels.

However, the area known as the **Gateway District** (roughly north and south of Charleston Boulevard to the west of Las Vegas Boulevard South) is slowly but surely gaining a name for itself as an actual artists' colony. Studios, small cafes, and other signs of life are springing up, and it is hoped this movement will last.

2 Getting Around

It shouldn't be too hard to navigate your way around. For the most part, you won't have to.

BY CAR

We highly recommend a rental car for Vegas tourists. The Strip is too spread out for walking, Downtown is too far away for a cheap cab ride, and public transportation is ineffective at best. Plus, further visits call for further exploration in still more parts of the city, and a car brings freedom. You should note that places with addresses some 60 blocks east or west from the Strip are actually less than a 10-minute drive—provided there is no traffic. However, if you plan to confine yourself to one part of the Strip (or one cruise down to it) or to Downtown, your feet will suffice.

Note: If you can, avoid driving during peak rush hours, especially if you have to make a show curtain. Parking is usually a pleasure, since all casino hotels offer valet service. That means that for a mere $1 tip you can park right at the door (though the valet usually fills up on busy nights.) Furthermore, though bus tours are available to nearby attractions, a car lets you explore at your own pace rather than according to a tour schedule. See "Renting a Car" in chapter 2 for information and toll-free numbers of companies with offices in Las Vegas.

Since driving on the outskirts of Las Vegas—for example, coming from California—involves desert driving, you must take certain precautions. It's a good idea to check your tires, water, and oil before leaving. Take at least five gallons of water in a clean container that can be used for either drinking or the radiator. Pay attention to road signs that suggest when to turn off your car's air conditioner. And don't push your luck with gas—it may be 35 miles, or more, between stations. If your car overheats, do not remove the radiator cap until the engine has cooled, and then remove it only very slowly. Add water to within an inch of the top of the radiator.

BY TAXI

Since cabs line up in front of all major hotels, an easy way to get around town is by taxi. Cabs charge $2.20 at the meter drop and 30¢ for each additional fifth of a mile. A taxi from the airport to the Strip will run you $8 to $12, from the airport to Downtown $15 to $18, and between the Strip and Downtown about $7 to $10. You can often save money by sharing a cab with someone going to the same destination (up to five people can ride for the same fare).

If you want to call a taxi, any of the following companies can provide one: **Desert Cab Company** (☎ **702/376-2688**), **Whittlesea Blue Cab** (☎ **702/384-6111**), and **Yellow/Checker Cab/Star Company** (☎ **702/873-2000**).

FAST FACTS: Las Vegas

Area Code   702.

Baby-Sitters   Contact **Around the Clock Child Care** (☎ **800/798-6768** or 702/365-1040). In business since 1985, this reputable company clears its sitters with the health department, the sheriff, and the FBI, and carefully screens references. Charges are $38 for 4 hours for one or two children, $7.50 for each additional hour, with surcharges for additional children and on holidays. Sitters are on call 7 days a week, 24 hours a day, and they will come to your hotel. Call at least 2 hours in advance.

Banks   Banks are generally open from 9 or 10am to 3pm, and most have Saturday hours. See also "Cash & Credit," below.

Cash & Credit   It's extremely easy, too easy, to obtain cash in Las Vegas. Most casino cashiers will cash personal checks and can exchange foreign currency, and just about every casino has a machine that will provide cash on a wide variety of credit cards.

Convention Facilities   Las Vegas is one of America's top convention destinations. Much of the action takes place at the **Las Vegas Convention Center,** 3150 Paradise Rd., Las Vegas, NV 89109 (☎ **702/892-0711**). The largest single-level convention center in the world, its 1.3 million square feet includes 89 meeting rooms. And this immense facility is augmented by the **Cashman Field Center,** 850 Las Vegas Blvd. N., Las Vegas, NV 89101 (☎ **702/386-7100**). Under the same auspices, Cashman provides another 98,100 square feet of convention space.

Currency Exchange   Most Las Vegas hotels can exchange foreign currency. There's also a currency exchange desk run by Travelex in the ticketing area on the first level of McCarran International Airport.

Dentists & Doctors   Hotels usually have lists of dentists and doctors should you need one. In addition, they are listed in the Centel Yellow Pages.

For dentist referrals you can also call the **Clark County Dental Society** (☎ **702/255-7873**), weekdays 9am to noon and 1 to 5pm; when the office is closed, a recording will tell you whom to call for emergency service.

For physician referrals, call **Desert Springs Hospital** (☎ **800/842-5439** or 702/733-6875). Hours are Monday to Friday 8am to 5pm.

Drugstores   **Sav-on** is a large 24-hour drugstore and pharmacy close to the Strip at 1360 E. Flamingo Rd., at Maryland Parkway (☎ **702/731-5373** for the pharmacy, 702/737-0595 for general merchandise). **White Cross Drugs,** 1700 Las Vegas Boulevard S. (☎ **702/382-1733**), open daily 7am to 1am, will make pharmacy deliveries to your hotel during the day.

Emergencies   Dial **911** to contact the police or fire departments or to call an ambulance.

Emergency services are available 24 hours a day at **University Medical Center,** 1800 W. Charleston Blvd., at Shadow Lane (☎ **702/383-2661**); the emergency room entrance is on the corner of Hastings and Rose streets. **Sunrise Hospital and Medical Center,** 3186 Maryland Pkwy., between Desert Inn Road and Sahara Avenue (☎ **702/731-8080**), also has a 24-hour emergency room. For more minor problems, if you are on the Strip, the Imperial Palace has a 24-hour urgent care facility, the **Resorts Medical Center,** an independently run facility on the 8th floor, with doctors and X-ray machines; it's located at 3535 Las Vegas Boulevard S., between Sands and Flamingo (☎ **702/731-3311**).

Highway Conditions   For recorded information, call ☎ **702/486-3116.**

Hot Lines   The **Rape Crisis Center** (☎ 702/366-1640), **Suicide Prevention** (☎ 702/731-2990), **Poison Emergencies** (☎ 800/446-6179).

Libraries   The largest in town is the **Clark County Library branch** at 1401 Flamingo Rd., at Escondido Street, on the southeast corner (☎ **702/733-7810**). Hours are Monday to Thursday 9am to 9pm, Friday and Saturday 9am to 5pm, Sunday 1 to 5pm.

Liquor and Gambling Laws   You must be 21 to drink or gamble. There are no closing hours in Las Vegas for the sale or consumption of alcohol, even on Sunday.

Newspapers and Periodicals   There are two Las Vegas dailies: the *Las Vegas Review Journal* and the *Las Vegas Sun.* The *Review Journal*'s Friday edition has a helpful "Weekend" section with a comprehensive guide to shows and buffets. There are two free alternative papers, with club listings and many unbiased restaurant and bar reviews. "City Life" is weekly and "Scope" is biweekly. And at every hotel desk, you'll find dozens of free local magazines, such as *Vegas Visitor, What's On in Las Vegas, Showbiz Weekly,* and *Where to Go in Las Vegas,* that are chock-full of helpful information—although probably of the sort that comes from paid advertising.

The **International Newsstand** carries a vast selection of virtually ever major U.S. city newspaper and many international ones; they probably don't have everything, but we tried and couldn't find one they had missed. They're in Citibank Plaza at 3900 Maryland Pkwy. (☎ **702/796-9901**). Open Monday to Sunday from 8:30am to 9pm.

Parking   Valet parking is one of the great pleasures of Las Vegas and well worth the dollar tip (given when the car is returned) to save walking a city block from the far reaches of a hotel parking lot, particularly when the temperature is over 100°. Another summer plus: The valet will turn on your air-conditioning, so you don't have to get in an "oven on wheels."

Police   For nonemergencies call ☎ **702/795-3111.** For emergencies call ☎ **911.**

Post Office   The most convenient post office is immediately behind the Stardust Hotel at 3100 Industrial Rd., between Sahara

---

Alert _____

The area northeast of Harmon and Koval has had increased gang activity of late, and should be avoided or at least approached with caution.

Avenue and Spring Mountain Road (☎ **800/297-5543**). It's open Monday to Friday 8:30am to 5pm. You can also mail letters and packages at your hotel, and there's a full-service U.S. Post Office in the Forum Shops in Caesars Palace.

Safety   In Las Vegas, vast amounts of money are always on display, and criminals find many easy marks. Don't be one of them. At gaming tables and slot machines, men should keep wallets well concealed and out of the reach of pickpockets, and women should keep handbags in plain sight (on laps). Outside casinos, popular spots for pickpockets and thieves are restaurants and outdoor shows, such as the volcano at the Mirage or the Treasure Island pirate battle. Stay alert. Unless your hotel room has an in-room safe, check your valuables in a safety-deposit box at the front desk.

Taxes   Clark County hotel room tax is 8%; the sales tax is 7%.

Time Zone   Las Vegas is in the Pacific time zone, 3 hours earlier than the East Coast, 2 hours earlier than the Midwest.

Weather and Time   Call ☎ **702/248-4800.**

Accommodations

*I*f there's one thing Vegas has, it's hotels. Big hotels. Here you'll find 19 of the 20 largest hotels in the world. And rooms: 110,000 rooms, to be exact—or at least exact at this writing. Every 5 minutes, or so it seems, someone is putting up a new giant hotel, or adding another 1,000 rooms to an already existing one. So finding a place to stay in Vegas should be the least of your worries. Or is it?

When a convention, a fight, or some other big event is happening—and these things are always happening—darn near all of those 110,000 rooms are going to be sold out. (Over the course of last year, the occupancy rate for hotel rooms in Las Vegas was about 90%.) A last-minute Vegas vacation can turn into a housing nightmare. If possible, plan in advance so you can have your choice.

But the bottom line is that with a few sometimes subtle differences, a hotel room is a hotel room. After you factor in location, price, and whether you have a pirate-loving kid, there isn't that much difference between rooms, except for perhaps size and the quality of their surprisingly similar furnishings. Price isn't even always a guideline; prices in Vegas are anything but fixed, so you will notice wild ranges (the same room can routinely go for anywhere from $60 to $250, depending on demand), and even that range is negotiable if it's a slow time (though such times are less and less common thanks to the influx of conventions).

1 Best Bets

- **Best for Conventioneers/Business Travelers:** The **Las Vegas Hilton,** 3000 Paradise Rd. (☎ **800/732-7117**), adjacent to the Las Vegas Convention Center and the setting for many on-premises conventions, offers extensive facilities along with helpful services such as a full business center.
- **Best Elegant Hotel:** Country club elegance is the keynote of the **Desert Inn Country Club Resort and Casino,** 3145 Las Vegas Blvd. S. (☎ **800/634-6906**). In its European-style casino, gaming tables are comfortably spaced; the glitzy glow of neon is replaced by the glitter of crystal chandeliers; and the scarcity of

Reservations Services

If you get harried when you have to haggle, use a free service offered by **Reservations Plus,** 2275 A Renaissance Dr., Las Vegas, NV 89119 (☎ **800/805-9528;** fax 702/795-8767). They'll find you a hotel room in your price range that meets your specific requirements. Because they book rooms in volume, they are able to get discounted rates. Not only can they book rooms, but they can arrange packages (including meals, transportation, tours, show tickets, car rentals, and other features) and group rates.

The **Las Vegas Convention and Visitors Authority** also runs a room reservations hot line (☎ **800/332-5334**), which can be helpful. They can apprise you of room availability, quote rates, contact a hotel for you, and tell you when major conventions will be in town.

For those of you hooked up to the Internet, a variety of online reservations systems can help you get a room and make all the appropriate travel arrangements for you.

- **www.180096hotel.com**
- **www.lasvegashotel.com**
- **www.lasvegasreservations.com**
- **www.lasvegasrooms.com**
- **www.lvholidays.com**

A couple of words of warning: a) Make sure they don't try to book you into a hotel you've never heard of before. Try to stick with the big names or ones listed in this book. b) Always get your information in writing and then make some phone calls just to confirm that you really have the reservations that they say they've made for you.

slot and video poker machines eliminates the usual noisy jangle of coins. Extensive facilities are complemented by attentive personal service. This is the most prestigious hotel address in town.
- **Best Archetypal Las Vegas Hotel:** By the end of 1998, there aren't going to be any. Las Vegas hotels are one and all doing such massive facelifts that the archetype is going to be but a memory. Still, despite some major changes, **Caesars Palace,** 3570 Las Vegas Blvd. S. (☎ **800/634-6666**), will probably continue to embody the excess and, well, downright silliness that used to characterize Vegas—and to a certain extent still does.

- **Best Swimming Pool:** The **Mirage,** 3400 Las Vegas Blvd. S. (☎ **800/627-6667**) and the **Flamingo Hilton,** 3555 Las Vegas Blvd. S. (☎ **800/732-2111**), probably tie for most stunning; both feature lushly landscaped areas, amor-phously shaped pools with water slides and waterfalls, plus kiddie pools, Jacuzzis, and, in the case of the Flamingo, swan- and duck-filled ponds and islands of flamingos and African penguins. Far more Vegas, however, is the **Tropicana,** 3801 Las Vegas Blvd. S.(☎ **800/ 634-4000**) where you'll also find a swim-up bar/blackjack table.

- **Best Health Club:** Like sumptuous swimming pools, deluxe state-of-the-art health clubs are the rule in Las Vegas hotels. Most exclusive (the fee is $20 per visit) and extensively equipped is the club at the **Mirage** (see above), offering a full complement of machines—some with individual TVs (headphones are supplied)— free weights, private whirlpool rooms as well as a large whirlpool and saunas, a thoroughly equipped locker room, and comfortable lounges in which to rest after your workout. An adjoining salon offers every imaginable spa service. Steve Wynn works out here almost daily, as do many celebrity guests.

- **Best Hotel Dining/Entertainment:** Food aficionados will be thrilled with the nationally renowned celebrity chefs at the **MGM Grand,** 3799 Las Vegas Blvd. S. (☎ **800/929-1111**). You'll find restaurants by Mark Miller, Emeril Lagasse, and Wolfgang Puck, as well as one of the best restaurants in Vegas: the Grand's gourmet room, Gatsby's. There's also a re-creation of Hollywood's famed Brown Derby here.

- **Best for Twentysomethings to Baby Boomers:** The **Hard Rock Hotel,** 4455 Paradise Rd. (☎ **800/473-ROCK**), which bills itself as the world's "first rock 'n' roll hotel and casino" and "Vegas for a new generation." Aficionados of Hard Rock clubs won't mind the noise level, but we aren't sure about everyone else.

- **Best Interior:** For totally different reasons, it's a tie between **New York New York,** 3790 Las Vegas Blvd. S. (☎ **800/ 693-6763**), and the **Mirage** (see above). The latter's tropical rain forest and massive coral-reef aquarium behind the registration desk may not provide as much relaxation as a Club Med vacation, but they're a welcome change from the general hubbub that is usual for Vegas. Speaking of hubbub, New York New York has cornered the market on it, but its jaw-dropping interior, with its extraordinary attention to detail (virtually every significant characteristic of New York City is re-created somewhere here) makes this a tough act to beat. Ever.

- **Best for Families:** It's a classic. **Circus Circus,** 2880 Las Vegas Blvd. S. (☎ **800/444-CIRC**), has almost unlimited activities for kids—ongoing circus acts, a vast video-game arcade, a carnival midway, and a full amusement park.
- **Best Rooms:** On the strip, they're at the **Mirage** (see above); downtown, they're at the **Golden Nugget,** 129 E. Fremont St. (☎ **800/634-3454**). The rooms actually look almost identical, though the former are done in more earth tones, while golds are the hallmark of the latter. In both hotels, each room has a marble entryway, a half-canopy bed, a dressing table with lighted lamp, comfortable overstuffed chairs in the single-bed rooms, and a lush (if average-sized) marbled bathroom. You feel special in them.
- **Best Noncasino Hotel:** The very upscale **Alexis Park Resort,** 375 E. Harmon Ave. (☎ **800/582-2228**), is the choice of many visiting celebrities and headliners. Many of its rooms have working fireplaces and/or Jacuzzis, and guests are cosseted with can-do concierge service.
- **Best Casinos:** Our favorite places to gamble are anywhere we might win. But we also like the **Mirage** (lively, beautiful, and not overwhelming), **Caesars Palace** (because the cocktail waitresses are dressed in togas), **New York New York** (because of the aforementioned attention to detail; it almost makes losing fun!), and **Main Street Station,** 200 N. Main St. (☎ **800/465-0711**) (because it's about the most smoke-free casino in town, and because it's pretty).
- **Best Downtown Hotel:** It's a tie. The upscale **Golden Nugget** (see above) is exceptionally appealing in every aspect. The **Main Street Station** (see above), which has done a terrific job of renovating an older space, now evokes turn-of-the century San Francisco, with great Victorian details everywhere, solidly good restaurants, and surprisingly nice rooms for an inexpensive price.
- **Best Views:** From high-floor rooms at the **Stratosphere,** 2000 Las Vegas Blvd. S. (☎ **800/99-TOWER**), you can see the entire city.

2 South Strip

EXPENSIVE

Due to open in early 1999 on the site of the old Hacienda, **Mandalay Bay,** Las Vegas Blvd. S. at Hacienda, named for the Rudyard Kipling poem, promises to be "1890s Burma"-themed. Plans include a Four Seasons on the top few floors, complete with its

South Strip Accomodations

Excalibur **6**	Mandalay Bay **9**	New York New York **3**
Holiday Inn Casino Boardwalk **1**	MGM Grand Hotel/Casino **4**	Orleans **5**
Luxor Las Vegas **8**	Monte Carlo Resort & Casino **2**	Tropicana Resort & Casino **7**

own separate entrance (and, presumably, rates), and a branch of the House of Blues nightclub. No more details were available at press time—though the building does look quite spiffy on the outside—but the name makes us think of southwest Asia in the days of the Raj, tigers, jungle, British colonial tea plantations, and political unrest. It does not, however, make us think of casinos, but time will tell.

✪ **MGM Grand Hotel/Casino.** 3799 Las Vegas Blvd. S. (at Tropicana Ave.), Las Vegas, NV 89109. ☎ **800/929-1111** or 702/891-7777. Fax 702/891-1112. www.mgmgrand.com. 5,005 units. A/C TV TEL. $69–$119 standard double; $79–$129 concierge floor double with breakfast; $99–$2,500 suite. Extra person $10. Children under 12 stay free in parents' room. AE, DC, DISC, MC, V. Free parking (self and valet).

The MGM Grand has recently completed one of the most amusing renovations in Vegas. When it first opened, the billion-dollar property, spread over 112 acres, had a *Wizard of Oz* theme. The outside was a shocking shade of emerald green, some door handles had "Oz" on them, rainbows were everywhere, and right in the center was a giant animatronic reenactment of MGM's most famous movie. Outside was a theme park, which initially charged an exorbitant entry fee.

That has changed. The outside is still green, but now the MGM Grand is The City of Entertainment, which means the theme is *all* MGM movies, not just one specific film beloved by children. Gone is the Oz attraction (though it may reappear at a later date in a different, less prominent part of the hotel), replaced by a Rain Forest Cafe and Studio 54, both of which are accessed through an ornate circular domed room, full of replicated '30s glamour, glitz, and gilded statues. Obviously, this is all more appealing to adults. The MGM did seem a bit cheesy (particularly if you contrast it to the even older, original MGM Grand, the elegant place that was destroyed in one of the worst hotel fires in history). As one of the world's largest hotels, it was also overwhelming and hard to navigate.

But the renovations sought to fix all that. The redesign will attempt to create some more intimate corners, and has already made navigating the still immense place somewhat easier. (It's actually kind of amusing how they are now backing away from bragging about their size and moving more toward trying to hide that fact.) And the staff, confirms a recent guest, couldn't be more helpful and friendly. Throughout, the theme of The City of Entertainment is repeated, as old movies are evoked in the decor (though considerable green and the odd rainbow still remain). In certain areas (like the restaurant row), the look is meant to suggest a behind-the-scenes view of a film studio back lot.

The rooms will give no cause for complaint. They are decorated in four distinct motifs. Most glamorous are the Hollywood rooms furnished in two-tone wood pieces (bird's-eye maple on cherry), with gold-flecked walls (hung with prints of Humphrey Bogart, Marilyn Monroe, and Vivien Leigh as Scarlett), gilded moldings, and beds backed by mirrors. Oz-themed rooms still have emerald-green rugs and upholstery, silver and gold star-motif wallpaper, bright poppy-print bedspreads, and tasseled green drapes; walls are hung with paintings of Dorothy and friends. In the Casablanca rooms—decorated in earth tones with shimmery fabrics and pecan/walnut furnishings and moldings—artworks depict Moroccan scenes such as an Arab marketplace. And the cheerful Old South rooms feature 18th-century–style furnishings and faux-silk beige damask walls hung with paintings of Southern belles and scenes from *Gone With the Wind.* All rooms offer gorgeous marble bathrooms.

Dining: MGM houses the most prestigious assemblage of dining rooms of any hotel in town. Four cutting-edge stars in the Las Vegas culinary galaxy—the **Wolfgang Puck Café,** Emeril Lagasse's **New Orleans Fish House, Gatsby's,** and Mark Miller's **Coyote**

Café—along with buffet offerings, are described in chapter 5. Indeed, Emeril's and Gatsby's vie for the honor of best restaurant in Vegas. The **Oz Buffet** is described in chapter 5. There are several other restaurants and lounges as well.

Amenities: 24-hour room service, foreign-currency exchange, guest-relations desk, shoe shine (in men's rooms), casino, MGM Grand Adventures Theme Park, full-service health spa and health club, full-service unisex hair/beauty salon, four night-lit tennis courts with pro shop (lessons available), huge, beach-entry swimming pool with waterfall, 30,000-square-foot video arcade (including virtual-reality games); carnival midway with 33 games of skill, business center, florist, shopping arcade, two wedding chapels (in the theme park), show/sports event ticket desks, car-rental desk, sightseeing/tour desks, America West airline desk.

The **MGM Grand Youth Center** is a first-rate facility for children ages 3 to 16 (☎ **702/891-3200** for details and prices).

Monte Carlo Resort & Casino. 3770 Las Vegas Blvd. S. (between Flamingo Rd. and Tropicana Ave.), Las Vegas, NV 89109. ☎ **800/311-8999** or 702/730-7777. Fax 702/730-7250. www.monte-carlo.com. 3,014 units. A/C TV TEL. Sun–Thurs $69–$199 double, Fri–Sat $99–$269; suites $139–$339. Extra person $15. Children under 12 stay free in parents' room. AE, CB, DC, DISC, MC, V. Free parking (self and valet).

The newest resort on the Strip, the massive Monte Carlo is the world's seventh-largest hotel. It's fronted by Corinthian colonnades, triumphal arches, splashing fountains, and allegorical (and slightly naughty) statuary, with an entranceway opening on a bustling casino. A separate entrance in the rear of the hotel leads to a splendid marble-floored, crystal-chandeliered lobby evocative of a European grand hotel. Palladian windows behind the registration desk overlook a salient feature: the hotel's 20,000-acre pool area, a lushly landscaped miniature water park with a 4,800-foot wave pool, a surf pond, waterfalls, and a "river" for tubing.

Spacious rooms with big marble baths exude a warmly traditional European feel. Striped tan wallpapers with fleur-de-lis friezes create a neutral backdrop for rich cherrywood furnishings and vivid floral-print fabrics and carpeting. Cable TVs are equipped with hotel-information channels, keno, and pay-movie options. A concierge level for VIPs is on the 32nd floor.

Dining: Restaurants include **Blackstone's,** the **Monte Carlo Pub and Brewery,** and the **Dragon Noodle Company.** In addition, the hotel has added a branch of the classic Downtown French restaurant **Andre's,** reviewed in chapter 5.

Amenities: 24-hour room service, foreign currency exchange, shoe shine, limo rental, casino, car-rental desk, four tennis courts, sightseeing/tour/show desk, barber/beauty salon, vast swimming pool, kiddie pool, whirlpool, water attractions, wedding chapel, full business center, large video-game arcade, large shopping arcade.

✪ **New York New York Hotel & Casino.** 3790 Las Vegas Blvd. S. (at Tropicana Ave.), Las Vegas, NV 89109. ☎ **800/693-6763** or 702/740-6969. Fax 702/740-6920. www.nynyhotelcasino.com. 2,034 units. A/C TV TEL. Sun–Thurs from $89 double, Fri–Sat from $129 double. Extra person $20. AE, CB, DC, DISC, MC, V. Free parking (self and valet).

Just when you think Las Vegas has it all and has done it all, they go and do something like this. New York New York is just plain spectacular. Even the jaded and horrified have to admit it. You can't miss the hotel, it's that little (Hah!) building on the corner of the Strip and Tropicana that looks like the New York City skyline: the Empire State Building, the Chrysler Building, the Public Library, down to the 150-foot Statue of Liberty and Ellis Island, all built to approximately one-third scale. And as if that isn't enough, they threw in a roller coaster running around the outside and into the hotel and casino itself.

And inside, it all gets better. There are details everywhere—so many, in fact, that the typical expression on the face of casino-goers is slack-jawed wonder. If you enter the casino via the Brooklyn Bridge (the walkway from the Strip), you find yourself in a replica of Greenwich Village, down to the cobblestones, the manhole covers, the tenement buildings, and the graffiti. (Yes, they even re-created that. You should see the subway station.) The main casino area is done as Central Park, complete with trees, babbling brooks, streetlamps, and footbridges. The change carts are little Yellow Cabs. The reception area and lobby are done in belle epoque, art deco, golden age of Manhattan style; you feel like breaking out into a 1930s musical number while standing there. It really is impossible to adequately describe the sheer mind-blowing enormity of the thing. So we are just going to leave it at: *Wow.* The word *subtle* was obviously not in the lexicon of the designers. It's hard to see how Vegas can ever top this, but then again that's been said before.

Rooms are housed in different towers, each with a New York–inspired name. There are 64 different styles of rooms, and they are all smashing. Each is done up in a hard-core art deco style: various shades of inlaid wood, rounded tops to the armoires and headboards, usually shades of brown and wood colors. However, some of the rooms are downright tiny (just like New York again!), and in those

---

👫 Family-Friendly Hotels

As repeatedly mentioned in their individual listings, most of the hotels are backing away from being perceived as a place for families. Still, anything with a serious theme and/or outlets for kids, as the following all have, is probably better than a regular hotel.

Circus Circus *(see p. 47)*   Centrally located on the Strip, this is our first choice if you're traveling with the kids. The hotel's mezzanine level offers ongoing circus acts daily from 11am to midnight, dozens of carnival games, and an arcade with more than 300 video and pinball games. And behind the hotel is a full amusement park.

Excalibur *(see p. 30)*   Also owned by Circus Circus, Excalibur features a whole floor of midway games, a large video-game arcade, crafts demonstrations, free shows for kids (puppets, jugglers, magicians), and thrill cinemas. It has child-oriented eateries and shows.

Luxor Las Vegas *(see p. 32)*   Another Circus Circus property. Kids will enjoy VirtualLand, an 18,000-square-foot video-game arcade that showcases Sega's latest game technologies. Another big attraction here is the "Secrets of the Luxor Pyramid," a high-tech adventure/thrill ride using motion simulators and IMAX film.

The MGM Grand Hotel, Casino, & Theme Park *(see p. 25)*   This resort is backed by a 33-acre theme park and houses a state-of-the-art video-game arcade and carnival midway. A unique offering here is a youth center for hotel guests ages 3 to 16, with separate sections for different age groups. Its facilities range from a playhouse and tumbling mats for toddlers to extensive arts and crafts equipment for the older kids.

---

all this massively detailed decoration could be overwhelming, if not suffocating. The bathrooms are also small, but with black, marble-topped sinks, which again lend a glamorous '20s image. And a mere 6 months after opening, hotel representatives announced they were doing so well they were planning to add another 1,000 rooms.

Dining: Restaurants include the **Motown Café, Il Fornaio, Chin-Chin,** and **Gallagher's Steak House.**

Amenities: Concierge, courtesy limo, currency exchange, dry cleaning, express check-out, laundry, newspaper delivery, room service, safety-deposit boxes, video rentals, valet and self-parking, beauty salon, car rental, casino, arcade, pool, tour desk. The spa is smaller than average and merely adequate, but at $15 a day it is slightly cheaper than spas at other major hotels.

Tropicana Resort & Casino. 3801 Las Vegas Blvd. S. (at Tropicana Ave.), Las Vegas, NV 89109. ☎ **800/634-4000** or 702/739-2222. Fax 702/739-2469. tropicana.lv.com. 1,874 units. A/C TV TEL. $79-$229 double. Extra person $15. Children under 18 stay free in parents' room. AE, CB, DC, DISC, MC, V. Free parking (self and valet).

This long-time denizen of the Strip is looking great since a major renovation in 1995. The entranceway is now a colorful Caribbean-village facade; there are nightly laser light shows on the Outer Island corner facing the Strip; pedestrian skywalks across the Strip link the Trop with the MGM Grand, the Excalibur, and the Luxor; and the resort's resident bird and wildlife population has dramatically increased. The Trop today comprises a lush landscape of manicured lawns, towering palms, oleanders, weeping willows, and crepe myrtles. There are dozens of waterfalls, thousands of exotic flowers, lagoons, and koi ponds. And flamingos, finches, black swans, mandarin ducks, African crown cranes, cockatoos, macaws, toucans, and Brazilian parrots live on the grounds. There's even a wildlife walk (home to pygmy marmosets, boa constrictors, and others) inside the resort itself.

Rooms in the Paradise Tower are traditional, with French provincial furnishings and turn-of-the-century wallpapers. Island Tower rooms are more befitting a tropical resort, and some have beds with mirrored walls and ceilings. Motel rooms out back can be tiny and oddly shaped. All Trop rooms have sofas and safes; TVs offer Spectravision movies, account review, video checkout, and channels for in-house information.

Dining: Restaurants include **Mizuno's, El Gaucho,** and **Papagayo's.**

Amenities: 24-hour room service, shoe shine, casino, health club (a range of machines, treadmills, exercise bikes, steam, sauna, Jacuzzi, massage, and tanning room), video-game arcade, tour and show desks, wedding chapel, car-rental desk, beauty salon and barbershop, business center, travel agent, shops (jewelry, chocolates, women's footwear, logo items, women's fashions, sports clothing, gifts, newsstand), and three swimming pools, including one with a swim-up bar/blackjack table.

MODERATE

Excalibur. 3850 Las Vegas Blvd. S. (at Tropicana Ave.), Las Vegas, NV 89109. ☎ **800/937-7777** or 702/597-7777. Fax 702/597-7040. www.excaliburcasino.com. 4,032 units. A/C TV TEL. $49–$119 for up to 4 people. Children under 17 stay free in parents' room, children over 17 pay $12. Rates are higher during holidays and convention periods. AE, CB, DC, DISC, MC, V. Free parking (self and valet).

Now this is kitsch. One of the largest resort hotels in the world, Excalibur (aka "the Realm") is a gleaming white, turreted castle complete with moat, drawbridge, battlements, and lofty towers. And it's huger than huge. Apparently, the creators thought there were a lot of Arthur and Guinevere wannabes out there. And probably they are right; but do we really need a medieval, forest-themed, knights-running-amok hotel in which to act out our fantasies?

And it is hilarious. What it is not, is comfortable, which is actually historically accurate since big castles were not traditionally warm, cozy, inviting places. Excalibur is just too darn big, a chaotic frenzy at all times. Even the must-see factor fades quickly.

The rooms maintain the Arthurian motif with walls papered to look like stone castle interiors. Guests who have stayed in Tower 2 have complained about the noise from the roller coaster across the street at New York New York. It shuts down at 11pm, so early birds should probably stay in a different part of the hotel.

Dining: Restaurants include **Camelot, Sir Galahad's, Wild Bill's,** and **Lance-a-Lotta Pasta.**

Amenities: 24-hour room service, free gaming lessons, shoe shine, foreign-currency exchange, casino, tour and show desks, state-of-the-art video-game arcade, wedding chapel (you can marry in medieval attire), unisex hairdresser, car-rental desk, a parking lot that can accommodate RVs, shops (see chapter 8). There are two large, beautifully landscaped swimming pools complete with waterfalls and water slides and an adjoining 16-seat whirlpool spa.

Holiday Inn Casino Boardwalk. 3750 Las Vegas Blvd. S. (between Harmon and Tropicana aves.), Las Vegas, NV 89109. ☎ **800/HOLIDAY,** 800/635-4581, or 702/735-2400. Fax 702/730-3166. www.hiboardwalk.com. 655 units. A/C TV TEL. $39–$109 double; $250–$495 1-bedroom suite, $495–$895 2-bedroom suite. Extra person $15. Rates may be higher during special events. Children 19 and under stay free in parents' room. AE, DC, DISC, JCB, MC, V. Free parking (self and valet).

This is just like a Holiday Inn, only in Vegas you *gotta* have a theme, and the hotel underwent an extensive renovation to give it a more attractive Coney Island and Boardwalk flavor, inside and especially out. At press time, Steve Wynn's Mirage Corp. had just purchased the property, with assurances that nothing will change for now.

Still, for the time being, it's a Holiday Inn, which means you know what you are getting in terms of quality, and the Strip location is a good one. Also, you don't have to walk through the casino to get to the lobby, which is a plus. On the other hand, it's a bit pricey, at the high end for what are standard Holiday Inn hotel rooms. The rooms in the new 16-story tower are perhaps a bit nicer than the older units. All offer cable TVs with pay-movie options. Irons and ironing boards are in the rooms.

Dining: Cyclone Coffee Shop, a 24-hour facility, has some of the best bargain meals in town (see chapter 5 for details).

Amenities: 24-hour room service, shoe shine, casino, two small swimming pools, shops, coin-op washers/dryers, video-game arcade and shooting gallery, sightseeing/show/tour desk, car-rental desk. Guests can use health club facilities nearby.

✪ **Luxor Las Vegas.** 3900 Las Vegas Blvd. S. (between Reno and Hacienda aves.), Las Vegas, NV 81119. ☎ **800/288-1000** or 702/262-4000. Fax 702/262-4452. www.luxor.com. 4,988 units. A/C TV TEL. Sun–Thurs $49–$259 double; Fri–Sat $99–$299 double; $179–$279 concierge level; $99–$329 Jacuzzi suite, $500–$800 for other suites. Extra person $10. Children under 12 stay free in parents' room. AE, CB, DC, DISC, MC, V. Free parking (self and valet).

Luxor has just completed a $300 million renovation and expansion. Cheese fans will be disappointed to learn that the Egyptian fantasma that set the pace for all others isn't all that tacky anymore. Oh sure, the main hotel is still a 30-story bronze pyramid, complete with a really tall, 315,000-watt light beam at the top. (The Luxor says that's because the Egyptians believed their souls would travel up from heaven in a beam of light; we think it's really because it gives them something to brag about: "The most powerful beam on earth!") Sure, replicas of Cleopatra's Needle and the Sphinx still grace the outside, but the interior redesign has been made much more inviting, classier, and functional.

The rooms have had a freshening-up in the pyramid. High-speed "inclinator" elevators run on a 39° angle, making the ride up to your room a bit of a thrill. Sloped window walls remind you you're in a pyramid. *Note:* In the pyramid, most bathrooms have showers only, no tubs. The rooms are probably better in the new tower. Featuring fine art deco and Egyptian furnishings, they are full of nice touches. Huge armoires house not only the TV but closet space. The marble bathrooms have phones, vanity mirrors, and hair dryers. This is one of the few rooms in Las Vegas that stands out. You know you are in the Luxor when you are in these rooms, as opposed to the cookie-cutter decor usually found in town. Especially desirable is a group of suites with glamorous art deco elements, private sitting rooms, refrigerators, and, notably, Jacuzzis by the window (enabling you to soak under the stars at night).

Dining: Restaurants include **Isis** and the **Sacred Sea Room.**

Amenities: 24-hour room service, foreign-currency exchange, shoe shine, casino, full-service unisex hair salon, complete spa and health club (with a full range of machines, free weights, steam, sauna, and Jacuzzi, massage, facials, herbal wraps, and other beauty treatments available), VirtuaLand (an 18,000-square-foot video arcade that showcases Sega's latest game technologies), car-rental desk, tour/show/sightseeing desks, five swimming pools.

INEXPENSIVE

✪ **Orleans.** 4500 W. Tropicana Ave. (west of Strip and I-15), Las Vegas, NV 89103. ☎ **800/ORLEANS** or 702/365-7111. Fax 702/365-7505. www.orleanscasino.com. 870 units. A/C TV TEL. $39–$89 standard double; $175–$225 1-bedroom suite. AE, DC, DISC, MC, V. Free parking (self and valet).

Just opened in December 1997, the Orleans is owned by the same company that owns the Barbary and Gold Coast casinos. It's a little out of the way, but with a 12-screen movie complex, complete with food court and day care center, this becomes an increasingly attractive option to staying on the hectic Strip.

If the prices hold true (as always, quotes vary), this hotel is one of the best bargains in town, despite the location. The rooms are particularly nice—the largest in town, so the hotel claims, next to the Rio's. They all have a definite New Orleans French feel. They are L-shaped with a seating alcove by the windows, and come complete with slightly turn-of-the-century–style overstuffed chair and sofa. The one drawback is that all these furnishings and the busy floral decorating theme make the room seem crowded, particularly down by the seating area in front of the bathrooms. Still, décor is meant to evoke a cozy, warm Victorian parlor, which traditionally is very overcrowded, so maybe it's successful after all.

Dining: Still to come are a number of restaurants, but right now the offerings include **Canal St. Grill** and **Don Miguel's.**

Amenities: Room service, safety-deposit boxes, courtesy bus to/ from airport and the Strip, casino, beauty salon, business center, game room/arcade, 70-lane bowling alley, wedding chapel, 40,000 square feet of meeting space (with more on the way), two swimming pools.

3 Mid-Strip

VERY EXPENSIVE

Bally's Las Vegas. 3645 Las Vegas Blvd. S. (at Flamingo Rd.), Las Vegas, NV 89109. ☎ **800/634-3434** or 702/739-4111. Fax 702/794-2413. www.ballyslv.com. 2,804 units. A/C TV TEL. $95–$135 double; $35 more for concierge floor (incl. breakfast); $300–$2,500 suite. Extra person $15. Children 18 and under stay free in parents' room. AE, CB, DC, JCB, MC, V. Free parking (self and valet).

Bally's recently completed a $72 million renovation, which included the construction of a monorail that whisks passengers from its downstairs shopping level (a bit of a hike from the casino) to the MGM Grand. More noticeable is its elaborate new facade, a plaza containing four 200-foot people movers that transport visitors to and from the Strip via a neon-lit arch surrounded by cascading waters and lush landscaping. Light, sound, and water shows take place here every 20 minutes after dark.

The large rooms all have sofas. TVs offer video checkout, not to mention cash-advance capability for your credit card. The 22nd floor is a concierge level.

Dining: Restaurants include **Seasons, Bally's Steakhouse** and **Al Dente.**

Amenities: 24-hour room service, guest-services desk, shoe shine, foreign-currency exchange, casino, tour and show desks, car-rental desk, small video-game arcade, shopping arcade (see chapter 8), wedding chapel, men's and women's hair salons, state-of-the-art health spa and fitness center, eight night-lit tennis courts and pro shop (lessons available), two basketball courts, and a swimming pool.

Bellagio. 3600 Las Vegas Blvd. S. (at the corner of Flamingo Rd.), Las Vegas, NV 89109. ☎ **888/987-6667**. www.bellagiolasvegas.com. 3,270 units. A/C TV TEL. $129–$499 double. Extra person $30. AE, CB, DC, DISC, MC, V. Free parking (self and valet).

Steve Wynn's latest amazing upscale resort is due to open in late 1998, on the site of the legendary Dunes Hotel. The $1.6 billion resort is inspired by the eponymous Italian village that overlooks Lake Como. For the price, it better be good. Knowing Wynn, it will be.

The front of the property, in keeping with Wynn hotels, is spectacular. It features an 8-acre lake, the setting for a choreographed water-ballet extravaganza (more free shows!) and a replica of an Italian village. The grounds will be some of the most lushly landscaped, with classical gardens, fountains, and pools. Rooms are to be appointed with "custom European-style furnishings, art and antiques" plus heavily marbled bathrooms. There will be a monorail to carry guests between Bellagio and Monte Carlo.

Dining: Plans are for a variety of dining options, from casual cafes and bistros to branches of the legendary **Le Cirque** and the famed Boston restaurant, **Olives.**

Bally's Las Vegas **11**
Barbary Coast Hotel & Casino **8**
Bellagio **10**
Caesars Palace **7**
Center Strip Inn **12**
Flamingo Hilton **6**

Harrah's Las Vegas **3**
Imperial Palace **5**
Mirage **4**
Rio Suites **9**
Treasure Island at the Mirage **1**
Vagabond Inn **2**

♣ **Caesars Palace.** 3570 Las Vegas Blvd. S. (just north of Flamingo Rd.), Las Vegas, NV 89109. ☎ **800/634-6661** or 702/731-7110. Fax 702/731-6636. www.caesars.com. 2,471 units. A/C TV TEL. From $99 standard double, $109–$500 "run of house deluxe" double; $549–$1,000 suite. Extra person $20. Children under 12 stay free in parents' room. AE, CD, DC, DISC, MC, V. Free parking (self and valet).

Since 1966, Caesars has stood as simultaneously the ultimate in Vegas luxury and the nadir (or pinnacle, depending on your values) of Las Vegas cheese. It's the most Vegasey of hotels you can find. Or at least it was. Caesars has completed a massive $300 million renovation, inside and out. Don't worry, the Roman theme remains. But as with everything else in Vegas, it has been upgraded to, let's say, a nicer neighborhood in Rome.

Past or future, Caesars remains spectacular. From the Roman temples, heroic arches, golden charioteers, and 50-foot Italian cypresses of its entrance, to the overwhelming interiors, it's the spectacle a good Vegas hotel should be.

Caesars is also known for its luxurious rooms and service. (Long lines at the reservation desk are sometimes relieved by gratis champagne.) You'll likely enjoy a lavish bathrooms with marble floor, European fixtures, and oversized marble tubs (about half are Jacuzzis). (*Note:* Some of the rooms have lavish tubs in the middle of the room, which can be uncomfortable if you want to shower and don't want this to turn into a spectator sport.) Furnishings tend to neoclassic styles; Roman columns, pilasters, and pediments are common. Many rooms have four-poster beds with mirrored ceilings, and all are equipped with three phones (bedside, bathrooms, and desk), cable TVs with HBO, a gaming instruction channel (with cameo appearances by hotel headliners like Natalie Cole and Johnny Mathis), and in-house information stations. All rooms have private safes, hair dryers, irons and ironing boards, and lighted closets.

In the brand-new 32-story Tower, rooms lack cutesy Roman touches, but supply additional luxury. Expect all the above touches, plus his-and-her baths and an eco-friendly, computer-programmed climate control system monitored at the front desk.

Dining: Caesars has a well-deserved reputation for superior in-house restaurants. Among our top recommendations are **Palace Court, Bacchanal,** and the sushi restaurant, **Hyakumi.**

Amenities: 24-hour room service, shoe shine, complimentary gaming lessons, valet and dry cleaning services, three casinos, two extensive shopping arcades, state-of-the-art video arcade, American Express office, show desks, car-rental desk, swimming pool, health spa. Also under construction are 113,000 square feet of meeting space and 250,000 square feet of additional retail space for The Fo-rum Shops. These should be finished by the time you read this.

EXPENSIVE

Flamingo Hilton. 3555 Las Vegas Blvd. S. (between Sands Ave. and Flamingo Rd.), Las Vegas, NV 89109. ☎ **800/732-2111** or 702/733-3111. Fax 702/733-3353. www.hilton.com. 3,999 units. A/C TV TEL. $69–$205 double; $250–$580 suite. Extra person $16. Children 18 and under stay free in parents' room. Inquire about packages and time-share suites. AE, CB, DC, DISC, JCB, MC, V. Free parking (self and valet).

The Flamingo has changed a great deal since Bugsy Siegel opened his 105-room oasis "in the middle of nowhere" in 1946. It was so luxurious for its time that even the janitors wore tuxedos. Jimmy Durante was the opening headliner, and the wealthy and famous flocked to the tropical paradise of swaying palms, lagoons, and waterfalls. While the Flamingo is a senior citizen on the Strip with a colorful history, a fresh, new look, enhanced by a recent $130 million renovation and expansion, has made Siegel's "real class joint"

better than ever. Still, reaching the outside world (the Strip and Flamingo competitors) can be difficult; there is a lot of casino between
you and the lobby, and then again between you and the street.

For those planning some leisure time outside the casino, the
Flamingo's exceptional pool area, spa, and tennis courts are a big
draw. One of the two best in Vegas, the pool is smashing, with
countless trees and foliage, live birds, two water slides, waterfalls, and
so forth. Rooms occupy six towers and are variously decorated.

Dining: Restaurants include **Beef Baron, Alta Villa, Peking
Market, Hamada of Japan,** and **Lindy's Deli.**

Amenities: 24-hour room service, guest services desk, translation
services (interpreters are available for more than 35 languages; gaming guides are available in six languages), casino, car-rental desk, tour
and show desks, full-service beauty salon/barber shop, wedding
chapel, four night-lit championship tennis courts with pro shop and
practice alley (tennis clinics and lessons are available), shopping arcade, five swimming pools, and a health club.

✪ **Harrah's Las Vegas.** 3475 Las Vegas Blvd. S. (between Flamingo Rd. and
Spring Mountain Rd.), Las Vegas, NV 89109. ☎ **800/HARRAHS** or 702/
369-5000. Fax 702/369-5008. www.harrahs.lv.com. 2,700 units. A/C TV TEL.
$75–$289 standard double, $99–$329 deluxe double; $195–$1,000 suite. Extra person $15. Children 12 and under stay free in parents' room. AE, CB, DC,
DISC, MC, V. Free parking (self and valet).

A recent radical face-lift has completely transformed Harrah's. It's
more elegant, with a European carnival theme. Overall, Harrah's has
done a terrific job with its remodeling, creating a comfortable and
fun environment while somehow eschewing both kitsch and the
haughtiness that follow in the wake of other hotel conversions' more
upscale images.

The rooms are light and festive, with marble fixtures and light
wood accents. All the rooms are larger than average; the points that
emerge from both the old and the new tower wings translate inside
into an extra triangle of space for a couch and table. In all rooms,
TVs offer hotel-information and keno channels, pay movies,
Nintendo, and video account review and checkout.

Dining: Restaurants include **Claudine's,** the **Range Steakhouse,**
and **Asia.**

Amenities: 24-hour room service (including a special pizza and
pasta menu), complimentary gaming lessons, casino, car-rental desk,
tour and show desks, nice-sized video-game arcade, coin-op laundry,
shops (see chapter 8 for details), unisex hair salon, health club, and
swimming pool.

✪ **Mirage.** 3400 Las Vegas Blvd. S. (between Flamingo Rd. and Sands Ave.), Las Vegas, NV 89109. ☎ **800/627-6667** or 702/791-7111. Fax 702/791-7446. www.themirage.com. 3,323 units. A/C TV TEL. Sun–Thurs $79–$399 double, Fri–Sat and holidays $159–$399 double; $250–$3,000 suite. Extra person $30. AE, CB, DC, DISC, MC, V. Free parking (self and valet).

We really like this place. Actually, ask around; most visitors and locals agree. Even if they haven't stayed here, the majority consider it the most beautiful hotel in Vegas. From the moment you walk in and breathe the faintly tropically perfumed air (we think it's vanilla) and enter the lush rain forest, you just know that you are on vacation. It's a totally different experience from most Vegas hotels, where you step inside the door and are immediately the victim of a sensory assault.

Occupying 102 acres, the Mirage is fronted by more than a city block of cascading waterfalls and tropical foliage centering on a very active "volcano," which, after dark, erupts every 15 minutes, spewing fire 100 feet above the lagoons below. (In passing, that volcano cost $30 million, which is equal to the entire original construction cost for Caesars next door.) The lobby is dominated by a 53-foot, 20,000-gallon simulated coral reef aquarium stocked with more than 1,000 colorful tropical fish, including six sharks.

To get to the casino and the rooms, you walk through the rain forest, which occupies a 90-foot domed atrium—a path meanders through palms, banana trees, waterfalls, and serene pools. The formerly tropical-themed rooms have been redone in varying neutrals, with liberal use of muted gold. A marble entryway, mirrors, vanity table, and canopy over the bed's headboard give even the standards a luxurious appearance. The bathrooms are marble and slightly on the small size, depending on the room. Oak armoires house 25-inch TVs, and phones are equipped with fax and computer jacks. Farther up the price scale are superdeluxe rooms with whirlpool tubs.

Off the casino is a habitat for Siegfried and Roy's white tigers, a plaster enclosure that allows for photo taking and "aaaahhhs." Out back is the pool, one of the nicest in Vegas (it has a ¼-mile shoreline), a tropical paradise of waterfalls, trees, water slides, and so forth. Behind the pool is the Dolphin Habitat and the new Siegfried and Roy's Secret Garden, which has a separate admission.

Dining: Restaurants include The **Noodle Kitchen, Kokomo's, Mikado, Moongate, Restaurant Riva,** and a **California Pizza Kitchen.**

Amenities: 24-hour room service, overnight shoe shine on request, morning newspaper delivery, casino, car-rental desk, shops, unisex hairdresser and salon offering all beauty services, video arcade, business-services center, swimming pool. A free tram travels between the Mirage and Treasure Island almost around the clock. The **Mirage Day Spa** is highly recommended.

Rio Suites. 3700 W. Flamingo Rd. (at I-15), Las Vegas, NV 89103. ☎ **800/ 752-9746** or 702/252-7777. Fax 702/252-0080. www.playrio.com. 2,582 units. A/C TV TEL. Sun–Thurs $95, Fri–Sat $149. Extra person $15. Inquire about golf packages. AE, CB, DC, MC, V. Free parking (self and valet).

The Rio Hotel confounded expectations by not only succeeding in an area somewhat removed from the Strip, but by thriving there. It recently completed an immediately popular $200 million addition: a new 41-story tower and the Masquerade Village. Diverging from the rest of the tropically themed hotel, this latter simulates a European village, complete with shops, restaurants, and a bizarre live action show in the sky. The addition is actually quite nice—not only is the architecture, in its faux way, aesthetically pleasing, but this part of the casino is much more airy, thanks to the very tall ceilings.

The rooms are touted because of their size; every one is a "suite," which does not mean two separate rooms, but rather one large one with a sectional, corner sofa and coffee table at one end. The dressing areas are certainly larger than average and feature a number of extra amenities, such as refrigerators (unusual for a Vegas hotel room), coffeemakers, and small snacks. Windows, running the whole length of the room, are floor to ceiling, with a pretty impressive view. The furniture does not feel like hotel room standard, but otherwise, the decor (shades of green) is fairly bland and nothing to get excited about.

Dining: Restaurants include **Fiore** (the Rio's premier restaurant, described in chapter 5), **Antonio's, Napa, Mask,** and the **Voodoo Cafe.**

Amenities: 24-hour room service, guest-services desk, foreign-currency exchange, shoe shine, complimentary shuttle bus to/from the MGM and the Forum Mall, casino, tour and show desks, unisex hair salon (all beauty services, including massage and facials), small video-game arcade, fitness room, shops, and three swimming pools.

✪ **Treasure Island at the Mirage.** 3300 Las Vegas Blvd. S. (at Spring Mountain Rd.), Las Vegas, NV 89177. ☎ **800/944-7444** or 702/894-7111. Fax 702/ 894-7446. www.treasureislandlasvegas.com. 2,891 units. A/C TV TEL. From $69 double; from $109 suite. Extra person $30. Inquire about packages. AE, DC, DISC, JCB, MC, V. Free parking (self and valet).

They will deny it now if you ask them, but Treasure Island was originally conceived (more or less) as the family alternative to the more grown-up Mirage. Why else would you build a hotel that is essentially a blown-up version of Disneyland's Pirates of the Caribbean? But that's all behind them. Sure, the pirate theme remains with a vengeance, complete with plenty of skulls, crossbones, treasure chests, pirate-ship figureheads, animatronic skeletons, and pirate nautical paraphernalia. But a $25 million face-lift has added more marble and gilded the bones, so to speak (actually, literally in some cases). It's still Pirates of the Caribbean, but with lots and lots of money thrown at it. Despite this, it still remains a top family choice and many kids are often running about, which some vacationers may not find desirable.

The rooms continue the Caribbean theme; in other words, expect a lot of sand. And parchment. It's not quite as opulent as the Mirage, but comfortable. Best of all, Strip-side rooms have a view of the pirate battle—views are best from the sixth floor on up.

Dining: The hotel's premier restaurant, the **Buccaneer Bay Club,** is described in chapter 5. Other restaurants include **Madame Ching's,** the **Plank,** and the **Black Spot Grille.**

Amenities: 24-hour room service, limo rental, foreign-currency exchange, shoe shine (in men's room in the lobby and casino), casino, tour and sightseeing desks, car-rental desk, travel agency, Mutiny Bay (an 18,000-square-foot, state-of-the-art video-game arcade and carnival midway; one highlight is a full-size Mazda Miata motion-simulator ride), two wedding chapels, full-service unisex salon (days of beauty are an option), shopping arcade, swimming pool, and health spa. A free tram travels between Treasure Island and the Mirage almost around the clock.

MODERATE

Barbary Coast Hotel & Casino. 3595 Las Vegas Blvd. S. (at Flamingo Rd.), Las Vegas, NV 89109. ☎ **800/634-6755** or 702/737-7111. Fax 702/737-6304. 200 units. A/C TV TEL. Sun–Thurs $39–$75 double, Fri–Sat and holidays $100. Extra person $10. Children under 12 stay free in parents' room. AE, CB, DC, DISC, JCB, MC, V. Free parking (self and valet).

Evoking the romantic image of turn-of-the-century San Francisco but not quite as nicely as Main Street Station downtown, the Barbary Coast enjoys a terrific Strip location. The casino is adorned with $2 million worth of magnificent stained-glass skylights, and the extremely charming, Victorian-style rooms make for an opulent setting. All accommodations include little sitting parlors with entrances framed by floral chintz curtains.

Dining: There are two restaurants in the hotel.

Amenities: 24-hour room service, shoe shine, casino, Western Union office, tour and show desks, gift shop.

Imperial Palace. 3535 Las Vegas Blvd. S. (between Sands Ave. and Flamingo Rd.), Las Vegas, NV 89109. ☎ **800/634-6441** or 702/731-3311. Fax 702/735-8328. www.imperialpalace.com. 2,700 units. A/C TV TEL. $49–$99 double; $79–$149 "luv tub" suite, $159–$299 other suites. Extra person $15. Inquire about packages. AE, CB, DC, DISC, MC, V. Free parking (self and valet).

Though appearing even older than its 17 years, the Imperial Palace has much more going for it than first impressions might give. The Strip location, right in the middle of the action, can't be beat. The standard rooms are just that, but they all have balconies, which is exceedingly rare in Vegas. The "luv tub" rooms are a great deal; for the price, you get a larger bedroom (with a mirror over the bed!) while the larger than usual bathroom features a 300-gallon sunken "luv tub" (with still more mirrors). A perfect Vegas hoot. Given the slightly larger size of the "luv tub" rooms, that $59 low-end fee plus the location make them one of the best bargains on the Strip. And the hotel also has a well-appointed 24-hour urgent care clinic, open to the public, which given the location—in the middle of the afore-mentioned action—is well worth knowing about.

Dining: The hotel has several restaurants, including **Embers** and the **Ming Terrace.**

Amenities: 24-hour room service, free gaming lessons, shoe shine in casino, casino, health club (machines, free weights, sauna, steam, massage, tanning, TV lounge), show and tour desks, car-rental desk, travel agency, unisex hairdresser, wedding chapel, shopping arcade, swimming pool.

INEXPENSIVE

Center Strip Inn. 3688 Las Vegas Blvd. S. (at Harmon Ave.), Las Vegas, NV 89109. ☎ **800/777-7737** or 702/739-6066. Fax 702/736-2521. 156 units. A/C TV TEL. Sun–Thurs $40–$50 double; Fri–Sat and holidays from $80 double; suites (for up to 4): Sun–Thurs $80, higher Fri–Sat and special events. Rates include continental breakfast. Mention you read about the Center Strip in Frommer's for a $5 discount Sun–Thurs. AE, DC, DISC, MC, V. Free parking at your room door.

This centrally located little motel is owned and operated by Robert Cohen, who is usually on the premises making sure guests are happy. He's a bit of an eccentric, and his hotel doesn't fit into any expected budget-property pattern. For example, the rooms have videocassette players, and a selection of about 1,000 movies can be rented for just $2 each. Local calls and use of a fax machine are free. There is a free continental breakfast, and free coffee is available in the lobby all day. A free pasta dinner is offered daily (subject to availability). There is no restaurant in the hotel. Facilities include a swimming pool and sundeck and a car-rental desk; the front desk can arrange tours.

Vagabond Inn. 3265 Las Vegas Blvd. S. (just south of Sands Ave.), Las Vegas, NV 89109. ☎ **800/828-8032,** 800/522-1555, or 702/735-5102. Fax 702/735-0168. 126 units. A/C TV TEL. Sun–Thurs $42–$95 standard double, $65–$125 king room; Fri–Sat $52–$110 standard double, $72–$150 king room. Rates include continental breakfast. AE, CB, DC, DISC, MC, V. Free self parking.

A central location just across the street from Treasure Island (a cool place from which to watch the pirate battle—drag out a lawn chair), plus clean, nicely decorated basic motel rooms, make this a viable choice. One-third of the rooms have patios or balconies, and all offer cable TVs with pay-movie options. King rooms have wet bars and refrigerators. A wide selection of complimentary bathroom amenities is available at the front desk, and free coffee is served in the lobby around the clock, as is a daily continental breakfast. Facilities include coin-op washers and dryers. There's a swimming pool, but no restaurant. A gratis airport shuttle and free local calls are pluses.

4 North Strip

VERY EXPENSIVE

☉ Desert Inn Country Club Resort & Casino. 3145 Las Vegas Blvd. S. (between Spring Mountain Rd. and Convention Center Dr.), Las Vegas, NV 89109. ☎ **800/634-6906** or 702/733-4444. Fax 702/733-4744. 702 units. A/C TV TEL. $175–$185 double; $215–$225 minisuite; $350–$555 suite. Extra person $35. Children under 12 stay free in parents' room. AE, CB, DC, DISC, JCB, MC, V. Free parking (self and valet).

The Desert Inn has long been the most glamorous and gracious of Vegas hotels; coming here means leaving the hectic Strip action behind. The Desert Inn considers itself more a resort than a hotel, and the property and prices reflect this. The property has just undergone a serious renovation. The look now reflects a turn-of-the-century Palm Beach resort, with elegant, clean, and spare lines. (Frankly, the time period of the decor is not turn-of-the-century in many parts, but let's not be picky.) As with most Vegas renovations, the look of everything is lighter, brighter, and cleaner—apparently, in the '90s, sand tone, rather than dark, means glamour. The clientele this attracts is middle to upper class, with a large convention crowd, thanks to their close proximity to the Sands Convention Center. Since this is more resort than hotel, expect first-rate service all the way.

The newly redone rooms (in light golds and greens) feel spacious, with comfortable armchairs and matching hassocks. The fluffy bed coverings appear lusher than usual, and the mattresses are very firm. Rooms have views of either the Strip or the golf course (the latter helps really give the feel of a getaway), and some even have small

North Strip Accommodations

Algiers Hotel **3**
Circus Circus Hotel/Casino **4**
Desert Inn Country Club
  Resort & Casino **8**
Riviera Hotel & Casino **6**
Sahara Hotel & Casino **2**
Stardust Resort & Casino **7**
Stratosphere Las Vegas **1**
Westward Ho Hotel & Casino **5**

balconies. Each room has a very big closet with an iron and ironing board. Business travelers will be pleased that the phone lines have modem connections. Cable TVs feature pay-movie options as well as gaming instruction and hotel-information channels. The bathrooms are perhaps the best in Vegas: beautiful and large, done in black and gray granite with double sinks, a separate enclosure for the toilet, and a glass shower separate from the tub. Amenities include a big basket of Neutrogena products, phone, and hair dryer.

Dining: See chapter 5 for details on the opulent **Monte Carlo Room.** There are several other restaurants, all better than average.

Amenities: 24-hour room service, concierge, shoe shine, golf course, five tennis courts, swimming pool (some suites have private swimming pools), day spa, casino, tour and show desks, car-rental

desk, beauty salon/barbershop, business center, shops, including golf
and tennis pro shops.

EXPENSIVE

Riviera Hotel & Casino. 2901 Las Vegas Blvd. S. (at Riviera Blvd.), Las
Vegas, NV 89109. ☎ **800/634-6753** or 702/734-5110. Fax 702/794-9451.
2,136 units. A/C TV TEL. $59–$95 double; $125–$500 suite. Extra person $20.
Inquire about "Gambler's Spree" packages. AE, CB, DC, MC, V. Free parking
(self and valet).

Opened in 1955 (Liberace cut the ribbon and Joan Crawford was
official hostess of opening ceremonies), at nine stories the Riviera
was the first "high-rise" on the Strip. Today, it tries to evoke the
Vegas of the good old days—"Come drink, gamble, and see a
show"—and while it is appropriately dark and glitzy, it's also very
crowded and has a confusing layout.

Rooms have recently been redone; gone are the dark tones and
heavy appointments in favor of muted florals, sandstone, and foam.
It's less old fashioned, but also has less character. Half the rooms
offer pool views. Amenities include in-room safes and cable TVs
with pay-movie options and in-house information stations.

Dining: A handful of restaurants plus a food court.

Amenities: 24-hour room service, shoe shine, casino (one of the
world's largest), large arcade with carnival and video games, well-
equipped health club, Olympic-size swimming pool, wedding chapel,
beauty salon/barbershop, comprehensive business-services center,
America West airlines desk, tour and show desks, car-rental desk,
shops, two Har-Tru tennis courts lit for night play. A unique feature
here: a wine-tasting booth operated by Nevada's only winery.

MODERATE

Sahara Hotel & Casino. 2535 Las Vegas Blvd. S. (at E. Sahara Ave.), Las
Vegas, NV 89109. ☎ **800/634-6666** or 702/737-2111. Fax 702/737-2027.
2,035 units. A/C TV TEL. $35–$55 standard double, $55–$85 deluxe double;
$200–$600 suite. Extra person $10. Children under 14 stay free in parents'
room. AE, CB, DC, DISC, MC, V. Free parking (self and valet).

One of the few venerable hotel casinos remaining in Vegas (it's come
a long way since it opened in 1952 on the site of the old Club
Bingo), the Sahara has just finished a major face-lift. The point is
not only to keep up with the Joneses—as the newer, glitzy hotels
make the old ones seem not just quaint but shabby—but also to
attempt to unify the theme.

Room decor suffers from overkill, with stars and stripes assault-
ing the eyes and not looking terribly Moroccan (but then again, neither does Morocco). The boldly striped bedspreads on the otherwise

comfortable beds are a particular mistake. The windows open, which is unusual for Vegas. It should be noted that the Sahara feels they are not as well-equipped for children as other hotels and discourage you from bringing yours.

Dining: Restaurants include **Sahara Steakhouse, Paco's Hideaway,** and the **Caravan Coffee Shop.**

Amenities: 24-hour room service, casino, beauty salon/barbershop, car-rental desk, tour and show desks, shops, video-game arcade, swimming pool.

Stardust Resort & Casino. 3000 Las Vegas Blvd. S. (at Convention Center Dr.), Las Vegas, NV 89109. ☎ **800/634-6757** or 702/732-6111. Fax 702/732-6257. www.stardustlv.com. 2,495 units. A/C TV TEL. Tower rooms and suites $60–$1,000; Motor Inn rooms $36–$200 (2-person max). Extra person $10. Children 12 and under stay free in parents' room. AE, CB, DC, DISC, JCB, MC, V. Free parking (self and valet).

Opened in 1958, the Stardust is a longtime resident of the Strip, its 188-foot starry sign one of America's most recognized landmarks. Today, fronted by a fountain-splashed exterior plaza, the Stardust has kept pace with a growing city. In 1991, it added a 1,500-room tower and a 35,000-square-foot state-of-the-art meeting and conference center, part of a comprehensive $300 million expansion and renovation project. It's a likable hotel, but has no personality, despite being the only star of *Showgirls*. (It was probably chosen for its oh-so-Vegas lightbulb-intensive facade.)

Rooms in the Towers are perfectly adequate, nice even, but frankly, completely forgettable. There are also Villa rooms in two-story buildings surrounding a large swimming pool. The least expensive rooms are in the Stardust's Motor Inn, set far back on the property. In the past, they were rundown motel rooms, but they now have more cheerful colors. A suite can be better, but it is a long walk to your hotel. Motor Inn guests can park at their doors. All Stardust accommodations offer in-room safes, and TVs have Spectravision movie options and in-house information channels.

Dining: Restaurants include **William B's, Tres Lobos, Ralph's Diner,** and a branch of **Tony Roma's.**

Amenities: 24-hour room service, shoe shine, free ice on every floor, casino, beauty salon/barbershop, video-game arcade, car-rental desk, show desk, shops (gifts, candy, clothing, jewelry, logo items, liquor), two swimming pools.

Stratosphere Las Vegas. 2000 Las Vegas Blvd. S. (between St. Louis St. and Baltimore Ave.), Las Vegas, NV 89104. ☎ **800/99-TOWER** or 702/380-7777. Fax 702/383-5334. www.grandcasinos.com. 1,500 units. A/C TV TEL.

Sun–Thurs $39–$93 double; Fri–Sat $59–$129; $69–$400 suites. Extra person $15. Children 18 and under stay free in parents' room. Rates may be higher during special events. AE, CB, DC, DISC, JCB, MC, V. Free parking (self and valet).

At 1,149 feet, it's the tallest building west of the Mississippi. In theory, this should have provided yet another attraction for visitors; climb (okay, elevator) to the top and gaze at the stunning view. But location—it's a healthy walk from anywhere—and the hefty price charged for the privilege of going up have conspired to keep the crowds away.

But in an effort to lure crowds back, prices have dropped and some changes have been made. The casino has been toned down (previously it was a World's Fair theme; now it's more temperate and adult-looking). The shopping arcade, again with a "major cities" theme, has been expanded slightly. You can still ride the incredible thrill rides (provided the wind isn't blowing too hard that day) on top of the tower, including the world's highest roller-coaster. Indoor and outdoor observation decks do offer the most stunning city views you will ever see, especially at night.

The rooms are furnished in handsome, Biedermeier-style cherrywood pieces with black lacquer accents. Ask for a high floor when you reserve to optimize your view.

Dining: Restaurants include the revolving **Top of the World,** plus some fast-food outlets.

Amenities: 24-hour room service, foreign-currency exchange, casino, guest services desk, tour and show desk, video-game arcade, shopping arcade, three wedding chapels (offering incredible views from the 103rd floor), car-rental desk. An exercise facility, child care center, and vast resort-style pool and sundeck are in the works.

INEXPENSIVE

Algiers Hotel. 2845 Las Vegas Blvd. S. (between Riviera Blvd. and Sahara Ave.), Las Vegas, NV 89109. ☎ **800/732-3361** or 702/735-3311. Fax 702/792-2112. 106 units. A/C TV TEL. Sun–Thurs from $40 double, Fri–Sat and holidays from $55 double. Extra person $10. Children under 12 stay free in parents' room. AE, CB, DC, DISC, MC, V. Free self parking at your room door.

A venerable denizen of the Strip, the Algiers opened in 1953. However, a recent multimillion-dollar renovation—including landscaping (note the lovely flower beds out back) and a new facade with a 60-foot sign—brought rooms and public areas up to date. There's no casino here, though you can play video poker in the bar. Neat two-story, aqua-trimmed peach stucco buildings house nice-sized rooms (with dressing areas) that are clean and spiffy looking. Free local calls are a plus. Facilities include a medium-size pool and palm-fringed sundeck.

✪ **Circus Circus Hotel/Casino.** 2880 Las Vegas Blvd. S. (between Circus Circus Dr. and Convention Center Dr.), Las Vegas, NV 89109. ☎ **800/444-CIRC,** 800/634-3450, or 702/734-0410. Fax 702/734-2268. www.circuscircus.com. 3,744 units. A/C TV TEL. Sun–Thurs $39–$79 double, Fri–Sat $59–$99. AE, CB, DC, DISC, MC, V. Free parking (self and valet).

Perhaps the strongest evidence that things are changing in Las Vegas is the massive remodeling and renovation of this classic hotel and casino. The circus theme remains, but Jumbo the Clown has been replaced by commedia dell'arte harlequins. In other words, like everyone else, even the venerable Circus Circus, once the epitome of kitsch, is trying to be taken more seriously. But don't come expecting an adult atmosphere; the circus theme remains and the kid appeal along with it. The midway level features dozens of carnival games, a large arcade (more than 300 video and pinball games), trick mirrors, and ongoing circus acts under the big top from 11am to midnight daily. According to the *Guinness Book of World Records,* it's the world's largest permanent circus.

The thousands of rooms here occupy sufficient acreage to warrant a free Disney World–style aerial shuttle (another kid-pleaser) and minibuses connecting its many components. Tower rooms have brand-new, just slightly better than average furnishings and offer safes and TVs with in-house information and gaming-instruction stations. The Manor section comprises five white, three-story buildings out back, fronted by rows of cypresses. Manor guests can park at their doors, and a gate to the complex that can be opened only with a room key assures security. These rooms are usually among the least expensive in town, but we've said before and we'll say again: You get what you pay for.

Dining: There are several different restaurants and casino bars.

Amenities: 24-hour room service (continental breakfast and drinks only), shoe shine, three casinos, wedding chapel, tour and show desks, car-rental desk, unisex hairdresser, two swimming pools, two video-game arcades, shops, Grand Slam Canyon Theme Park (see chapter 6).

Adjacent to the hotel is **Circusland RV Park,** with 384 full-utility spaces and up to 50-amp hookups. It has its own 24-hour convenience store, swimming pools, saunas, Jacuzzis, kiddie playground, fenced pet runs, video-game arcade, and community room. The rate is $12 Sunday to Thursday, $16 Friday and Saturday, $18 holidays.

Westward Ho Hotel & Casino. 2900 Las Vegas Blvd. S. (between Circus Circus Dr. and Convention Center Dr.), Las Vegas, NV 89109. ☎ **800/634-6803** or 702/731-2900. 777 units. A/C TV TEL. $37–$56 double; $76 suite. Extra person $10. MC, V. Free parking at your room door.

Located next door to Circus Circus, the Westward Ho is fronted by a vast casino, with rooms in two-story buildings that extend out back for several city blocks. In fact, the property is so large that a free bus shuttles regularly between the rooms and the casino 24 hours a day. There are three swimming pools. The rooms are clean and adequately furnished motel units. A good buy here: two-bedroom suites with 1$\frac{1}{2}$ baths, living rooms with sofa beds, and refrigerators; they sleep up to six people.

There's a 24-hour restaurant in the casino under a stained-glass skylight dome. Other facilities include a tour desk, free airport shuttle, gift shop, and casino lounge.

5 East of the Strip

In this section we've covered hotels close to the Convention Center, along with those farther south on Paradise Road, Flamingo Road, and Tropicana Avenue.

VERY EXPENSIVE

Alexis Park Resort. 375 E. Harmon Ave. (between Koval Lane and Paradise Rd.), Las Vegas, NV 89109. ☎ **800/582-2228** or 702/796-3300. Fax 702/796-4334. 500 units. A/C MINIBAR TV TEL. $99–$139 1-bedroom suite, $175–$250 1-bedroom loft suite, $350–$1,500 larger suite. Extra person $15. Children 18 and under stay free in parents' room. AE, CB, DC, DISC, JCB, MC, V. Free parking (self and valet).

A low-key atmosphere, luxurious digs, and superb service combine to make Alexis Park the hotel choice of many showroom headliners and visiting celebrities.

Spacious suites are decorated in light resort colors with taupe lacquer furnishings. Loft suites have cathedral ceilings. All are equipped with refrigerators, wet bars, two-line phones (one in each room of your suite) with computer jacks, and TVs (also one in each room) with HBO and pay-movie options. More than a third of the suites have working fireplaces and/or Jacuzzi tubs.

Dining: There are two restaurants.

Amenities: 24-hour room service, concierge, gift shop, unisex hair salon, health club, swimming pool.

Courtyard Marriott. 3275 Paradise Rd. (between Convention Center Dr. and Desert Inn Rd.), Las Vegas, NV 89109. ☎ **800/321-2211** or 702/791-3600.

Accommodations East of the Strip

Alexis Park Resort **9**

Best Western Mardi Gras Inn **4**

Courtyard Marriott **3**

Emerald Springs Holiday Inn **6**

The Hard Rock Hotel & Casino **8**

La Quinta Inn **5**

Las Vegas Hilton **1**

Motel 6 **10**

Residence Inn by Marriott **2**

Super 8 Motel **7**

Fax 702/796-7981. www.marriott.com. 159 units. A/C TV TEL. Sun–Thurs $109 double, Fri–Sat $119; $119–$129 suite. Convention rates can be higher. AE, CB, DC, DISC, MC, V. Free parking at your room door.

The Courtyard is a welcome link in the Marriott chain. Although the services are limited, don't picture a no-frills establishment. This is a beautiful hotel, with a pleasant, plant-filled lobby and very nice rooms indeed.

Like its public areas, the rooms, most with king-size beds, still look spanking new. Decorated in shades of gray-blue, mauve, and burgundy, with sofas and handsome mahogany furnishings (including large desks), they offer TVs with multiple On-Command movie options. All rooms have balconies or patios.

Dining: There is one restaurant and one lounge.

Amenities: Room service 4 to 10pm, complimentary airport shuttle, small exercise room, medium-size swimming pool with adjoining whirlpool, picnic tables and barbecue grills, coin-op washers/dryers.

✪ **The Hard Rock Hotel & Casino.** 4455 Paradise Rd. (at Harmon Ave.), Las Vegas, NV 89109. ☎ **800/473-ROCK** or 702/693-5000. Fax 702/693-5010. www.hardrock.com. 340 units. A/C TV TEL. Sun–Thurs $75–$250 double, Fri–Sat $145–$300; from $250 suite. Extra person $25. Children 12 and under stay free in parents' room. AE, DC, MC, V. Free parking (self and valet).

Everything here is rock-themed, from the Stevie Ray Vaughan quote over the entrance ("When this house is a rocking, don't bother knocking, come on in") to the vast collection of music memorabilia displayed in public areas. The casino features piano-shaped roulette tables and guitar-neck-handle slot machines. Even the walls of the bell desk are lined with gold records.

Large, attractive rooms, decorated in earth tones with photographs of rock stars adorning the walls, have beds with leather headboards and French windows that actually open to fresh air (a rarity in Las Vegas). Uncharacteristically large 27-inch TVs offer pay movie options and special music channels. A new expansion is underway, due to be finished in 1999, that should double the size of the hotel.

Dining: The hotel has several restaurants, including the **Hard Rock Cafe.**

Amenities: 24-hour room service, concierge, casino, small video-game arcade, gift/sundry shop and immense Hard Rock retail store, show desk (for **The Joint** only; tickets to other shows can be arranged by the concierge), health club, swimming pool.

✪ **Las Vegas Hilton.** 3000 Paradise Rd. (at Riviera Blvd.), Las Vegas, NV 89109. ☎ **800/732-7117** or 702/732-7111. Fax 702/732-5790. www. vhilton.com. 3,479 units. A/C TV TEL. $95–$279 double. Extra person $25. Children of any age stay free in parents' room. Inquire about attractively priced golf and other packages. CB, DC, DISC, ER, MC, V. Free parking (self and valet).

Elvis played here. Do you really need to know anything more?

Oh, all right. This is quite a classy hotel, which is probably why so many business travelers prefer it. (That, and the location next to the convention center.) There are quite a few terrific restaurants, plus the largest hotel convention and meeting facilities in the world. A serious renovation has added a number of new shops, plus **Star Trek: The Experience,** a themed attraction and accompanying space-themed casino (see chapter 6). They want to start attracting more of a leisure crowd, but you do have to wonder how all these additions might change the otherwise high-rent atmosphere.

The newly remodeled rooms have partly marble floors and slightly larger marble bathtubs. Each has a small dressing area outside the bathroom. The rooms are nothing particularly special in terms of decor, but they are very comfortable. Some have views of the adjacent 18-hole golf course. They do feature automatic checkout on the TV and a hot-line number on the phone that sends you directly to housekeeping.

Dining: The hotel has a number of terrific restaurants, including **Bistro Le Montrachet,** the **Seafood Grille, Benihana,** and **Andiamo.**

Amenities: 24-hour room service, foreign-currency exchange, two casinos, car-rental desk, tour desk, travel agency, shops, small video-game arcade, business service center (faxing and express mail), beauty salon/barbershop, jogging trail, 18-hole golf course, swimming pool, tennis courts, health club.

EXPENSIVE

La Quinta Inn. 3970 Paradise Rd. (between Twain Ave. and Flamingo Rd.), Las Vegas, NV 89109. ☎ **800/531-5900** or 702/796-9000. Fax 702/796-3537. www.laquinta.com. 181 units. A/C TV TEL. $85–$95 standard double, $89–$99 executive double; $115–$125 suite. Rates include continental breakfast; inquire about seasonal discounts. AE, CB, DC, DISC, MC, V. Free parking (self).

A remodeling process to be completed in 1999 may remove some of the pleasant grounds of this mission-style hotel. Nonetheless, it's still a tranquil alternative to Strip hubbub which features a court-yard, a charming stone fountain, rustic benches, lawn games (croquet, badminton, volleyball), barbecue grills, and picnic tables. The staff is terrific—friendly and incredibly helpful. The rooms are immaculate and attractive. Ground floor accommodations have patios, and all accommodations feature baths with oversized whirlpool tubs. TVs offer satellite channels and HBO.

Dining: The restaurant is called the **Patio Café,** and offers complimentary continental breakfast.

Amenities: Car rentals/tours arranged at the front desk, coin-op washers/dryers, medium-size swimming pool and adjoining whirlpool. A free 24-hour shuttle offers pickup and return to and from the airport and several Strip casino hotels.

✪ **Residence Inn by Marriott.** 3225 Paradise Rd. (between Desert Inn Rd. and Convention Center Dr.), Las Vegas, NV 89109. ☎ **800/331-3131** or 702/796-9300. www.marriott.com. 192 units. A/C TV TEL. $89–$169 studio; $109–$219 penthouse. Rates include continental breakfast. AE, CB, DC, DISC, MC, V. Free parking (self).

Staying here is like having your own apartment in Las Vegas. The property occupies seven acres of perfectly manicured lawns, tropical foliage, and neat flower beds. It's a great choice for families and business travelers. Monday to Friday, they offer a free light dinner with beer, wine, and soda.

Accommodations, most with working fireplaces, are housed in condolike, two-story wood and stucco buildings, fronted by little gardens.

Dining: A big continental buffet breakfast is served each morning. Weekday evenings from 5:30 to 7pm, there's a complimentary buffet with beverages.

Amenities: Local restaurants deliver food, and there's also a complimentary food-shopping service. Maids wash your dishes. Car-rental desk, barbecue grills, coin-op washers/dryers, sports court (paddle tennis, volleyball, basketball), swimming pool, health club next door.

MODERATE

Best Western Mardi Gras Inn. 3500 Paradise Rd. (between Sands Ave. and Desert Inn Rd.), Las Vegas, NV 89109. ☎ **800/634-6501** or 702/731-2020. Fax 702/733-6994. 315 units. A/C TV TEL. $40–$125 double. Extra person $8. Children 18 and under stay free in parents' room. AE, CB, DC, DISC, JCB, MC, V. Free parking at your room door.

Opened in 1980, this well-run little casino hotel is a block from the convention center and close to major properties.

Accommodations are all spacious, queen-bedded minisuites with sofa-bedded living room areas and eat-in kitchens, the latter equipped with wet bars, refrigerators, and coffeemakers. All are attractively decorated and offer TVs with HBO and pay-movie options. Staying here is like having your own little Las Vegas apartment.

Dining: A pleasant restaurant/bar off the lobby serves typical coffee-shop fare.

Amenities: Free transportation to/from airport and major Strip hotels, small casino (64 slots/video poker machines), small video-game arcade, car-rental desk, tour and show desks, coin-op washers/dryers, unisex hairdresser, gift shop, RV parking, swimming pool.

Emerald Springs Holiday Inn. 325 E. Flamingo Rd. (between Koval Lane and Paradise Rd.), Las Vegas, NV 89109. ☎ **800/732-7889** or 702/732-9100. Fax 702/731-9784. 150 units. A/C TV TEL. $69–$99 studio; $99–$129 Jacuzzi suite, $129–$175 hospitality suite. Extra person $15. Children 18 and under stay free in parents' room. AE, CB, DC, DISC, MC, V. Free parking (self).

Emerald Springs offers a friendly, low-key alternative to the usual glitz and glitter. Typical of the inn's hospitality is a bowl of apples for the taking at the front desk. And weeknights from 10:30pm to midnight you can "raid the icebox" at the **Veranda Café,** which offers complimentary cookies, peanut butter and jelly sandwiches, and coffee, tea, or milk. Although your surroundings here are serene, you're only three blocks from the heart of the Strip.

Even the smallest accommodations (studios) offer small sofas, desks, and armchairs with hassocks. You also get two phones (desk and bedside), an in-room coffeemaker (with gratis coffee), and a wet bar with refrigerator.

Dining: The hotel has a coffee shop and bar.

Amenities: Concierge, complimentary limousine transportation to and from the airport and nearby casinos between 6:30am and 11pm (van service available 11pm to 6:30am), room service, business services, gratis newspapers available at the front desk, fitness room, swimming pool.

INEXPENSIVE

Motel 6. 195 E. Tropicana Ave. (at Koval Lane), Las Vegas, NV 89109. ☎ **800/4-MOTEL-6** or 702/798-0728. Fax 702/798-5657. 602 units. A/C TV TEL. Sun–Thurs $34 single, Fri–Sat $52 single. Extra person $6. Children under 17 stay free in parents' room. AE, CB, DC, DISC, MC, V. Free parking at your room door.

Las Vegas's Motel 6 is the largest in the country and happens to be a great budget choice, quite close to major Strip casino hotels (the MGM is nearby). The rooms, in two-story cream stucco buildings, are clean and attractively decorated. Some rooms have showers only,

Note

At press time, there were plans to turn a portion or all of this property into a new 1940s gangster-themed hotel called Bugsy's. A portion of the Motel 6 may still be operating or it may be entirely closed by the end of 1999.

others, tub/shower bathrooms. Local calls are free and your TV offers HBO.

Three restaurants (including a pleasant 24-hour family restaurant called **Carrows**) adjoin. On-premises facilities include a large, well-stocked gift shop, vending machines, a tour desk, two swimming pools, a whirlpool, and coin-op washers/dryers.

Super 8 Motel. 4250 Koval Lane (just south of Flamingo Rd.), Las Vegas, NV 89109. ☎ **800/800-8000** or 702/794-0888. 290 units. A/C TV TEL. Sun–Thurs $41–$43 double, Fri–Sat $56–$58 double. Extra person $8. Children 12 and under stay free in parents' room. Pets $8 per night (one pet only). AE, CB, DC, DISC, MC, V. Free parking (self).

"The world's largest Super 8 Motel." Coffee is served gratis in a pleasant little lobby furnished with comfortable sofas and wing chairs. Rooms are clean and well maintained. Some have safes, and TVs offer free movie channels.

Dining: Ellis Island Restaurant, open 24 hours, offers typical coffee-shop fare.

Amenities: Limited room service via Ellis Island, free airport transfer, casino (actually located next door at Ellis Island; race book and 50 slot/poker/21 machines), small pool/sundeck and adjoining whirlpool, car-rental desk, coin-op washers/dryers.

6 Downtown

EXPENSIVE

✪ **Golden Nugget.** 129 E. Fremont St. (at Casino Center Blvd.), Las Vegas, NV 89101. ☎ **800/634-3454** or 702/385-7111. Fax 702/386-8362. www.mirageresorts.com. 1,907 units. A/C TV TEL. $49–$299 double; $275–$500 suite. Extra person $20. AE, CB, DC, DISC, MC, V. Free parking (self and valet).

The Golden Nugget opened in 1946, the first building in Las Vegas constructed specifically for casino gambling. Steve Wynn took it over as his first major project in Vegas, in 1973. He gradually transformed the Old West/Victorian interiors (typical for downtown) into something more high-rent. The whole package seems considerably more resortlike and genuinely luxurious, especially for Downtown.

Accommodations Downtown

California Hotel/
Casino & RV Park **3**

El Cortez Hotel
& Casino **8**

Fitzgeralds Casino
Holiday Inn **7**

Four Queens **6**

Golden Nugget **4**

Jackie Gaughan's
Plaza Hotel/Casino **2**

Lady Luck Casino Hotel **5**

Main Street Station **1**

If the decor of the Mirage sounded appealing to you and you want to stay Downtown, come here, since the same people own them and the rooms look almost identical.

Dining: Hotel restaurants include the **California Pizza Kitchen** and the **Carson Street Cafe.**

Amenities: 24-hour room service, shoe shine, concierge, casino, car-rental desk, full-service unisex hair salon, shops (gifts, jewelry, designer fashions, sportswear, logo items), video-game arcade, swimming pool, health club.

MODERATE

✪ **Fitzgeralds Casino Holiday Inn.** 301 Fremont St. (at 3rd St.), Las Vegas, NV 89101. ☎ **800/274-LUCK** or 702/388-2400. Fax 702/388-2181. 652 units. A/C TV TEL. $40–$85 double; $60–$105 suite. Extra person $10. Children under 19 stay free in parents' room. AE, CB, DC, DISC, MC, V. Free parking (self and valet).

Fitzgeralds recently became a Holiday Inn franchise and has upgraded all its rooms to fit said chain's code. The result is attractive and received an award for Best Redesign from the Governor's Conference. Fitzgeralds has the only balcony in Downtown from which you can watch the Fremont Street Experience.

The look in the rooms is clean and comfortable, standard hotel room decor, done in shades of green (no, the leprechaun theme does not follow in here). Because this is the tallest building in Downtown (34 stories), you get excellent views: either snowcapped mountains, Downtown lights, or the Strip. Jacuzzi tub rooms are $20 more and are slightly larger with wrap-around windows. All rooms offer safes and 25-inch TVs with pay-movie options.

Dining: Limericks is an upscale Irish pub. There are two other restaurants, a **McDonald's,** and three casino bars.

Amenities: 24-hour room service, complimentary gaming lessons, casino, tour and show desks, car-rental desk, gift shop, jewelry shop.

✪ **Four Queens.** 202 Fremont St. (at Casino Center Blvd.), Las Vegas, NV 89101. ☎ **800/634-6045** or 702/385-4011. Fax 702/387-5122. www.savenet.com/702/4queen.htm. 700 units. A/C TV TEL. $29–$179 double; $119–$350 suite. Extra person $15. AE, CB, DC, DISC, MC, V. Free parking (self and valet).

Opened in 1966 with a mere 120 rooms, the Four Queens (named for the owner's four daughters) has evolved over the decades into a major Downtown property occupying an entire city block. You just know you are in old Las Vegas. And are glad. As the staff says, this is the place to stay if you just want to gamble.

Notably nice rooms, decorated in basic hotel room style, are located in 19-story twin towers. Especially lovely are the North Tower rooms, decorated in a Southwestern motif and, in most cases, offering views of the Fremont Street Experience. Some rooms are equipped with small refrigerators and coffeemakers.

Dining: Hugo's Cellar is the best of the Four Queens' offerings.

Amenities: 24-hour room service, gift shop, car-rental desk, tour and show desks, small video-game arcade, plus a basic workout room that is free.

INEXPENSIVE

California Hotel/Casino & RV Park. 12 Ogden Ave. (at 1st St.), Las Vegas, NV 89101. ☎ **800/634-6255** or 702/385-1222. Fax 702/388-2660. 855 units. A/C TV TEL. Sun–Thurs $50 double; Fri–Sat $60, holidays $70. Extra person $5. Children 12 and under stay free in parents' room. AE, CB, DC, DISC, MC, V. Free parking (self and valet).

This is a hotel with a unique personality. California-themed, it markets mostly in Hawaii, and since 85% of the guests are from the "Aloha State," it offers Hawaiian entrees in several of its restaurants and even has an on-premises store specializing in Hawaiian foodstuff.

The rooms, however, reflect neither California nor Hawaii. Decorated in contemporary-look burgundy/mauve or apricot/teal color schemes, they have mahogany furnishings and attractive marble bathrooms. In-room safes are a plus, and TVs offer pay-per-view movies and keno channels.

Dining: Restaurants include **Redwood Bar and Grill,** the **Pasta Pirate,** and the rather charming **Market Street Café.**

Amenities: Room service (breakfast only), casino, car-rental desk, car wash, small rooftop pool, small video-game arcade, shops (gift shop, chocolates). A food store carries items popular with Hawaiians.

El Cortez Hotel & Casino. 600 Fremont St. (between 6th and 7th sts.), Las Vegas, NV 89101. ☎ **800/634-6703** or 702/385-5200. 428 units. A/C TV TEL. $32 double; $40 minisuite. Extra person $3. AE, CB, DC, DISC, JCB, MC, V. Free parking (self and valet).

This small hotel is popular with locals for its casual, "just folks" downtown atmosphere and its frequent big-prize lotteries. The nicest accommodations are the enormous minisuites in the newer, 14-story tower. Some are exceptionally large king-bedded rooms with sofas; others have separate sitting areas with sofas, armchairs, and tables, plus small dressing areas. The rooms in the original building are furnished more traditionally and with less flair, and they cost less. There are two restaurants.

On-premises facilities include a small video-game arcade, beauty salon, gift shop, and barbershop.

Jackie Gaughan's Plaza Hotel/Casino. 1 Main St. (at Fremont St.), Las Vegas, NV 89101. ☎ **800/634-6575** or 702/386-2110. Fax 702/386-2378. 1,037 units. A/C TV TEL. $40–$120 double; $80–$150 suite. Extra person $8. Children under 12 stay free in parents' room. AE, DC, DISC, MC, V. Free parking (self and valet).

Built in 1971 on the site of the old Union Pacific Railroad Depot, the Plaza, a double-towered, 3-block-long property, permanently altered the downtown skyline. Las Vegas's Amtrak station (currently unused) is right in the hotel, and the main Greyhound terminal adjoins it. Fremont Street literally ends right at the Plaza's front door, so you can't fault the location.

Accommodations are spacious and attractively decorated, with king rooms offering plush sofas. The suites in particular are huge, and the two-bedroom would be a terrific option for a large party of friends to share. Rooms in the North Tower look down on the Fremont Street Experience.

Dining: The **Center Stage Restaurant** offers fabulous views of Glitter Gulch and the Fremont Street Experience.

Amenities: Guest-services desk (also handles in-house shows), tour desk, casino, car-rental desk, shops, wedding chapel, beauty salon/barbershop, swimming pool, quarter-mile outdoor jogging track, and four Har-Tru tennis courts.

Lady Luck Casino Hotel. 206 N. 3rd St. (at Ogden Ave.), Las Vegas, NV 89101. ☎ **800/523-9582** or 702/477-3000. Fax 702/382-2346. www. lady-luck.com. 792 units. A/C TV TEL. $40–$155 double; Sun–Thurs $55–$75 junior suite, Fri–Sat $70–$105. Extra person $8. AE, CB, DC, DISC, JCB, MC, V. Free parking (self and valet).

Lady Luck opened in 1964 as a five-employee casino, but now is a major downtown player taking up an entire city block. What it retains from earlier times is a friendly atmosphere, one that has kept customers coming back for decades. Eighty percent of Lady Luck's clientele is repeat business.

Tower rooms are larger, brighter, and lighter than you might expect (though again, a variation on familiar hotel room decor). Rooms also have full-length mirrors. The bathroom amenities come in a red plastic, heart-shaped container. All rooms are equipped with small refrigerators and TVs with pay-per-view movie options. The original Garden Rooms are a little smaller and less spiffy-looking in terms of decor; on the plus side, they're right by the pool, which is not heated (but there aren't a lot of pools in the Downtown area).

Dining: Restaurants include the **Burgundy Room** and **Marco Polo.**

Amenities: 24-hour room service, multilingual front desk, complimentary airport shuttle, casino, tour and show desks, car-rental desk, gift shop, unheated swimming pool, and sundeck.

✪ **Main Street Station.** 200 N. Main St. (between Fremont St. and I-95), Las Vegas, NV 89101. ☎ **800/465-0711** or 702/387-1896. Fax 702/386-4466. 406 units. A/C TV TEL. Sun–Thurs $45 double, Fri–Sat $55, holidays and conventions $65. AE, CB, DC, DISC, MC, V. Free parking (valet and self).

Though not actually on Fremont Street, the Main Street Station is just two short blocks away, barely a 3-minute walk. Considering how terrific it is, this is hardly an inconvenience. In our opinion, this is one of the nicest hotels in Downtown and one of the best bargains in the city. The overall look is, admittedly as usual for Downtown, turn-of-the-century San Francisco. Outside, gas lamps flicker on wrought-iron railings and stained-glass windows. Inside are hammered tin ceilings, ornate antique-style chandeliers, and lazy ceiling fans. The small lobby is filled with wood panels, long wooden benches, and a front desk straight out of the Old West with an old-timey key cabinet with beveled glass windows. Even the cashier cages look like antique brass bank teller's cages. Over the casino bar, rattan blade fans rotate horizontally rather than vertically. It's all very Victorian, and even though faux it feels authentic. It's also incredibly appealing and just plain pretty.

The long and narrow rooms are possibly the largest in Downtown. The simple but not unattractive furniture is vaguely French provincial, done in medium-tone neutrals. It's all clean and in good taste. It should be noted that rooms on the north side overlook the freeway, and the railroad track is nearby. The soundproofing seems quite strong—we couldn't hear anything when inside. A few guests have complained about noise in these rooms, but the majority have had no problems. If you are concerned, request a room on the south side. Each room has Nintendo for a charge and movies for free.

Dining: The excellent buffet is described in chapter 5. There are two other restaurants, including a cigar club.

Amenities: Dry cleaning and laundry service, in-room massage, safety-deposit boxes, casino, gift shop, show desk, shopping and game room arcade at California Hotel accessible via connecting walkway.

5

Dining

*A*mong the many images that people have of Las Vegas is cheap food deals, bargains so good the food is practically free. They think of the buffets, all a small country can eat, only $3.99!

All that is true, but frankly, eating in Las Vegas is no longer something you don't have to worry about budgeting for. The buffets are certainly there—no good hotel would be without one—as are the cheap meal deals, but you get what you pay for. Some of the cheaper buffets, and even the more moderately priced ones, are mediocre at best, ghastly and inedible at worst. And we don't even want to think about those 69¢ cup of beef stew specials.

As for quality restaurants, little by little they have been sneaking into Las Vegas. Wolfgang Puck's **Spago** and **Chinois,** Emeril Lagasse's **Emeril's New Orleans Fish House** (serving stunning Creole seafood), **Gatsby's** (the MGM Grand's gourmet restaurant, which even hard-core foodie snobs say serves some of the best food they've ever eaten), and Mark Miller's **Coyote Cafe** all would be standouts in any other major city. Reliable small chains such as **Lawry's** and **Il Fornaio** have crept in during the last year. The **Enigma Cafe,** located in the slowly burgeoning Gateway artists' district (right between the Strip and Downtown, so it's accessible to both), offers up healthful, interesting food at prices comparable to some of the best hotel meal deals in town.

There are tricks to surviving dining in Vegas. If you can, make reservations in advance, particularly for the better restaurants. Eat as often as you can during off hours, which admittedly are hard to find. But you know that noon to, say, 1:30 or 2pm is going to be prime for lunch, and 5:30 to 8:30pm (and just after the early shows get out) for dinner. And give yourself plenty of time, particularly if you have to catch a show.

1 Best Bets

- **Best All-Around:** It's a toss-up between **Gatsby's** (☎ 702/ 891-7337) and **Emeril's** (☎ 702/891-7374), both located on the South Strip in the MGM Grand, and both of which vie for the unofficial "Best Restaurant in Vegas" title. Emeril's features Creole seafood, while Gatsby's is nouvelle and slightly Asian-influenced. Both are superb dining experiences.

- **Best Buffet:** For the Strip, it's **The Mirage** (☎ 702/791-7111). Not at all the cheapest in town, but the quality goes up accordingly. Downtown, the new **Main Street Station,** 200 N. Main St. (☎ 702/387-1896), has an incredible buffet; all live-action stations, wood-fired brick oven pizzas, fresh lovely salsas and guacamole in the Mexican section, and better than average desserts. Nowhere else in Downtown comes even close.

- **Best Sunday Champagne Brunch:** It's Mid-Strip's **Bally's** lavish **Sterling Sunday Brunch** (☎ 702/739-4111), where display tables embellished with floral arrangements and ice sculptures are laden with everything from mounds of fresh shrimp to sushi and sashimi, and fancy entrees include the likes of roast duckling with black-currant and blueberry sauce.

- **Best Graveyard Dinner Deal:** Downtown, **Binion's Horseshoe,** 128 E. Fremont St., at Casino Center Boulevard (☎ 702/382-1600), offers a complete New York steak dinner served with potato, roll, and salad for just $3 from 10pm to 5:45am.

- **Best Cheap Breakfast:** Make your first stop of the day at the South Strip's **Cyclone Coffee Shop,** 3750 Las Vegas Blvd. S., at the Holiday Inn Casino Boardwalk, where a $1.29 breakfast includes two eggs, bacon or sausage, hash browns, and toast. It's served around the clock.

- **Best Spot for a Romantic Dinner:** In Mid-Strip, the Rio's warmly elegant **Fiore** (☎ 702/252-7702), with its gorgeous interior and arched windows overlooking the palm-fringed pool, is the most simpatico setting for a leisurely romantic dinner. Brilliant cuisine, a great wine cellar, and superb service combine to create a memorable evening.

- **Best Spot for a Celebration:** On the South Strip at the Tropicana, **Mizuno's** (☎ 702/739-2713) teppanyaki grills are ideal for small parties, with the chef's theatrics comprising a tableside show. Additionally, the elegant **Gatsby's** (see above) with its superlative food would make a fine spot for a wedding supper.

- **Best Free Show at Dinner:** At Treasure Island's **Buccaneer Bay Club** (☎ 702/894-7350) everyone rushes to the window when the ship battle begins.

- **Best Wine List:** The distinguished cellar at **Gatsby's** (see above) houses 600 wines in all price ranges and has a friendly master sommelier on hand to guide you in your selections. Trust him; he knows his stuff.
- **Best View:** See all of Las Vegas from the revolving **Top of the World** (☎ 702/380-7711), at the Stratosphere, North Strip, 106 stories up.
- **Best California Cuisine:** Wolfgang Puck's **Spago** (☎ 702/369-6300) didn't invent California cuisine (or did it?) but it might as well have. Find it Mid-Strip at Caesars.
- **Best Chinese Cuisine: Chin's,** 3200 Las Vegas Blvd. S. (☎ 702/733-8899), where piano bar music enhances an ambience of low-key elegance, offers scrumptious and authentic Cantonese fare, including some original creations such as deep-fried battered chicken served with strawberry sauce and fresh strawberries.
- **Best Deli:** The **Stage Deli** (☎ 702/893-4045) in Caesars will give no cause for complaints. You might also try the new deli in **New York New York,** which has been winning raves.
- **Best Healthy/Veggie Conscious:** The **Enigma Cafe,** 918¹/₂ S. 4th St. (☎ 702/386-0999), in the Gateway District, which makes it convenient for both the Strip and Downtown, offers a large selection of really cheap sandwiches, salads, and smoothies, all fresh and interesting.
- **Best Italian Cuisine:** The chain **Il Fornaio** (☎ 702/650-6500) in New York New York is the best for a moderately priced meal, and **Fiore** (see above) in the Rio for something quite a bit more dear.
- **Best New Orleans Cuisine:** One of Las Vegas's newest celebrity chef venues, **Emeril's New Orleans Fish House** (see above) at the MGM Grand offers total authenticity combined with culinary brilliance.
- **Best Southwestern Cuisine:** The fact that it's the only notable Southwestern restaurant in town doesn't make the MGM Grand's **Coyote Cafe** (☎ 702/891-7349) any less impressive. Superstar Santa Fe chef Mark Miller brings contemporary culinary panache to traditional Southwestern cookery, and the results are spicy and spectacular.
- **Best Steak and Seafood: Lawry's The Prime Rib,** 4043 Howard Hughes Pkwy. (☎ 702/893-2223), has such good prime rib, it's hard to ever imagine having any better.

2   South Strip

VERY EXPENSIVE

❂ **Coyote Cafe.** The MGM Grand, 3799 Las Vegas Blvd. S. ☎ **702/ 891-7349.** Reservations recommended for the Grill Room, not accepted for the Cafe. Grill Room main courses $15–$32. Cafe main courses $7.50–$17.50 (many are under $10). AE, CB, DC, DISC, JCB, MC, V. Grill Room daily 5:30– 10pm. Cafe daily 7:30am–11pm. SOUTHWESTERN.

In a town where restaurant cuisine often seems stuck in a 1950s time warp, Mark Miller's Coyote Cafe evokes howls of delight. His robust regional cuisine combines elements of traditional Mexican, Native American, Creole, and Cajun cookery with cutting-edge culinary trends. The main dining room is fronted by a lively cafe/bar, in which an exhibition-cooking area houses a *cazuela* (casserole) oven and *comal* grill under a gleaming ceramic tile hood. The adobe-walled Grill Room offers a more tranquil setting.

The Grill Room menu changes monthly. If you're lucky, you might find the heavenly "painted soup"—half garlicky black bean, half beer-infused smoked Cheddar—"painted" with chipotle cream and garnished with salsa fresca and de árbol chili powder. A reliable main course is the salmon fillet crusted with ground pumpkin seeds and corn tortillas topped with roasted chile/ pumpkin-seed sauce and presented on a bed of spinach-wrapped spaghetti squash studded with pine nuts, corn kernels, scallions, and morsels of sun-dried tomato. Desserts include chocolate banana torte served on banana crème anglaise and topped with a scoop of vanilla ice cream. The wine list includes many by-the-glass selections, including champagnes and sparkling wines, which nicely complement spicy Southwestern fare; Brazilian daiquiris are a house specialty.

The Cafe menu offers similar but somewhat lighter fare. Southwestern breakfasts ($6 to $9.50) range from *huevos rancheros* to blue-corn pancakes with toasted pine nuts, honey butter, and real maple syrup

❂ **Emeril's New Orleans Fish House.** The MGM Grand, 3799 Las Vegas Blvd. S. ☎ **702/891-7374.** Reservations suggested. Main courses $12–$18 lunch, $18–$28 dinner (more for lobster). AE, CB, DC, DISC, MC, V. Daily 11am–3pm, 5:30–10:30pm. CONTEMPORARY CREOLE.

Tucked into an almost unseen corner of the MGM Grand is one of the very finest restaurants in the city. Chef Emeril Lagasse of New Orleans's Emeril's and NOLA (and an extremely popular TV chef on cable's Food Network) has brought his cuisine to town. The restaurant's quiet and comforting decor provides the stage for creative, exciting, "BAM!" food.

Although Lagasse caters to the tastes of everyone from poultry lovers to vegetarians, seafood is the specialty here, flown in from Louisiana or from anywhere he finds the quality of the ingredients to be the very finest. We started off with the most recent edition of Lagasse's legendary savory "cheesecakes," the Lobster Cheesecake with tomato-tarragon coulis, topped with a dollop of succulent Louisiana choupique caviar. It's a heady, rich appetizer that may be completely unlike anything you've ever had. Oysters on the half-shell are also a favorite, served with two tangy dipping sauces. And try the barbecue shrimp, which come in a garlic herb butter sauce that will have you mopping your plate with bread.

Our entrees did not fail to elicit a "Wow!" from everyone at the table. A Creole-seasoned seared ahi steak was stuffed with Hudson Valley foie gras and served in a bed of Lagasse's famous "smashed" potatoes, creamy and rich, with roasted shallots and a part-shallot reduction—absolutely luxurious. A medley of seafood, from caviar to shrimp to mussels and clams, came over pasta in a delicious and very spicy broth. And in a dish that bordered on the sinful, there was a marvelously seasoned filet mignon stuffed with a crawfish dressing and topped with Bordelaise sauce with crawfish tails and sliced andouille sausage. Meat eaters will also be very happy with the utterly tender and flavorful filet of beef with tasso Hollandaise sauce and homemade Worcestershire.

It would be difficult to recommend one particular dessert from the vast menu since they're all fabulous, but if it's your first visit, a slice of the Banana Cream Pie with banana crust and caramel drizzle is one of the finest desserts you will ever have. And if your capacity for rich food is depleted by the end of your meal, there's a trio of house-made sorbets, which provide a lovely finish to your meal without necessarily pushing you over the edge of the abyss. If you're feeling adventurous, don't miss the Chef's Degustation, a seven-course tasting menu. It usually features smaller portions (thank heavens) of the most exciting dishes from the regular menu, plus some specials of the evening.

✪ **Gatsby's.** The MGM Grand, 3799 Las Vegas Blvd. S. ☎ **702/891-7337.** Reservations suggested. Jackets suggested for men. Main courses $29–$58. Degustation (tasting) menu $75, $95 with selected wines accompanying each course. AE, CB, DC, DISC, MC, V. Wed–Mon open at 6pm, last seating at 9:30pm. EURASIAN.

Restaurants
All Star Café ❷
Country Star ❶
Coyote Café ❺
Emeril's New Orleans
  Fish House ❺
Gatsby's ❺

Mizuno's ❼
Monte Carlo Pub
  & Brewery ❸
Motown Café ❹
Rain Forest Café
  (in MGM Grand) ❺
Wolfgang Puck Café ❺

Buffets
Excalibur's Round Table Buffet ❻
Luxor Pharoah's Pheast Buffet ❽
Tropicana Island Buffet ❼

This is a very expensive restaurant, but on par with the swankiest establishments in more food-oriented cities. Gatsby's chef de cuisine, Terence Fong, has quite a conundrum to solve: How do you please the generally food-conservative Las Vegas customer and offer an innovative, exciting dining experience that invigorates everyone involved? Provide the expected but don't let it dictate preparation; combine familiar ingredients with more unusual ones to subtly educate the unadventurous; use only fresh, lovely, seasonal items. This means, for example, that Fong's lobster bisque, a rich soup you'll find on many a local menu, presented here with perhaps two lumps of divinely sweet meat and a few bites of equally sugar-rich roasted corn, awakens one to the difference between the ordinary and the extraordinary. It means starting with aromatic yet familiar jasmine and basmati rice, but adding toasted orzo, wheat berries, and quinoa (a rather trendy but very healthful and tasty grain) to produce a delicious confetti of flavors rather than a safe side dish. It means that the gracious wait staff brings unexpected treats to tease diners into anticipation, such as tiny cilantro crepe purses of beluga caviar and vodka crème fraîche, or perfectly smoked salmon on 50¢-sized blini.

Anything from this kitchen that includes foie gras is worth ordering. This delicacy might show up on the menu in more than one guise, accompanied with pan-roasted stuffed quail and a lentil-corn salad, or with Perigourd truffles and organic greens dressed in a port wine vinaigrette. Maine lobster might be simply sautéed and served with lobster-ginger butter to gild the already sumptuous meat; ahi tuna gets an Asian preparation with a sesame seed crust and a spicy wasabi butter. Fans of exotic meats, or anyone curious to try ostrich or buffalo, are in the right place. The grilled domestic ostrich, bathed in a red wine-shallot reduction and served with wild mushroom risotto, is a lovely dish, tender and not the least bit gamy. Duck is well treated here, as well. It's slow roasted, so the slices are as tender and lean as possible, garnished with an Asian-style sauce and pretty little vegetables. Vegetarians will find dinner just as lush. Along with the chef's vegetable plate, replete with couscous or risotto or that wonderful rice confetti and lots of recently plucked delicacies, vegetable broth-based soups, a couple of salads, and appetizers such as the vegetable spring rolls will profoundly satisfy your appetite and expectations.

It's painful to recall the dessert menu, living so far from the source. Melanie Bonnano, the pastry chef, takes great delight in whimsical presentations like a Cup of Java, a treat that fulfills coffee and chocolate lovers on a number of levels. Her coffee-and-cream granita-laden chocolate cup will have you examining your freezer in a new light. Soufflés available in five flavors are a house specialty, but chocolate cake mysteriously filled with fresh raspberries and wrapped in filo pastry is a feast for the eyes and tongue.

Everything, from the lavish crackers and bread to the sorbets presented in the center of ice flowers, is made in-house. It's also possible to request a special tasting menu ($75), which will truly give you a sense of the restaurant's possibilities. For an extra $30, the enthusiastic sommelier will pair wines from the luxuriously stocked cellar with each course.

EXPENSIVE

Mizuno's. Tropicana Resort and Casino, 3801 Las Vegas Blvd. S. ☎ **702/ 739-2713.** Reservations suggested. Full Samurai dinners mostly $15–$20, Shogun combination dinners $25–$39. AE, CB, DC, DISC, MC, V. Daily 5–10:30pm. JAPANESE.

This stunning, marble-floored restaurant is filled with authentic Japanese artifacts. A meandering glass "stream" is lit by tiny twinkling lights to suggest running water, and cut-glass dividers are etched with graceful cherry blossoms, irises, and plum trees. Food is prepared at marble teppanyaki grill tables where you're seated with other patrons. This being Las Vegas, the chef's dazzling display of dexterity is enhanced by a flashing light show over the grill.

Entrees comprised of tasty morsels of New York strip steak, filet mignon, shrimp, lobster, chicken, or shrimp and vegetable tempura, and various combinations of the above, come with miso soup or consommé (get the tastier miso), salad with ginger dressing, an array of crispy flavorful vegetables stir-fried with sesame seeds and spices, steamed rice, and tea. Though it's a lot of food, an appetizer of shrimp and mushrooms sautéed in garlic butter with lemon soy sauce merits consideration. And a bottle of warm sake is recommended. Ginger or red bean ice cream make for a fittingly light dessert. A great bargain here: a full early-bird dinner served from 5 to 6pm for just $10.

MODERATE

See also the listing for **Coyote Cafe** (p. 63), an expensive restaurant fronted by a more moderately priced cafe.

All Star Cafe. 3785 Las Vegas Blvd. S. (at Tropicana Ave. in the Showcase Mall, right next to the MGM Grand). ☎ **702/795-8326.** Reservations accepted. Main courses $6–$18. AE, DC, DISC, JCB, MC, V. Sun–Thurs 11am–midnight, Fri–Sat 11am–1am. AMERICAN.

This is the sports theme restaurant, filled with memorabilia from hundreds of different sports legends, covering just about every sport you can imagine. Buffs should be pleased. The co-owners are Vegas resident Andre Agassi, Monica Seles, Wayne Gretzky, Ken Griffey Jr., Joe Montana, Shaquille O'Neal, and Tiger Woods. The menu is "All American" and includes pasta specialties, salads, and the usual hamburgers and hot dogs.

Country Star. 3724 Las Vegas Blvd. S. (at Harmon Ave.) ☎ **702/740-8400.** Reservations for large parties only. Main courses $6–$22 (most under $14). AE, MC, V. Sun–Thurs 11am–10pm, Fri–Sat 11am–11pm. BARBECUE/ SOUTHWESERN.

This would be the country music entry, attempting to cash in on the success of the Hard Rock. Restaurant principals include Reba McEntire and Vince Gill. It's more low key and friendly than, say, Hard Rock or Planet Hollywood. Dozens of video monitors, including several embedded in the entranceway floor, play nonstop C&W music videos. The food here is pretty good and the barbecue sauce is terrific (bottles are on the tables).

Motown Cafe. New York New York Hotel, 3790 Las Vegas Blvd. S. ☎ **702/ 740-6440.** Reservations not accepted. Main courses $7–$18. AE, DISC, JCB, MC, V. Sun–Thurs 7:30am–11:30pm, Fri–Sat 7:30am–2am. SOUTHWESTERN.

The menu at this tribute to Motown record label artists features light Southern cuisine (jambalaya, shrimp Creole) probably because no one could figure out what the indigenous cuisine of Detroit was. (This is in addition to the basic burgers and so forth). They also offer a breakfast buffet. And as we all know, Motown music is just about the best there is for dancing, so the Cafe stays open for dancing until 3am on weekdays and 4am on weekends.

Rain Forest Cafe. MGM Grand, 3799 Las Vegas Blvd. S. ☎ **702/891-8580.** Reservations not required. Main courses $9–$13 breakfast, $10-19 dinner. AE, DC, DISC, JCB, MC, V. Mon–Thurs 7am–midnight, Fri–Sat 7am–1am, Sun 7am–11pm. CALIFORNIA.

If you've always wanted to eat a meal in the Jungle Cruise ride at Disneyland, here's your chance. Decor-wise, this is possibly the best of the many theme restaurants in town. It's full of faux foliage, flowers, giant butterflies, and so forth. The food is tasty and imaginative, if somewhat busy variations on the usual pastas, sandwiches, and whatnot. The veggie burgers did earn serious raves from connoisseurs. Kids will love the sights and the children's menu. You won't love trying to steer them through the gift shop entrance.

✪ **Wolfgang Puck Café.** MGM Grand, 3799 Las Vegas Blvd. S. ☎ **702/ 895-9653.** Reservations not accepted. Main courses $9–$15. AE, DC, MC, V. Sun–Thurs 8am–11pm, Fri–Sat 8am–midnight. CALIFORNIA.

A brightly colored riot of mosaic tiles and other experiments in geometric design, the Wolfgang Puck Café stands out in the MGM Grand. It's more or less Spago Lite: downscaled salads, pizzas, and pastas, all showing the Puck hand, and while perhaps a little more money than your average cafe, the food is comparably better, if sometimes not *that* special. However, it's all very fresh nouvelle cuisine, which makes a nice change of pace. The specialty pizzas are fun; constructed on crusts topped with fontina and mozzarella cheeses, they're brushed with pesto and layered with embellishments such as spicy jalapeño-marinated sautéed chicken, leeks, and cilantro. (And no, it's not just like eating the Puck brand sold in the frozen food section.) It's always a thrill to get a good salad in Vegas, and there are quite a few on this menu. Worth noting is the signature Chinois chicken salad tossed with crispy fried wontons, julienned carrots, cabbage, and green onions in a Chinese honey-mustard sauce. For something cheap, try the surprisingly large baby greens salad with the goat cheese toast—that and the very fine herb bread (that comes gratis) is $5, which fills you up in a fairly healthy way for not a lot of money. Desert highlights include a caramel cheesecake, a warm chocolate soufflé, and a hot chocolate truffle cake with chocolate sauce. There does tend to be a line, particularly after EFX lets out just across the casino.

INEXPENSIVE

Monte Carlo Pub & Brewery. Monte Carlo Resort, 3770 Las Vegas Blvd. S. (between Flamingo Rd. and Tropicana Ave.) ☎ **702/730-7777.** Reservations not accepted. Main courses $6–$8. AE, CB, DC, DISC, MC, V. Sun–Thurs 11am–1am, Fri–Sat 11am–3am. PUB FARE.

This is a favorite lunch spot and after-work hangout for local businesspeople. A working microbrewery (you can view the copper holding tanks and vats through large windows), it has a high-ceilinged warehouse/industrial interior, with exposed-brick and rusty corrugated-tin walls, track lighting, and a network of exposed pipes overhead. An ornate mahogany backbar with beveled mirrors adds a note of elegance. The Pub is cigar-friendly (maintaining a humidor), and rock videos blare forth from a large screen and 40 TV monitors around the room.

The menu features somewhat sophisticated versions of pub fare, doled out in enormous portions. We like the pizza topped with lamb, grilled eggplant, and goat cheese. Other choices include penne pasta with wild mushrooms in garlic cream sauce, a sample platter of sausages served with warm potato salad and whole-grain mustard, sandwiches, burgers, and barbecued baby back ribs. A microbrew with your meal (or a sampler of five) is de rigueur. Desserts include bread pudding with butterscotch rum sauce and creamy peanut butter pie. After 9pm, only pizza is served, and dueling pianos provide dance music and entertainment.

3 Mid-Strip

VERY EXPENSIVE

Bacchanal. Caesars Palace, 3570 Las Vegas Blvd. S. (just north of Flamingo Rd.) ☎ 702/731-7110. Reservations essential. Fixed-price $69.50, plus tax and gratuity. AE, CB, DC, DISC, MC, V. Tues–Sat 6–11pm with seatings at 6, 6:30, 9, and 9:30pm. CONTINENTAL.

This is the quintessential Vegas restaurant experience, where the food is considerably less important than the spectacle. You will be expected to accept a massage from a wine goddess (the toga-clad waitresses who dispense alcohol) or Hercules, be enticed by the belly dancers, show respect and honor for Caesar and Cleopatra, and for pity's sake, eat and drink your fair share. Not for the introverted or inhibited. Giggling is allowed. Being aloof and above it all is not. The six-course meal (entree, soup, salad, pasta, crudites, and dessert) is certainly plentiful and satisfactory—but you really don't come for the food. You come for the show, the royal service, the personalized greeting by Caesar and Cleopatra, the belly dancing, and of course, the wine goddesses, who keep your glass ever full.

✪ **Buccaneer Bay Club.** Treasure Island, 3300 Las Vegas Blvd. S. ☎ **702/ 894-7350.** Reservations required. Main courses $16–$26. AE, CB, DC, DISC, JCB, MC, V. Daily 5–10:30pm. AMERICAN/CONTINENTAL.

This is a little-known gem (at least, outside of Treasure Island guests) that features a laudable menu more innovative than the standard found at other equivalent hotel restaurants. And it's certainly considerably cheaper.

A meandering layout creates a series of intimate dining nooks (perfect for quiet conversations) all done in a posh pirate theme with a low-beamed ceiling and stucco walls adorned with daggers and pistols. The whole thing overlooks the hotel's "bay" where a pirate battle is waged every 90 minutes. This probably isn't the best place to view it (the windows are smallish, and you're behind the action), but the wait staff does notify you at show time and will hold your food service until it's through if you have chosen to watch. It's fun to watch everyone rush to the windows when they announce, "Pirates are on!"

Speaking of the service, it is among the best we've experienced, with an efficient team of friendly, knowledgeable, and almost prescient servers at every table (they anticipated a woman's desire for another glass of wine before she even had finished wistfully vocalizing it).

Appetizers come in both hot (shrimp Jamaica, escargot brioche) and cold (shrimp cocktail, Parma prosciutto) varieties with the savory celery-root flan and the quail being the true standouts. Regarding the latter, it was not on the menu, so be sure to ask about specials. Favorites here are the Pheasant Charles, which comes with pan-seared, thyme-roasted wild mushroom risotto and is served in a Merlot lingonberry sauce. There's also Colorado Buffalo Prime Rib, which is roasted and grilled over mesquite wood and served with creamy horseradish potatoes. It's hard to get over the thought of eating a buffalo at first, but if you can, it'll be one of the best pieces of meat you'll ever taste. Desserts include apple binets, white

Restaurants
Bacchanal ◆
Buccaneer Bay Club ◆
Chinois ◆
Fiore ◆
The Noodle Kitchen ◆

Palace Court ◆
The Palm ◆
Planet Hollywood ◆
Spago ◆
Stage Deli ◆

Buffets
Bally's Big Kitchen Buffet ◆
Bally's Sterling Brunch Buffet ◆
Caesars Palace Palatium Buffet ◆

Flamingo Hilton Paradise Garden Buffet ◆
Mirage Buffet ◆
Rio's Carnival World Buffet ◆

chocolate cheesecake with raspberry sauce, and the house specialty apricot or harlequin (Grand Marnier, white and dark chocolate) minisoufflés.

Chinois. 3570 Las Vegas Blvd. S. (in the Forum Shops at Caesars Palace). ☎ **702/737-9700.** Reservations recommended. Main courses $11–$16.50 cafe, $19.75–$28 restaurant. AE, JCB, MC, V. Restaurant daily 6–10:30pm, cafe 11:30am–midnight. EURASIAN.

From Wolfgang Puck, the man who brought you Spago and gourmet frozen pizzas, comes another entry in the world of fine dining and innovative cuisine. Demonstrating both modern and Southwestern influences, food and decor could be called nouvelle—or would it be nuevo?—Asian. Food is served family style, which helps spread the rather high prices around some. There are specials every night, but you can count on Chinois "classics" every evening. Appetizers include Szechuan pancakes with stir-fried Peking duck, spring veggies and wild mushrooms—everything combines into one new savory taste. Always free to spend your money, we also recommend the lovely sautéed foie gras with rhubarb compote (it has a citrus zing to it) and a sauce made from port wine, figs, and spices. More budget-minded is the whole sizzling catfish, which along with a couple of appetizers will easily feed two people. The Cantonese duck with divine sesame crepes is also superb, a light, nearly perfect rendering of that difficult fowl. Skip the ordinary Mongolian lamb chops but save room for the scrumptious chocolate mint gateau dessert.

Fiore. Rio Suite Hotel, 3700 W. Flamingo Rd. (at I-15.) ☎ **702/252-7702.** Reservations recommended. Main courses $26–$48. AE, CB, DC, DISC, MC, V. Daily 5 –11pm. ITALIAN/PROVENÇALE.

Fiore offers a deliciously simpatico setting for the brilliantly innovative cuisine of chef Kolachai Ngimsangaim. We love the interior space, but it's also tempting to dine alfresco on the flower-bordered flagstone terrace (heated in winter, mist-cooled in summer).

Ngimsangaim's seasonally changing menus complement the culinary elegance of northern Italy with the earthy exuberance of southern France. For an appetizer we've had the sautéed herb-crusted prawns in a buttery mustard/anise sauce. This was followed by an entree of barbecued Atlantic salmon in honeyed hickory sauce, served with grilled polenta, portobello mushrooms, roasted roma tomatoes, and grilled asparagus spears. Fiore's thoughtful list of more than 400 wines in several price ranges is international in scope and includes 45 premium by-the-glass selections. Consult knowledgeable sommelier Barrie Larvin for suggestions. Dine slowly, and consider including a cheese course—excellent cheeses are served with seasonal fruits. But do save room for dessert—perhaps a warm chocolate torte on crème anglaise embellished with raspberry stars and chocolate hearts. In addition to an extensive listing of cognacs, ports, and dessert wines, hand-rolled cigars elegantly presented in a mahogany humidor are a postprandial option on the terrace.

✪ **Palace Court.** Caesars Palace, 3570 Las Vegas Blvd. S. (just north of Flamingo Rd.) ☎ **702/734-7110.** Reservations essential. Main courses $29–$55. AE, MC, V. Daily sittings 6, 6:30, 9, 9:30pm. FRENCH.

The Palace Court has long been considered one of the finest restaurants in town; when it went through a brief slump, foodies were disheartened. It's still not cheap, but it is back up to its original standards and is worth the expense again.

It's hard to know where to begin with the lavish menu. The delicious tuna appetizer comes with the perfect amount of ginger plus tender, paper-thin radishes. Sautéed fresh scallops, accompanied by baby asparagus, are perfect, tender with no grit, covered in a light and most mellow tarragon sauce that might have you licking your plate to get the last drop. If red snapper is offered on a special, skip it. Instead, go right to the rack of lamb with fresh goat cheese; "absolutely fabulous" was the comment that followed this amazing combo. Do consider a selection from the vast and beautifully chosen wine list.

The Palm. The Forum Shops at Caesars Palace, 3500 Las Vegas Blvd. S. ☎ **702/732-7256.** Reservations recommended. Main courses $8.50–$14 lunch, $15–$35 dinner. AE, CB, DC, MC, V. Daily 11:30am–11pm. STEAK/SEAFOOD.

A branch of the now wide-reaching venerable New York eatery, which attracts a star-studded clientele fond of the reliable, if not terribly exciting, hearty bill of fare. (The famous may also be hoping to find their faces among the many caricatures that cover the walls.) This is plain, but filling Boy food, but at Manly prices. Red-meat lovers will be happy with the high-quality steaks found here, though those on a budget will shudder in horror. The tendency is to give them a good charring, so if you don't like your meat blackened, you might want to start with it less well done, and send it back for more if necessary. If you hit a jackpot, your money will be well spent on one of the Palm's Buick-sided lobsters, utterly succulent and outrageously priced, but given their size—they start at 3 pounds—they can easily be shared. If you are worried it can't be enough, add one of the delicious appetizers (plump but high-priced shrimp cocktails, or perfect prosciutto with melon), or toss in a side of crispy deep-fried onions. Desserts are similarly heavy and unspectacular.

✪ **Spago.** The Forum Shops at Caesars Palace, 3500 Las Vegas Blvd. S. ☎ **702/369-6300.** Reservations recommended for the dining room; not accepted at the cafe. Dining room main courses $14–$28. Cafe main courses $8.50–$16.50. AE, CB, DC, DISC, JCB, MC, V. Dining room Sun–Thurs 6–10pm, Fri–Sat 5:30–10:30pm. Cafe daily 11am–midnight. AMERICAN/ASIAN.

Wolfgang Puck's landmark L.A. restaurant provides a rare foodie oasis in Vegas. However, though one of the few truly innovative restaurants in Vegas, Spago has been riding a bit on its reputation. While anything you get here is going to be better and more interesting than what you'd get at the vast majority of Vegas restaurants, you get the feeling they've been far ahead of the pack for just long enough to get comfortable. Which is not to say Spago is not worth the cost—it just means that others have caught up with them (and in some cases, though it may be considered heresy to say it, may have surpassed Puck's baby), and they are no longer the only foodie game in town.

But it's still an experience going there—call it California casual elegance. The postindustrial interior is the very model of a modern major restaurant, while the exterior cafe on the Forum Shops is more relaxed, and provides an opportunity for people watching as fine as at any European sidewalk cafe. It's probably not as star-heavy as the celebrated L.A. original, but it's safe to say that any Hollywood muck-a-muck in town would probably be inclined to eat here.

When Nomi Malone, who appeared in the film *Showgirls,* came to eat at the cafe, she peevishly said she didn't "know what any of this stuff is." She must not get out much; the cafe menu features such familiar items as meat loaf and pizza, although glamorized versions—this isn't Country Kitchen, and so this pizza features smoked salmon. Not to mention crème fraîche. It sounds like an unholy hybrid of Italian and deli, but it's sublime. Other cafe specialties include Puck's signature Chinois chicken salad and a superb mesquite-fried salmon served with a tangy toss of soba noodles and cashews in a coconut-sesame-chili paste vinaigrette nuanced with lime juice and Szechuan mustard. The inside menu changes seasonally; examples of potential choices include scallops with a divine basil risotto, an appetizer of tuna sashimi in hot olive oil and sesame, or porcini mushrooms with a truffle sauce. The "signature" dish is a Chinese-style duck, moist but with a perfectly crispy skin. It's about as good as duck gets. It is served with a doughy steamed bun and Chinese vegetables. Desserts range from fresh fruit sorbets in surprising flavors (cantaloupe, honeydew), to a luscious brownie topped with homemade chocolate, whipped cream, and ice cream. The wine list is impressive, but the house wine was a disappointment and possibly not worth the cost.

MODERATE

See also the listing for **Spago** and **Chinois** (both above), expensive restaurants fronted by more moderately priced cafes.

The Noodle Kitchen. Mirage, 3400 Las Vegas Blvd. S. (between Flamingo Rd. and Sands Ave.) ☎ **800/456-4564.** Reservations not accepted. Main courses $8–$22.75 (many under $10). AE, CB, DC, DISC, MC, V. Daily 11am–4am. CHINESE.

The Mirage designed The Noodle Kitchen to serve its sizable clientele of Asian high rollers, a clientele desirous of authentic, non-Americanized Chinese fare. Most of the diners here are Asian, but American and European food aficionados will also appreciate the Kitchen's high-quality cuisine. It's really not so much a separate establishment as a section of the hotel's lushly tropical Caribe Café.

Start off with clear soup, flavored with Chinese cilantro and replete with thin egg noodles and dumplings filled with minced shrimp and ear mushrooms. A combination plate of soy chicken slices, roast pork, and tender crisp-skinned roast duck with plum sauce makes a marvelous entree choice, especially when accompanied by delicious al dente steamed vegetables (Chinese broccoli or choy sum) in oyster sauce. If you like to spice things up, you'll find three hot sauces on the table. There are Asian desserts (such as red bean ice delight), but as these are an acquired taste, you might prefer fresh-baked cakes and pies from the Caribe Café menu. Or skip dessert altogether in favor of sweet Vietnamese iced coffee mixed with condensed milk, coconut milk, and shaved ice. All bar drinks, including Chinese and Japanese beers, are available.

Planet Hollywood. Forum Shops at Caesars Palace, 3500 Las Vegas Blvd. S. ☎ **702/791-STAR.** Reservations not accepted. Main courses $8–$20 (most under $13). AE, DC, MC, V. Sun–Thurs 11am–midnight, Fri–Sat 11am–1am. CALIFORNIA.

Arnold, Sly, Bruce, and Demi joined forces with some finance buddies to create a movie version of the Hard Rock. It was an instant success and a sure sign of the decline of Western civilization. Some of the objects displayed are worthless, others are sort of amusing—Barbara Eden's genie bottle, chariot wheels from *Ben Hur,* the side of beef Stallone sparred with in Rocky, the *Star Trek* control tower. Video monitors are everywhere. Further reluctant credit is given for the more imaginative- than average-theme restaurant menu: blackened shrimp served with Creole mustard sauce; linguine tossed with Thai shrimp, peanuts, and julienned vegetables in spicy sweet chili sauce; white chocolate bread pudding drenched in whiskey sauce and topped with white chocolate ice cream.

Stage Deli. Forum Shops at Caesars Palace, 3500 Las Vegas Blvd. S. ☎ **702/ 893-4045.** Reservations accepted for large parties only. Main courses $10–$14, sandwiches $6–$14. AE, DC, DISC, JCB, MC, V. Sun–Thurs 7:30am–10:30pm, Fri–Sat 7:30am–midnight. DELI.

This is a branch of the New York City institution, which has been slapping pastrami on rye for more than half a century. The deli is often not crowded. In addition to being handy for Caesars guests, if you are staying next door at the Mirage, it's easy to pop over, making it a satisfying breakfast alternative to often overcrowded, overpriced, and not very good hotel joints in the area. The huge (we mean it) menu means finding something for even the pickiest of eaters.

Most of the fare—including fresh-baked pumpernickel and rye, meats, chewy bagels, lox, spicy deli mustard, and pickles—comes in daily from New York. The Stage dishes up authentic 5-inch-high sandwiches stuffed with pastrami, corned beef, brisket, or chopped liver. Maybe overstuffed is a better description. Unless you have a hearty appetite, are feeding two, or have a fridge in your room for leftovers, you might want to try the half sandwich and soup or salad combos. Other specialties here include matzo ball soup, knishes, kasha varnishkes, cheese blintzes, kreplach, pirogen, and smoked fish platters accompanied by bagels and cream cheese. Or you might prefer a full meal consisting of pot roast and gravy, salad, homemade dinner rolls, potato pancakes, and fresh vegetables. Desserts run the gamut from rugelach cheesecake to Hungarian-style apple strudel, and available beverages include wine and beer, milk shakes, Dr. Brown's sodas, and chocolate egg creams.

4   North Strip

VERY EXPENSIVE

The Monte Carlo Room. Desert Inn, 3145 Las Vegas Blvd. S. (between Desert Inn Rd. and Sands Ave.) ☎ **702/733-4444.** Reservations recommended. Jackets for men required. Main courses $28–$80. AE, CB, DC, DISC, JCB, MC, V. Thurs–Mon 6–11pm. FRENCH.

The delightful Monte Carlo Room is equally renowned for its sub-lime setting and fine French cuisine. Excellent appetizer choices include seafood ravioli with champagne-caviar sauce or a terrine of fresh goose liver. We also love the thick, velvety, cognac-laced lobster bisque, full of rich flavor, served in a scooped-out round loaf of bread. For your entree, consider a classic French entrecôte au poivre or duck à l'orange served with apple- and pine nut–studded wild rice. A mélange of vegetables and a potato dish (perhaps pommes soufflés) accompany entrees. There's an extensive wine list; consultthe sommelier for suggestions. Flaming tableside preparations are a specialty, including desserts such as crêpes Suzette and cherries jubilee.

Top of the World. Stratosphere Las Vegas Hotel, 2000 Las Vegas Blvd. S. (between St. Louis St. and Baltimore Ave.) ☎ **702/380-7711.** Reservations required. Main courses $13–$21 lunch, $21–$29 dinner. AE, CB, DC, DISC, JCB, MC, V. Daily 11am–3:45pm; Sun–Thurs 4–11pm, Fri–Sat 4pm–midnight. AMERICAN/CONTINENTAL.

Okay, revolving restaurants are the very definition of kitsch. But you know what? We like 'em. And when you've got views like these, well, there is a difference between having good taste and being made of stone.

Big Sky ❸
Chin's ❺
Dive! ❻
Liberty Cafe at the
   Blue Castle Pharmacy ❷
The Monte Carlo Room ❹
Rincon Criollo ❶
Top of the World ❸

Because you are 869 feet in the air, Vegas is stretched out before you in a glittering palette. Who knew this town could be so beautiful? This proves the Stratosphere is good for something. The Top of the World restaurant may not have the best food in Vegas (though some things are actually pretty good), but it has hands down the best view. You will be so busy admiring the Strip, noticing that Vegas goes on much farther than you thought, wondering which casino that particular cluster of lights is, and trying to spot your hotel, that you won't even notice what you are eating. It's one of the most romantic spots in town to dine.

But it's expensive, and the entrees, at least, are not worth the cost. Having anticipated that customers might want to fill up tables just ordering a small snack, there is a $15 per person minimum. Here's what you do: Order the generous-sized appetizers and desserts—only. You won't be disappointed, and you can easily make the minimum. The menu changes, but recent appetizers included Southwestern spring rolls (think of a cross between an egg roll and a fajita) filled with chicken and veggies, slightly deep fried to a nice crunch, and served with a fine guacamole. It's tart, crunchy, messy, and fattening, which means it has to be good. There was also an oversized (to the point of silliness) bruschetta (chopped tomato, basil, and garlic covered in olive oil on huge toasted slices of bread) that was tasty if hard to eat. The salads are overpriced and overly fussy, while the entrees are not terribly imaginative. (The fillet of almond-crusted salmon did get a thumbs-up on an earlier visit.) The desserts were stellar, with the stand-out being the expensive ($9) but easily shared by two (it's huge and rich) Chocolate Stratosphere Tower. Yep, a chocolate replica of the very building you are sitting in; the top part is filled with a terrific chocolate mousse, and the whole thing gets covered in chocolate sauce, poured by your waiter with great ceremony. Additional happiness came with towering *vacherin,* layers of hazelnut meringue filled with Bavarian cream, garnished with fresh berries, and served with crème anglaise and kiwi and raspberry sauces. The service was also impeccable.

EXPENSIVE

✪ **Chin's.** 3200 Las Vegas Blvd. S. (in the Fashion Show Mall, turn at the Frontier sign). ☎ **702/733-8899.** Reservations recommended. Main courses $10–$12 lunch, $10–$30 dinner. AE, DC, MC, V. Mon–Sat 11:30am–9:30pm, Sun noon–9:30pm. CHINESE.

Chin's has been a Vegas fixture for nearly 20 years and is consistently voted by locals in the *Las Vegas Review* as their favorite Chinese restaurant. It is certainly a surprise for anyone who knows Chinese food solely through take-out or strip malls. The simple, stark decor produces an ambience of low-key elegance. The prices will surprise you, too. This is not $1 Chinese food. But as owner Mr. Chin points out, Chinese food takes so much time to prepare (all that chopping, dicing, splicing, and what not) and to present in the traditionally stylish way (no steam trays here) that it's a wonder anyone would ever charge just a couple of dollars for a dish.

Chin is justly proud of his achievements, but he adds as much to his restaurant as the food. You will see him moving from table to table, greeting regulars by name; do try to have him visit with you, if you can. He's full of stories, like how Jerry Lewis and Neil Sedaka are regulars, with a special dish created just for the latter (shrimp with lobster in lobster sauce, no vegetables).

However, anyone with broad experience with Chinese food won't find anything terribly surprising here. Experiments with more radical dishes failed (too-timid tourists?), and so the menu is on the safe side. Which is not to say it isn't good. Stand-outs include strawberry chicken (think lemon chicken but with a different fruit; Chin's created this twist on a familiar dish, and other local restaurants have copied it); an appetizer of sinful deep-fried shrimp puffs (stuffed with minced shrimp and mildly curried cream cheese); splendid spring rolls; and barbecue pork-fried rice that strikes that tricky, careful balance between dry and greasy.

MODERATE

DIVE! 3200 Las Vegas Blvd. S. (in the Fashion Show Mall.) ☎ **702/369-DIVE.** Reservations for large parties only. Main courses $7–$14. AE, CB, DC, DISC, MC V. Sun–Thurs 11:30am–10pm, Fri–Sat 11:30am–11pm. AMERICAN.

Notable for being one of the few theme restaurants not devoted to memorabilia, DIVE! was partly created by Steven Spielberg and movie exec Jeffrey Katzenberg. The outside is admittedly quite fun: a yellow submarine crashing through a 30-foot wall of water that cascades into an oversized pool erupting with depth-charge blasts. Its gunmetal-gray interior replicates the hull of a submarine with vaulted cylindrical ceilings, porthole-shaped (albeit neon-accented, since this is Vegas) windows, exposed conduits that burst with steam, sonar screens, and working periscopes. Every hour a high-tech show projected on a 16-cube video wall (and 48 additional monitors throughout the restaurant) simulates a fantasy submarine dive. And overhead, a luxury ocean liner, a manta ray research vessel, exotic fish, a fighting shark, and model subs circumnavigate the room on a computerized track. It's all whimsical and imaginative. Surprise—they serve submarine sandwiches (among other choices). Kids should love it and adults will find it slightly less annoying than, say, Chuck E. Cheese (and with somewhat more sophisticated food).

INEXPENSIVE

Big Sky Steak House. Stratosphere Las Vegas Hotel, 2000 Las Vegas Blvd. S. (between St. Louis St. and Baltimore Ave.) ☎ **702/780-7777.** Complete steak dinners from $10, all-you-can-eat barbecue dinner $13, children under 6 free. AE, CB, DC, DISC, JCB, MC, V. Sun–Thurs 5–11pm, Fri–Sat 5pm–midnight. BARBECUE.

Food bargains abound in Las Vegas, and this is one of the best. Big Sky offers a suitably rustic setting for hearty all-you-can-eat family-style feasts. Country music helps set the tone, and service is down home and friendly.

Entree choices include prime rib with creamed horseradish sauce and a barbecue combination (beef brisket, St. Louis ribs, Carolina-pulled pork, and fried chicken), and steaks. Whatever you select, it will come with a huge salad, scrumptious corn muffins (don't fill up on them; there's lots more food coming), corn on the cob, seasoned steak fries, coleslaw, Texas toast, and baked beans with pork. And when you've eaten your fill, you can waddle over to the dessert table and help yourself to apple cobbler, fresh berries and cream, and bread pudding with rum sauce. There's a full bar.

✪ **Liberty Cafe at the Blue Castle Pharmacy.** 1700 S. Las Vegas Blvd. ☎ **702-383-0101.** Reservations not accepted. Nothing over $6.50. No credit cards. 24 hours. DINER.

You can go to any number of retro soda fountain replicas (such as Johnny Rockets) and theme restaurants that pretend to be cheap diners, but why bother when the (admittedly, decidedly unflashy) real thing is just past the end of the Strip? The soda fountain/lunch counter at the Blue Castle Pharmacy was Las Vegas's first 24-hour restaurant, and it has been going strong for 60 years. Plunk down at the counter, and watch the cooks go nuts trying to keep up with the orders. The menu is basic comfort food: standard grill items (meat loaf, ground round steak, chops), fluffy cream pies, and classic breakfasts served "anytime"—try the biscuits and cream gravy at 3am. They also serve gyros and the like. But the best bet is a $1/3$-pound burger and "thick creamy shake," both the way they were meant to be and about as good as they get. At around $5, this is half what you would pay for a comparable meal at the Hard Rock Cafe. And as waitress Beverly says, "This is really real."

Rincon Criollo. 1145 Las Vegas Blvd. S. ☎ **702-388-1906.** Reservations not accepted. Main courses $6.50–$10, paella (for 3) $20. AE, DISC, MC, V. Tues–Sun 11am–10pm. CUBAN.

Located beyond the wedding chapels on Las Vegas Boulevard, Rincon Criollo has all the right details for a good, cheap ethnic joint: full of locals and empty of frills. It's not the best Cuban food ever, but it gets the job done. The main courses (featuring Cuban pork and chicken specialties) are hit and miss; try the marinated pork leg or, better still, ask your server for a recommendation. Paella is offered, but only for parties of three or more (and starts at $20). The side-course *chorizo* (a spicy sausage) is excellent, and the Cuban sandwich (roast pork, ham, and cheese on bread, which is then pressed and flattened out) is huge and tasty. For only $3.50, the latter makes a fine change-of-pace meal.

5 East of the Strip

In this section we've covered restaurants close by the Convention Center, along with those farther south on Paradise Road, Flamingo Road, and Tropicana Avenue.

VERY EXPENSIVE

Bistro Le Montrachet. Las Vegas Hilton, 3000 Paradise Rd. ☎ **702/ 732-5111.** Reservations suggested. Main courses $23–$46. AE, CB, DC, DISC, JCB, MC, V. Wed–Mon 6–10:30pm. FRENCH.

Dishes are exquisitely presented and prepared at this ultra-elegant French restaurant. You might begin with chilled foie gras served on toast points. Also noteworthy are creamy lobster bisque and the salad "Le Montrachet," a refreshing mélange of Belgian endive, watercress, julienned beets, and enoki mushrooms in a Gorgonzola/walnut oil dressing. Entree choices range from roasted breast of Muscovy duck (served with white and black beans and currants in a crème de cassis sauce) to broiled live Maine lobster removed from the shell and served atop herbed Moroccan couscous with crab dressing and drawn butter. Among desserts, we're partial to the rich crème brûlée complemented by seasonal fruits, berries, and petits fours. The restaurant's wine cellar stocks more than 400 wines from vineyards spanning the globe.

Pegasus. Alexis Park Resort, 375 E. Harmon Ave. (between Koval Lane and Paradise Rd.) ☎ **702/796-3300.** Reservations recommended. Main courses $13–$19. AE, DC, DISC, MC, V. Daily 6–10pm. MEDITERRANEAN/ITALIAN.

This low-key luxury resort attracts many visiting celebrities and Strip headliners, and its premier restaurant is a fitting venue for such an upscale clientele. A new menu features Mediterranean and Italian dishes, all with a gourmet flair. Options include Italian pasta and bean soup, lobster won ton and shrimp eggroll (very Italian!), and California-style pizzas (all under $10). Main courses include fresh ahi tuna, fresh salmon fillet grilled or poached laced with a citrus and dill beurre blanc, chicken ravioli, and steak. There's an extensive wine list (including many Italian wines) with choices in varying price ranges.

The Tillerman. 2245 E. Flamingo Rd. (at Channel 10 Dr., just west of Eastern Ave.). ☎ **702/731-4036.** Reservations recommended. Main courses $20–$39. AE, CB, DC, DISC, MC, V. Daily 5–11pm, bar/lounge until midnight. STEAK/ SEAFOOD.

The Tillerman is on any number of local "best of Vegas" lists, and while we agree the food is terrific, the high prices and somewhat snooty attitude make us feel we can spend our money better elsewhere. Portions are immense, so appetizers are really not necessary, but then again, they're too good to pass up. Especially notable: crab cake garnished with carrot chips, superb filet medallions in a spicy red sauce, and yellowfin tuna blackened and served almost rare in spicy mustard sauce. For entrees, regulars most often order the crab legs, which are excellent, as is the swordfish and halibut. Try also the shrimp in garlic cream sauce. The wine list is huge, but expensive; the cheapest glass of wine is $8.

EXPENSIVE

✪ **Lawry's The Prime Rib.** 4043 Howard Hughes Pkwy. (at Flamingo, between Paradise and Koval). ☎ **702/893-2223.** Reservations recommended. Main courses $20–$30. AE, DC, DISC, JCB, MC, V. Sun–Thurs 5–10pm, Fri–Sat 5–11pm. STEAK/SEAFOOD.

If you love prime rib, come here, because Lawry's does one thing, and it does it better than anyone else. Lawry's first opened in Los Angeles in 1938 and still remains an always packed tradition. Over the years, it has added three branches, the most recent landing in Las Vegas at the beginning of 1997. Yes, you can get prime rib all over town for under five bucks. But that's a tuna fish sandwich to Lawry's caviar (if one may mix food metaphors).

Eating at Lawry's is a ceremony, with all the parts played the same for the last 60 years. Waitresses in brown and white English maid uniforms, complete with starched white cap, take your order. For side dishes, that is. The real decision, what cut of rib you are going to have, comes later. Anyway, you tell the waitress what side dishes you want (sublime creamed spinach, baked potato) for an extra price. Later, she returns with a spinning salad bowl (think salad preparation as Busby Berkeley musical number). The bowl, resting on crushed ice, spins as she pours Lawry's special dressing in a stream from high over her head. Tomatoes garnish. Applause follows. Eventually, giant metal carving carts (designed after the original ones) come to your table, bearing the meat. You name your cut (the regular Lawry's, the extra large Diamond Jim Brady, only for serious carnivores, and the wimpy thin English cut), rare, medium, well done. It comes with terrific Yorkshire pudding, nicely browned and not soggy, and some creamed horseradish that is combined with fluffy whipped cream, simultaneously sweet and tart. You eat.

And it's so good. This will be the best prime rib you will ever have. Flavorful, tender, perfectly cooked, lightly seasoned; it just has to be tasted to be believed. You can finish off with a rich dessert (English trifle is highly recommended), but it almost seems pointless.

Dining East of the Strip

Allie's ❹

Bistro Le Montrachet ❸

Celebrity Deli ⓬

Ginza ❷

Hard Rock Café ⓫

Lawry's The Prime Rib ❾

Mamounia ⓯

Marrakesh ❽

Mediterranean Café & Market ⓭

Pamplemousse ❶

Pegasus ⓰

Ricardo's ⓱

Shalimar ❼

The Tillerman ⓮

Toto's ⓰

Z Tejas Grill ❻

Buffet

Las Vegas Hilton Buffet
of Champions ❺

Have You Heard the One About the Belly Dancer?

If you have never tried Moroccan food, you should. Not only are you in for some new taste treats, but the action-packed presentation and gluttonous portions are very appropriate to Vegas. Vegas has two notable Moroccan establishments: **Marrakech,** 3900 Paradise Rd., at Howard Hughes Drive (☎ **702/737-5611**), where a six-course meal will cost you $25 per person (reservations recommended; AE, DISC, DC, MC, V accepted; open Monday to Sunday 5:30 to 11pm); and **Mamounia,** 4632 S. Maryland Pkwy., between Harmon and Tropicana avenues (☎ **702/597-0092**), where a Moroccan feast will set you back $23 per person (reservations recommended; AE, DISC, MC, V accepted; open daily 5 to 11pm).

Both rooms are covered, floor to ceiling, with Moroccan (or Moroccan style) rugs, furnished with low tables made of intricately inlaid wood (from the town of Essaouira). There is some simple tile work on the walls at Marrakech. It all adds up to that Arabian Nights den of thieves feel. Diners sit on cushions on the floor or on very low cushioned benches.

Oh, and you eat with your fingers. Yep, that's part of the fun. A waiter comes out and pours water into a brass bowl so you can wash your hands and passes out huge towels for your lap. You then start a multicourse feast, beginning with a trio of cold salads: marinated carrots, eggplant and tomato and cucumber. Use the bread supplied from a big basket to scoop

Pamplemousse. 400 E. Sahara Ave. (between Santa Paula Dr. and Santa Rita Dr., just east of Paradise Rd.) ☎ **702/733-2066.** Reservations essential. Main courses $17.50–$24.50. AE, CB, DC, DISC, MC, V. Seatings daily at 6–6:30pm and 9–9:30pm. FRENCH.

Evoking a cozy French countryside inn, Pamplemousse is a catacomb of low-ceilinged rooms and intimate dining nooks with rough-hewn beams. It's all very charming and un-Vegasy. There's additional seating in a small garden sheltered by a striped tent. The restaurant's name, which means grapefruit, was suggested by the late singer Bobby Darin, one of the many celebrity pals of owner Georges La Forge.

The menu, which changes nightly, is recited by your waiter. The meal always begins with a large complimentary basket of crudités, it up. The salads sound and are relatively simple, and are supremely tasty. This is followed by shrimp in a garlic sauce that seems more Italian than Moroccan (peculiarly, both restaurants feature this out-of-place item). But if you like garlic and shrimp, you won't complain too much. Next is *b'stilla*, a truly amazing dish if done right. Layers of filo are interspersed with chicken, eggs, and nuts; the whole thing is topped with powdered sugar and cinnamon. The uninitiated raise their eyebrows at it, while their more informed companions dig in. After you try it, you will fight for more than your fair share too. The final course is some kind of fowl (chicken or Cornish game hen), usually in a wonderful lemon and olive sauce. You finish up with some sweet mint tea, poured with great ceremony. Then the belly dancer comes out to dazzle you with her gravity-defying shimmy skills, getting the crowd going in a conga line (or, unfortunately, the Macarena) and accepting a tip or two.

This experience is roughly the same at the two restaurants, but the food at Marrakech is considerably better. However, they found that the b'stilla was too strange for many patrons, so they turned it into a dessert with a fruit filling; they will make it with chicken if you ask when ordering; trust us and do. In its favor, the Mamounia offers à la carte items (Marrakech is considering this), so you can try other Moroccan specialties such as *tajines*, which are delicious stews cooked in clay pots.

a big bowl of olives, and a basket of hard-boiled eggs (a nice country touch). From there, you might proceed to an appetizer of lightly floured bay scallops sautéed in buttery grapefruit sauce, followed by an entree of crispy duck breast and banana in a sauce of orange honey, dark rum, and crème de banane. Filet mignon, New York steak, and rack of lamb are always featured. For dessert, perhaps there'll be homemade dark chocolate ice cream with pralines in a sabayon sauce. An extensive, well-rounded wine list complements the menu.

MODERATE

✪ **Allie's.** 325 Convention Center Dr. (in Marriott Suites). ☎ **702/650-2000**. Main courses $8.25–$15, sandwiches $6–$9.25. AE, CB, DC, DISC, MC, V. Mon–Fri 6:30am–10:30pm, Sat–Sun 7am–10pm. SOUTHWESTERN.

👥 Family-Friendly Restaurants

Buffets *(see p. 95)*   Cheap meals for the whole family. The kids can choose what they like, and there are sometimes make-your-own sundae machines.

DIVE! *(see p. 79)*   Housed in a submarine and featuring a zany high-tech show every hour projected on a video wall, this is the most fun family-oriented spot of all.

Rain Forest Cafe *(see p. 68)*   This is like eating in the Jungle Book Ride at Disneyland. Animals howl, thunder wails, everywhere is something to marvel at. There is a decent kids' menu and they might even learn a little bit about ecology and the environment.

Hard Rock Cafe *(see p. 87)*   Kids adore this restaurant, which throbs with excitement and is filled with rock memorabilia.

Planet Hollywood *(see p. 75)*   This popular chain houses a veritable museum of movie memorabilia, and the action on numerous video monitors keeps kids from getting bored.

Don't miss this little treasure. Tucked away on the other side of the bar in the Marriott Suites, Allie's is a coffee shop at breakfast time, but for lunch and dinner it turns into a cafe with a delightful menu that can be best described as nouveau Southwestern. Check out the chicken portobello quesadilla appetizer, or the Pacific Rim yellow-fin tuna salad—tuna on crispy Asian vegetables. The salmon BLT is a seared salmon steak over an inch thick with delicious maple pepper bacon, Grey Poupon sauce, and lovely leafy lettuce on a toasted brioche. Served with french fries and a cilantro coleslaw, it was a delicious, inventive take on an old favorite. There is a lovely dessert menu featuring a genuine root beer float.

Ginza. 1000 E. Sahara Ave. (between State St. and Maryland Pkwy.) ☎ **702/732-3080.** Reservations for large parties only. Main courses $12.55–$17.50. AE, DC, MC, V. Tues–Sun noon–10pm. JAPANESE.

For almost 2 decades, this charming little restaurant has attracted a devoted clientele of local Japanese and Japanese food aficionados.

You might begin with a shared appetizer of tempura shrimp and vegetables. Entrees such as beef, chicken, or salmon sprinkled with sesame seeds in a thick teriyaki sauce come with soup (miso or egg flower), salad, and green tea. Sushi is a highlight, and there are about 30 à la carte selections from which to choose. Be sure to try an appetizer or entree portion of Ginza's unique Vegas rolls: salmon, tuna, yellowtail, and avocado rolled with seaweed in sesame-studded rice and quickly deep-fried so the sesame seeds form a crunchy crust. It's served with lemon soy sauce. Also delicious are seaweed-wrapped California rolls. The fish is extremely fresh, and everything here is made from scratch. A bottle of sake is recommended. For dessert there's lemon sherbet or ginger and green tea ice creams.

Hard Rock Cafe. 4475 Paradise Rd. (at Harmon Ave.) ☎ **702/733-8400.** Reservations not accepted. Main courses $9–$17; burgers and sandwiches $7.60–8.75. AE, DC, MC, V. Sun–Thurs 11am–11:30pm, Fri–Sat 11am–midnight. AMERICAN.

The original Hard Rock Cafe opened in London as a meeting place for American expatriates and homesick exchange students dying for a good burger. Now Hard Rocks are everywhere. But this is the only Hard Rock (so far) attached to a hotel and a truly extraordinary casino, so let's cut this branch some slack. The menu offers some good salads in addition to the burgers. An inexpensive children's menu is a plus for families. Don't be frightened by the line outside—it's usually not for the restaurant but the on-premises Hard Rock merchandise store. The Hard Rock Hotel and Casino is next door (see chapter 4).

Ricardo's. 2380 Tropicana Ave. (at Eastern Ave., northwest corner). ☎ **702/ 798-4515.** Reservations recommended. Main courses $7.50–$13; lunch buffet $7.25; children's plates $3–$4, including milk or soft drink with complimentary refills. AE, CB, DC, DISC, MC, V. Sun–Thurs 11am–10pm, Fri–Sat 11am–11pm. MEXICAN.

This hacienda-style restaurant is a great favorite with locals. Start off with an appetizer of deep-fried battered chicken wings served with melted cheddar (ask for jalapeños if you like your cheese sauce hotter). Nachos smothered with cheese and guacamole are also very good here. For an entree, you can't go wrong with chicken, beef, or pork fajitas served sizzling on a hot skillet atop sautéed onions, mushrooms, and peppers; they come with rice and beans, tortillas, a selection of salsas, guacamole, and tomato wedges with cilantro. All the usual taco/enchilada/tamale combinations are also listed. A delicious dessert is *helado* Las Vegas: ice cream rolled in corn flakes and cinnamon, deep-fried, and served with honey and whipped cream. Be sure to order a pitcher of Ricardo's great margaritas. The same menu is available all day, but a buffet is offered at lunch. The kids' menu on a place mat with games and puzzles features both Mexican and American fare.

⚫ **Shalimar.** 3900 S. Paradise Rd. (in the Citibank Plaza). ☎ **702/796-0302.**
Reservations suggested. Lunch buffet $7.50; dinner main courses $10.50–$16.
AE, DISC, MC, V. Mon–Fri 11:30am–2:30pm, 5:30–10:30pm; Sat–Sun 5:30–
10:30pm. INDIAN

In a town full of buffet deals, it's hard to get excited about another
one, but on the other hand, all those other buffet deals offer pretty
much the identical food: carving stations, various cafeteria hot
dishes, and so forth. Here at Shalimar, a lunch buffet means about
two dozen different North Indian–style dishes. All for about seven
bucks. It's not as colorful or huge (in fact, it's just a table covered
with steam trays) as those buffets up the street, but it is far more interesting and different. It's also a great deal and one of the first places
to run to if you are sick of Strip food. Just ask the locals who vote
it their favorite ethnic restaurant in the *Las Vegas Review Journal's*
annual poll.

The buffet usually includes *tandoori* (chicken marinated in spiced
yogurt cooked in a clay oven), *marsala* (tandoori in a curry sauce),
naan (the flat Indian bread), and various vegetable dishes. (Vegetarians will find plenty to eat here—they offer special veggie dishes
daily.) One stand-out at a recent visit was the *Bengan Bharta* (eggplant diced fine and cooked with onions, tomatoes, and spices).
There was also a yellow squash curry that was outrageously good.
The tandoori chicken was perfect, tender, and moist. (Tandoori, by
the way, is a very low-fat way of preparing chicken.) In the evening,
a full Indian menu, with *vindaloo* (an especially hot curry in which
the meat is marinated in vinegar), flavored naans (try the garlic or
onion), and other Indian specialties are offered à la carte. They will
spice to order: mild, medium, hot, or very hot. If you make a mistake, you can always order *raita* (yogurt mixed with mild spices and
cucumber); it cools your mouth nicely.

Z Tejas Grill. 3824 Paradise Rd. (between Twain Ave. and Corporate Dr.)
☎ **702/732-1660.** Reservations recommended. Main courses $7.25–$12 at
lunch, $8.75–$17 at dinner. AE, CB, DC, DISC, JCB, MC, V. Daily 11am–11pm.
TEX-MEX.

This Austin, Texas-based restaurant's rather odd name came about because its original chef, a Frenchman, kept referring to it as "zee" Tejas
Grill. There is a vine-covered patio for outdoor dining, rare for Vegas,
with misters for summer and a fireplace and heaters for winter.

In particular, we like the generously portioned grilled fish tacos,
which come wrapped in fresh tortillas, stuffed with all kinds of
veggies and served with a spicy Japanese sauce. Not your usual
drippy, fattening tacos. Less of a bargain, but mighty tasty, is the

tender and piquant black sesame tuna with a black peppercorn vinaigrette and a soy mustard sauce. There is a larger version of this among the entrees, called "Voodoo Tuna"—it's not quite as good. A better choice would be the spicy grilled Jamaican jerk chicken, nuanced with lime and served with peanut sauce and rum-spiked coconut-banana ketchup; it comes with two side dishes—when we were there, garlic mashed potatoes and a corn casserole-soufflé. You might also consider downing some large and excellent margaritas at the newly enlarged, very lively bar, particularly on weeknights, when happy hour (4 to 7pm) finds all starters half-price.

INEXPENSIVE

Celebrity Deli. 4055 S. Maryland Pkwy. (at Flamingo). ☎ **702/733-7827.** Reservations not accepted. Main courses $7–$12. AE, MC, V. Mon–Sat 9am– 8pm, Sun 9am–4pm. DELI.

A basic, solid New York deli, lacking the mammoth portions of the Stage Deli (though perhaps that's a good thing) but lacking also the occasionally mammoth prices of same. And you won't go hungry. Don't look for anything vegetarian here; instead, you got your pastrami on rye, your matzo ball soup, chopped liver, tongue, meat loaf, lox and bagel. Desserts are a bit sparse for a deli, but you can't go wrong with the black and white cookies. Go ahead—have a nosh.

✪ **Mediterranean Café & Market.** 4147 S. Maryland Pkwy. (at Flamingo Rd.), in the Tiffany Square strip mall. ☎ **702/731-6030.** Reservations not accepted. Main courses $4–$13 (all sandwiches under $5). AE, MC, DISC, V. Mon–Sat 11am–9pm, closed Sunday. MEDITERRANEAN.

It is an immeasurable thrill to find this totally authentic, mom-and-pop Middle Eastern restaurant in Las Vegas, where high-quality ethnic eateries are scarce.

Everything here is homemade and delicious. You might order up a gyro (slivers of rotisseried beef and lamb enfolded into a pita with lettuce and tomato). Other good choices are a phyllo pie layered with spinach and feta cheese, served with hummus; skewers of grilled chicken and vegetable kabobs with lavash bread and hummus; and a combination platter of hummus, tabouli, stuffed grape leaves, and felafel. All entrees come with pita bread and salad. Try a side order of *bourrani* (creamy yogurt dip mixed with steamed spinach, sautéed garlic, and slivered almonds). Finish up with baklava and rich Turkish coffee. Wine and beer are available. You can also come by in the morning for Middle Eastern breakfasts. A Mediterranean market adjoins.

Toto's. 2055 E. Tropicana Ave. ☎ **702/895-7923.** Reservations not required. Main courses $6.25–$14.25. AE, DISC, MC, V. Mon–Thurs 11am–2pm, Fri–Sat 11am–11pm, Sun 9am–10pm. MEXICAN.

A family-style Mexican restaurant favored by locals, with enormous portions and quick service, this is good value for your money. Perhaps even more so; with all that food, you could probably split portions and still be satisfied. Chicken tamales got a thumbs up, while the veggie burrito was happily received by non-meat eaters; though not especially healthy, all the ingredients were fresh, with huge slices of zucchini and roasted bell peppers. The operative word here is "huge"; the burritos are almost the size of your arm. The generous portions continue with dessert—a piece of flan was practically pie-sized. The Sunday Margarita brunch is quite fun, and the drinks are large (naturally) and yummy.

6 West Las Vegas

EXPENSIVE

Cafe Nicolle. 4760 W. Sahara at Decatur (in the Sahara Pavilion). ☎ **702/870-7675.** Reservations recommended for large parties. Main courses $7–$15 at lunch; $16–$25 at dinner. AE, DC, MC, V. Mon–Sat 11am–10:30pm. CONTINENTAL.

Cafe Nicolle is a local favorite, a place to go for either a special occasion or just to hang out on the lovely patio, which features a cooling mist on hot summer nights. There are no surprises on the menu—pastas, crepes, chicken, veal—but everything is prepared beautifully and served attractively with generous portions. They have extremely good, fresh fish, presented very simply, but so the fish's own flavor is able to shine, not overwhelmed with sauces. The Florentine crepe is made with lots of fresh spinach and not too much cheese in the sauce. Be sure to dip your fresh bread in the excellent garlic and rosemary olive oil found on the table.

MODERATE

Cathay House. 5300 W. Spring Mountain Rd. (in Spring Valley). ☎ **702/876-3838.** Reservations recommended. Main courses $6.75–$19. AE, CB, DC, DISC, JCB, MC, V. Daily 11am–10:30pm. CHINESE.

Las Vegas actually has a Chinatown—a very large strip mall (naturally) on Spring Mountain Road near Wynn. There are several Asian restaurants there, including the average Plum Tree Inn, which serves dim sum, but ask locals who look like they know, and they will send you instead farther up Spring Mountain Road to the Cathay House (on the opposite side of the street). This only looks far from the Strip on a map; it's really about a 7-minute drive from Treasure Island.

Ordering dim sum, if you haven't experienced it, is sort of like being at a Chinese sushi bar, in that you order many individual, tasty little dishes. Of course, dim sum itself is nothing like sushi. Rather, it's a range of potstickers, panfried dumplings, *baos* (soft, doughy buns filled with meat like barbecued pork), translucent rice noodles wrapped around shrimp, sticky rice in lotus leaves, chicken feet, and so forth. Some of it's steamed, some is fried—for that extra good grease! You can make your own dipping sauce by combining soy sauce, vinegar, and hot pepper oil. The Chinese eat this for breakfast; the rest of us probably can't handle it until a bit later in the day. The wait staff pushes steam carts filled with little dishes; point, and they will attempt to tell you what each one is. Each dish ranges from approximately $1 to $3; each server makes a note of what you just received, and the total is tallied at the end. (For some reason, it almost always works out to about $9 a person.) Dim sum is usually available only until mid-afternoon.

The stand-out at the Cathay House was a vegetable bao that included Chinese glass noodles. Lightly browned and not overly doughy like many baos, it was slightly sweet and utterly delicious. The shrimp wrapped in rice noodles were big and plump, while anything that was fried was so good we decided to ignore our arteries for awhile. Cathay House (which features quite a good view through the windows on one side) also has a full dinner menu, which includes the strawberry chicken invented by Chin's; it's considerably cheaper here.

Viva Mercados. 6182 W. Flamingo (at Jones). ☎ **702/871-8826.** Reservations for large parties only. Main courses $8–$17. AE, DISC, MC, V. Sun–Thurs 11am–10pm, Fri–Sat 11am–11pm. MEXICAN.

Ask any local about Mexican food in Vegas, and almost certainly they will point to Viva Mercados as the best in town. That recommendation, plus the restaurant's health-conscious attitude, makes this worth the roughly 10-minute drive from the Strip.

Given all those warnings lately about Mexican food and its heart attack–inducing properties, Viva Mercados's approach to food is nothing to be sniffed at. No dish is prepared with or cooked in any kind of animal fat. Nope, the lard so dear to Mexican cooking is not found here. The oil used is an artery-friendly canola. Additionally, this makes the place particularly appealing to vegetarians, who will also be pleased by the regular veggie specials. Everything is quite fresh, and they do particularly amazing things with seafood. Try the Maresco Vallarta, which is orange roughy, shrimp, and scallops cooked in a coconut tomato sauce, with capers and olives. They have all sorts of noteworthy shrimp dishes, and 11 different salsas, ranked 1 to 10 for degree of spice. (Ask for advice first.) The staff is friendly (try to chat with owner Bobby Mercado) and the portions hearty.

INEXPENSIVE

✪ **Enigma Cafe.** 918¹/₂ S. 4th St. (at Charleston Blvd.) ☎ **702/386-0999.** Reservations not accepted. No items over $6. No credit cards. Mon 7am–3pm, Tues–Fri 7am–midnight, Sat–Sun 9am–midnight. CALIFORNIA/ MEDITERRANEAN.

Finding the Enigma Cafe is almost as good as finding a breeze on a really hot Vegas day. Or maybe it's more like suddenly finding yourself transported out of Vegas and into California. Owners Julie and Len have taken two 1930s-era cottages and turned them into a cafe/coffeehouse/art space that, during the day, is a restful, garden patio setting (orders are taken inside one house, inside the other is the art gallery, with more seating) with folk and classical music playing. At night the space blooms with candles, live music, and poetry readings.

The menu is a huge relief: healthful, interesting sandwiches ("Mossy Melt" is tuna salad "revved up with" horseradish and havarti, toasted open-face) and familiar ones (ham and Swiss, but well garnished), salads (again with a range from the ordinary green variety to "Dr. Bombay's" curried chicken breast with veggies) to hummus burritos and the "Tippy Elvis Supreme" (named after a local polka band/art project), which is peanut butter and bananas (what else?). You can get a side platter of hummus, feta cheese, veggies, and pita, or have a thick fruit smoothie. And that doesn't even begin to cover their wide range of coffee drinks. Best of all, it's cheap. Considering the soothing affect it has on your mind, spirit, wallet, and stomach, Enigma is like a vacation from your vacation. This is actually very close to both the Strip and Downtown, particularly the latter, where good (and healthful) food is hard to find.

7 Downtown

VERY EXPENSIVE

Andre's. 401 S. 6th St. (at Lewis Ave., a few blocks south of Fremont St.) ☎ **702/385-5016.** Reservations required. Main courses $19.75–$33. AE, CB, DC, MC, V. Daily from 6pm; closing hours vary. FRENCH.

Owner-chef Andre Rochat has created a rustic country-French setting in a converted 1930s house in Downtown Las Vegas. In addition to a catacomb of cozy interior rooms, there's a lovely, ivy-walled garden patio under the shade of a mulberry tree. This is

Andre's ❼
Binion's Horseshoe
  Coffee Shop ❸
Carson Street Café ❷
Limerick's ❻
Second Street
  Grill ❹

Buffets
Golden Nugget
  Buffet ❷
Lady Luck Banquet
  Buffet ❺
Main Street Station
  Garden Court ❶
Sam Boyd's Fremont
  Paradise Buffet ❹

a major celebrity haunt where you're likely to see Strip headliners. One night, Tom Hanks, Steven Spielberg, and James Spader were all spotted joining some pals for a bachelor party.

The menu changes seasonally. On a recent visit, appetizers included jumbo sea scallops rolled in a crunchy macadamia nut crust with citrus beurre blanc and red beet coulis. And among the entrees, a fan of pink, juicy slices of sautéed duck came with a confit of port wine and onions. A medley of vegetables—perhaps pommes lyonnaise, asparagus, broccoli hollandaise, and baby carrots—accompanies each entree, and sorbets are served between courses. For dessert, there are Andre's classic fruit tarts, flaky butter crusts layered with Grand Marnier custard and topped with fresh, plump berries. An extensive wine list (more than 900 labels) is international in scope and includes many rare vintages; consult the sommelier.

EXPENSIVE

Limerick's. Fitzgeralds Casino Holiday Inn, 301 Fremont St. (at 3rd St.) ☎ 702/388-2400. Reservations recommended. Main courses $14–$21. AE, DISC, MC, V. Daily 5:30–10:30pm. STEAK/SEAFOOD.

An extensive renovation in 1996 turned a down-at-the-heels eatery into a posh steakhouse. Decorated in the classic Olde English gentlemen's club style, Limerick's is meant to be an oasis of gracious dining away from hectic casino life, and the overall effect is comforting and moderately womblike, particularly in the cozy booths at the back. Unfortunately, casino "ca-chings" still creep in, but it's not overly bothersome. The menu is classic, upscale steakhouse: beef, chops, some lobster, and chicken. The portions are Vegas-sized (the small prime rib was 14 ounces), so bring an appetite (and a love of red meat), or take your leftovers back to the room to feed the kids for a couple days. The filet mignon was tender enough to cut with a fork, while the lamb chops came with a pecan mustard glaze. Patrons who don't eat red meat might want to try the apricot chicken. Appetizers are mostly seafood, though there is a fine-sounding baked Brie with strawberry preserves. "Chef's choice" desserts change nightly, and the wine list is good and extensive.

✪ **Second Street Grill.** Fremont Hotel, 200 E. Fremont St. ☎ **702/ 385-3232.** Main courses $17–$23. Reservations recommended. AE, DC, DISC, MC, V. Sun–Thurs 5–11pm, Fri–Sat 5am–midnight. INTERNATIONAL.

One of the better kept secrets of Las Vegas, this is a Downtown jewel. A lovely bit of romantic, cozy class tucked away inside the Fremont Hotel, with excellent food to boot. For starters, try the unusual lemon chicken potstickers and the duck confit. Entrees include lobster, ahi tuna, and filet mignon, but the whole fish (opakapaka on a recent visit), served in a bowl with a giant tea-leaf lid, is the best bet. It comes with sautéed mushrooms that will melt in your mouth. Other notable side dishes include some fabulous pesto mashed potatoes. Tiramisu fans should be pleased with the Grill's version of that ubiquitous dessert; it's light on the alcohol and more like an airy cheesecake. But don't skip the Chocolate Explosion: a piece of chocolate cake topped with chocolate mousse, covered with a rich chocolate shell.

INEXPENSIVE

Binion's Horseshoe Coffee Shop. Binion's Horseshoe, 128 E. Fremont St. (at Casino Center Blvd.) ☎ **702/382-1600.** Reservations not accepted. Main courses $4.25–$15 (most under $8). AE, CB, DC, DISC, MC, V. Daily 24 hours. AMERICAN.

Down a flight of steps from the casino floor, this is no humble hotel coffee shop. It's heralded by a gorgeous stained-glass dome and entered via doors embellished with antique beveled glass panels. The interior is equally impressive, with a magnificent, pressed copper ceiling, rich oak paneling, walls hung with original oil paintings you'll wish you owned, and displays of antiques, turn-of-the-century magazine covers, and black-and-white photographs of the Old West. Notice, too, an exhibit of vintage playing cards that depict real kings and queens (Henry VIII and Anne Boleyn).

The menu lists all the traditional Las Vegas coffee-shop items: sandwiches, burgers, Southern-fried chicken, steak and seafood entrees, along with breakfast fare. And you can't beat Binion's specials: two eggs with an immense slab of grilled ham, home fries, toast, and tea or coffee ($3 from 6am to 2pm); a 10-ounce New York steak dinner with baked potato, salad, and roll and butter ($4 from 10pm to 5:45am); a 7-ounce New York steak with eggs, home fries, and toast ($3 from 10pm to 5:45am); a 10-ounce prime rib dinner, including soup or salad, potato, and vegetables ($5.25 from 5 to 9:45pm)—$6.25 for a 16-ounce T-bone steak instead of prime rib. All bar drinks are available, and there's peanut butter cream pie for dessert.

Carson Street Café. Golden Nugget, 129 E. Fremont St. (between 1st St. and Casino Center Blvd.) ☎ **702/385-7111.** Reservations not accepted. Main courses $6–$15. AE, CB, DC, DISC, MC, V. Daily 24 hours. AMERICAN.

Las Vegas has many delightful 24-hour hotel restaurants. The Golden Nugget's is reminiscent of an elegant street cafe on the Champs-Elysées, albeit one overlooking a gorgeous hotel lobby instead of a Paris street. Its jewel-toned interior, under a white-fringed green awning, has murals of park scenes and topiary, white latticing, and seating amid potted orange trees and planters of greenery—it couldn't be lovelier.

And the food is notably excellent. A wide-ranging menu offers terrific salads (such as Oriental chicken), overstuffed deli sandwiches, burgers, Mexican fare (chicken burritos, fajita sandwiches), numerous breakfast items, and entrees running the gamut from filet mignon to country fried steak with mashed potatoes and vegetables. From 4 to 11pm, a 10-ounce prime rib dinner (with baked potato and vegetable) is $10. And from 11pm to 7am an 8-ounce grilled ham steak with eggs, hash browns, and toast costs $4. There's a full bar. Desserts include fresh-baked eclairs, strawberry shortcake, and hot fudge or butterscotch sundaes.

8 Buffets & Sunday Brunches

Lavish, low-priced buffets are a Las Vegas tradition, designed to lure you to the gaming tables and make you feel like you got such a bargain for your meal you can afford to drop more money. They're a gimmick, and we love them. Something about filling up on too much prime rib and shrimp just says "Vegas" to us. Of course, there is quite a range, from some perfunctory steam table displays and salad bars heavy on iceberg lettuce, to unbelievably opulent spreads with caviar and free-flowing champagne. Some are quite beautifully presented, as well. Some of the food is awful, some of it merely works as fuel, some of it is memorable.

Note: Buffet meals are extremely popular, and reservations are usually not taken (we've indicated when they are accepted, and in all those cases, they are highly recommended). Arrive early (before opening) or late to avoid a long line, especially on weekends.

SOUTH STRIP
MODERATE

Tropicana Island Buffet. 3801 Las Vegas Blvd. S. ☎ **702/739-2222.** Sat/Sun brunch $10, dinner $12. AE, CB, DC, DISC, MC, V. Daily 7am–1pm and 5–10pm.

This buffet is served in a large and delightful dining room. Dinners here feature an extensive salad bar and peel-and-eat-shrimp.

INEXPENSIVE

✪ **Excalibur's Round Table Buffet.** 3850 Las Vegas Blvd. S. ☎ **702/597-7777.** Breakfast $5, lunch $6, dinner $8. AE, CB, DC, DISC, MC, V. Daily 7–11am, 11am–4pm, and 4–10pm.

This strikes the perfect balance of cheap prices, mandatory, tacky decor, and adequate food. This is what you want in a cheap Vegas buffet. But on a recent trip they didn't have mashed potatoes or macaroni salad, which are essential for an archetypal buffet. The plates are large, so you don't have to make as many trips to the buffet tables.

✪ **The Luxor Pharaoh's Pheast Buffet.** 3900 Las Vegas Blvd. S. ☎ **702/262-4000.** Breakfast $6, lunch $7.50, dinner $10. AE, CB, DC, DISC, MC, V. Daily 6:30–11:30am, 11:30am–4pm, and 4–11pm.

The food is better than at most cheap buffets, including a Mexican station with some genuinely spicy food, Chinese stir-fry, and different Italian pastas. Desserts were disappointing. A beer and wine cart makes the rounds. Word has probably gotten out, unfortunately, because the lines are always enormous.

MID-STRIP
VERY EXPENSIVE

✪ **Bally's Sterling Sunday Brunch.** 3645 Las Vegas Blvd. S. ☎ **702/739-4111.** Reservations recommended. Brunch is $40. AE, CB, DC, JCB, MC, V. Sunday only 9:30am–2:30pm.

This brunch is served in the clubby elegant precincts of Bally's Steakhouse. Flower arrangements and ice sculptures grace lavish buffet spreads tended by white-hatted chefs. There's a waffle and omelet station, a sushi and sashimi bar, and a brimming dessert table. You might choose smoked fish with bagels and cream cheese or help yourself from a mound of fresh shrimp. Entrees vary weekly. On a recent visit the possibilities included rolled chicken stuffed with pistachios and porcini mushrooms, beef tenderloin, steak Diane, seared salmon with beet butter sauce and fried leeks, roast duckling with black currant and blueberry sauce, penne Florentine with pine nuts, and smoked chicken in vodka sauce. Of course, there are deli and breakfast meats, vegetables and scrumptious salads, cheeses, raw bar offerings, seasonal fruits and berries, and side dishes such as stuffed potatoes with caviar and sour cream. Champagne flows freely.

MODERATE

✪ **Bally's Big Kitchen Buffet.** 3645 Las Vegas Blvd. S. ☎ **702/739-4111.** Breakfast $9, brunch $10, dinner $14. AE, CB, DC, JCB, MC, V. Daily 7–11am, 11am–2:30pm, and 4 –10pm.

Everything is extremely fresh and of the highest quality. There's always a bountiful salad bar, a good choice of fruits and vegetables, entrees (perhaps seafood casserole in a creamy dill sauce, baked red snapper, pork chops sautéed in Cajun spices, barbecued chicken, and broiled steak in peppercorn sauce), pastas, rice and potato dishes, cold cuts, and a vast array of fresh-baked desserts. The brunch buffet includes breakfast fare and all-you-can-eat shrimp, while the dinner buffet adds Chinese selections.

✪ **Caesars Palace Palatium Buffet.** 3570 Las Vegas Blvd. S. ☎ **702/731-7110.** Breakfast $8, lunch $10, dinner $15; Sat/Sun brunch (includes unlimited champagne) $14 adults, children 4 to 12 half price, under 3 free. AE, CB, DC, DISC, MC, V. Mon–Fri 7:30–11:30am, 11:30am–3:30pm, and 4:30–10pm; Sat–Sun 8:30am–3:30pm and 4:30–10pm.

Selections at lunch and dinner include elaborate salad bars, fresh-baked breads, and much, much more. The evening meal includes a cold seafood station. Especially lavish are weekend brunches with omelet stations (in addition to egg dishes), breakfast meats, fresh-squeezed juices, potatoes prepared in various ways, pastas, rice casseroles, carved meats, cold shrimp, smoked salmon, and a waffle and ice-cream sundae bar in addition to two dessert islands spotlighting cakes and pastries. That's not the half of it.

✪ **Mirage Buffet.** 3400 Las Vegas Blvd. S. ☎ **702/791-7111.** Breakfast $7.50, lunch $9, dinner $13; Sun brunch $14; reduced prices for children ages

4–10, children under 4 free. AE, CB, DC, DISC, MC, V. Mon–Sat 7–10:45am, 11am–2:45pm, and 3–10pm; Sun 8am–9:30pm.

The Mirage offers lavish spreads in a lovely garden-themed setting with palm trees, a plant-filled stone fountain, and seating under verdigris eaves and domes embellished with flowers. You pay somewhat more here than at other buffets, but you certainly get what you pay for. The salad bars alone are enormous, filled with at least 25 different choices such as Thai beef, seafood, salad Niçoise, tabbouleh, Chinese chicken, Creole rice, and tortellini. At brunch champagne flows freely, and a scrumptious array of smoked fish is added to the board, along with such items as fruit-filled crepes and blintzes. And every meal features a spectacular dessert table (the bread pudding in bourbon sauce is noteworthy). For healthful eating there are many light items to choose from, including sugar- and fat-free puddings. And on Sundays a nonalcoholic sparkling cider is a possible champagne alternative.

INEXPENSIVE

Flamingo Hilton Paradise Garden Buffet. 3555 Las Vegas Blvd. S. ☎ **702/733-3111.** Breakfast $6.75, lunch $8, dinner $10. AE, CB, DC, DISC, JCB, MC, V. Daily 6am–noon, noon–2pm, and 4:30–10pm.

At dinner, there is an extensive international food station (which changes monthly) presenting French, Chinese, Mexican, German, or Italian specialties. A large salad bar, fresh fruits, pastas, vegetables, potato dishes, and a vast dessert display round out the offerings. Lunch is similar, featuring a mix of international cuisines as well as a stir-fry station and a soup/salad/pasta bar. At breakfast, you'll find all the expected fare, including a made-to-order omelet station and fresh-baked breads.

✪ **Rio's Carnival World Buffet.** 3700 W. Flamingo Rd. ☎ **702/252-7777.** Breakfast $7, lunch $9, dinner $11. AE, CB, DC, MC, V. Daily 8:30–10:30am, 11am–3:30pm, 3:30–11pm.

This is an excellent buffet with cheerfully decorative food booths set up like stations in an upscale food court. A barbecued chicken and ribs station offers side dishes of baked beans and mashed potatoes. Other stations offer stir-fry (chicken, beef, pork, and vegetables), Mexican taco fixings and accompaniments, Chinese fare, a Japanese sushi and teppanyaki grill, a Brazilian mixed grill, Italian pasta and antipasto, and fish and chips. There's even a diner setup for hot dogs, burgers, fries, and milk shakes. All this is in addition to the usual offerings of most Las Vegas buffets. Everything is fresh and beautifully prepared and presented.

EAST OF THE STRIP
MODERATE

✪ **Las Vegas Hilton Buffet of Champions.** 3000 Paradise Rd. ☎ **702/ 732-5111.** Breakfast $8, lunch $9, dinner $13; weekend brunch $12 (includes unlimited champagne). Children 12 and under half price. CB, DC, DISC, ER, MC, V. Mon–Fri 7–10am, 11am–2:30pm, and 5–10pm; Sat–Sun 8am–2:30pm and 5–10pm.

The fare is fresh and delicious. Dinner additionally features all-you-can-eat crab and shrimp.

DOWNTOWN
MODERATE

✪ **The Golden Nugget Buffet.** 129 E. Fremont St. ☎ **702/385-7111.** Breakfast $5.75, lunch $7.50, dinner $10.25; Sun brunch $11. AE, CB, DC, DISC, MC, V. Mon–Sat 7–10:30am, 10:30am–3pm, and 4–10pm; Sun 8am–10pm.

This buffet has often been voted number one in Las Vegas. The buffet tables are also laden with an extensive salad bar (about 50 items), fresh fruit, and marvelous desserts including Zelma Wynn's (Steve's mother) famous bread pudding. Every night fresh seafood is featured. Most lavish is the all-day Sunday champagne brunch, which adds such dishes as eggs Benedict, blintzes, pancakes, creamed herring, and smoked fish with bagels and cream cheese. *Note:* This stunning buffet room is also the setting for a $3 late-night meal of steak and eggs with home fries and biscuits with gravy; it's served 11pm to 4am.

INEXPENSIVE

Lady Luck Banquet Buffet. 206 N. 3rd St. ☎ **702/477-3000.** Breakfast $5, lunch $5.50, dinner $7.75. AE, CB, DC, DISC, JCB, MC, V. Daily 6–10:30am, 10:30am–2pm, and 4–10pm.

Dinner includes all-you-can-eat prime rib and frequent Chinese, Polynesian, and Italian specialties as well. Offerings additionally include an extensive salad bar, a make-your-own-sundae bar, an array of fresh-baked pies and cakes, and beverages.

✪ **Main Street Station Garden Court.** 200 N. Main St. ☎ **702/ 387-1896.** Breakfast $5, lunch $7, dinner $9; Fri seafood buffet $13; Sat and Sun champagne brunch $8; children 3 and under free. AE, CB, DC, DISC, MC, V. Mon–Fri 7–10:30am, 11am–3pm, and 4–10pm; Sat–Sun 7am–3pm and 4–10pm.

The Main Street Station Garden Court buffet is one of the best in town, much less in Downtown. Featuring nine live-action stations (meaning you can watch your food being prepared), it includes a

wood-fired brick oven pizza (delicious), many fresh salsas at the
Mexican station, a barbecue rotisserie, fresh sausage at the carving
station, Chinese food, Hawaiian food, and a selection of Southern
specialties (soul food and the like). On Friday nights, they have all
this plus countless kinds of seafood all the way up to lobster.

✪ **Sam Boyd's Fremont Paradise Buffet.** 200 E. Fremont St. ☎ **702/
385-3232.** Breakfast $5, lunch $6, dinner $9 ($14 for Seafood Fantasy);
Sun brunch $8. AE, CB, DC, DISC, JCB, MC, V. Mon–Sat 7–10:30am and 11am–
3pm; Mon, Wed, Thurs 4–10pm (Sat until 11pm); Seafood Fantasy Sun and
Tues 4–10pm (Fri until 11pm); Sun 7am–3pm.

Meals here are on the lavish side. Sunday, Tuesday, and Friday
nights the buffet is renamed the Seafood Fantasy, and food tables,
adorned with beautiful ice sculptures, are laden with lobster claws,
crab legs, shrimp, raw oysters, smoked salmon, clams, and entrees
such as steamed mussels, shrimp scampi, and scallops Provençale—
all in addition to the usual meat-carving stations and a few other
entrees. It's great! And finally, the Fremont has a delightful champagne Sunday brunch served by "island girls" in colorful Polynesian
garb. It includes not only unlimited champagne, but a full carving
station, lox with bagels and cream cheese, an omelet station, and
desserts.

What to See & Do in Las Vegas

*Y*ou aren't going to lack for things to do in Las Vegas. More than likely, you have come here for the gambling, which should keep you pretty busy (we say with some understatement). But you can't sit at a slot machine forever. (Or maybe you can.) In any event, it shouldn't be too hard to find ways to fill your time between poker hands.

Just walking on the Strip and gazing at the gaudy, garish, absurd wonder of it all can occupy quite a lot of time. This is the number-one activity we recommend in Vegas; at night, it is a mind-boggling sight like no other. But if you need something else to do, or if you are trying to amuse yourself while the rest of your party gambles away, this chapter will guide you. Don't forget to check out the free attractions, such as the Mirage's volcano and white tiger exhibit, Treasure Island's pirate battle, and the new Masquerade Show at the Rio Hotel.

But there's much more to a Las Vegas vacation than gaming action and headliner entertainment. Nearby **Hoover Dam** is a major sightseeing attraction, and Lake Mead is one of several pristinely beautiful recreation areas. In our opinion, the ideal Las Vegas vacation combines the glitz and glitter of casino hotels with explorations of the area's natural beauty. Be sure to take a look at attractions listed for children, many of which may also interest adults.

1 Las Vegas Attractions

✪ **Caesars Magical Empire.** Caesars Palace, 3570 Las Vegas Blvd. S. ☎ **800/445-4544** or 702/731-7333. Reservations necessary. Admission (including a three-course meal and wine, tax, and gratuities) $75 adults, children half price. Fri–Tues 4:30–11:30pm, closed Wed–Thur. Children must be at least 10 years of age.

Caesars spent a lot of money constructing this facility, and it shows. It's an impressive place of tunnels, grottos, revolving rooms, theaters, and so forth, with a surprise around every corner. Upon arrival, you are assigned to a group of no more than 24, which is escorted through catacombs by centurion guards to a private dining room. There, you are treated to an intimate magic show by your own private magician. Assisted by some very funny wait staff, a little story is usually played out as you eat your dinner. Up-close magic is performed between courses. Afterwards, you are taken through the rest of the Cavern (beware the Forbidden Crypt of Ramses if you have anything even remotely resembling motion sickness—they ask only if you have "balance problems"); you'll end up in a seven-story dome, with massive Egyptian columns and sculptures, where you can see several other magic shows ranging in size. Here, you can experience **Lumineria,** a 5-minute show combining smoke, dancing fire, and high-tech lighting effects (cover your eyes before the finale—it's nearly blinding), or chat with some skeletons (Habeas and Corpus) on the walls and, best of all, request songs from "Invisibella," the player-piano ghost with a nearly unlimited repertoire and a great sense of humor. All throughout are additional spots with some kind of trick to them; be sure to ask the bartenders for advice. (And look for ghosts in the bathroom mirrors.)

The three-course dinner isn't bad (salad and dessert were pretty good, main course average, though it featured a tasty polenta), and the whole experience is playful and genuinely fun. You can stay as long as you want, even after you have seen all the shows (though that could take a while as they rotate performers in the venues). There are two different bars inside, with video poker in case you are jonesing. You could hang out for hours in the Grotto Bar, making requests to Invisibella. Allow yourself at least 3 hours to see everything once. Considering how much show, spectacle, food, and just plain entertainment you get, this is one of the best values in the city.

Caesars OMNIMAX Theatre. Caesars Palace, 3570 Las Vegas Blvd. S. ☎ **800/634-6698** or 702/731-7901. Admission $7 adults; seniors, children 2–12, hotel guests, and military personnel $5. Show times vary. You must purchase tickets at the box office (open daily 9am–11pm) on the day of the performance.

If you've never seen one of these 3-D-like films, you're in for a treat. The OMNIMAX Theatre here is housed in a geodesic dome, a space-age environment with 368 seats that recline 27°, affording a panoramic view of the curved 57-foot screen. The movies, projected via 70mm film (which is 10 times the frame size of ordinary 35mm film), offer an awesome visual display enhanced by a state-of-the-art sound system (89 speakers engulf the audience in sound). Depending on the film being shown, viewers might soar over the Rocky

Las Vegas Attractions

To Salt Lake City & Valley of Fire

To Reno & Mt. Charleston

Bonanza Rd.

To Hoover Dam

Ogden Ave.
Fremont St.

DOWNTOWN

To Laughlin

Bonneville Ave.

Gateway District

Charleston Blvd.

To Red Rock Canyon

Stratosphere

Sahara Ave.

Karen Ave.

Circus Circus Dr.

Circus Circus

NORTH STRIP

Las Vegas Country Club

Stardust Rd.

Convention Center Dr.

Las Vegas Convention Center

Desert Inn Country Club

Desert Inn Rd.

Sands Ave.

Mirage

MID-STRIP

Twain Ave.

Caesars Palace

Imperial Palace

Tropicana Wash

Flamingo Rd.

University of Nevada Las Vegas

Harmon Ave.

Flamingo Wash

MGM Grand

Excalibur

Luxor

SOUTH STRIP

Tropicana Ave.

Reno Ave.

Hacienda Ave.

To Hoover Dam

Russell Rd.

Russell Rd.

McCarran International Airport

0   1 mi
    1.61 km

To Los Angeles

Caesars Magical Empire ⑫
Caesars Omnimax Theatre ⑫
Fremont Street Experience ④
Grand Slam Canyon ⑧
Imperial Palace Auto Collection ⑬
Las Vegas Motor Speedway ①
Las Vegas Natural History Museum ③
Liberace Museum ⑰
Lied Discovery Children's Museum ②
Luxor IMAX Theatre/ Secrets of the Luxor Pyramid ⑯
Magic & Movie Hall of Fame ⑭
MGM Grand Adventures Theme Park ⑮
Mirage Dolphin Habitat ⑪
Race for Atlantis ⑫
Scandia Family Fun Center ⑩
Secret Garden of Siegfried & Roy ⑪
Speedworld @ Sahara ⑥
Star Trek: The Experience ⑨
Stratosphere Thrill Rides ⑤
Wet 'n' Wild ⑦

P-0047

Note

A good place to view the Sky Parade light show is from the balcony at Fitzgeralds Hotel.

Mountains, plummet down steep waterfalls, ride the rapids, travel into outer space, or perch at the rim of an erupting volcano. Shows change frequently, but whatever you see will be stupendous.

○ **Fremont Street Experience.** Fremont St. (between Main St. and Las Vegas Blvd. in Downtown Las Vegas). Shows nightly. Free admission. www.vegasexperience.com.

For some years, Downtown Vegas has been losing ground to the Strip. But thanks to a $70 million revitalization project, that is starting to change. Fremont Street, the heart of "Glitter Gulch," has been closed off and turned into a pedestrian mall. The Fremont Street Experience is a 5-block open-air pedestrian mall, a landscaped strip of outdoor cafes, vendor carts, and colorful kiosks purveying food and merchandise. Overhead is a 90-foot-high steel-mesh "celestial vault"; at night, it is the **Sky Parade,** a high-tech light and laser show (the canopy is equipped with more than 2.1 million lights) enhanced by a concert hall quality sound system, which takes place four times nightly. But there's music between shows as well. Not only does the canopy provide shade, it cools the area through a misting system in summer and warms you with radiant heaters in winter. The difference this makes cannot be overemphasized; what was once a ghost town of tacky, rapidly aging buildings, in an area with more undesirables than not, is now a bustling (at least at night), friendly, safe place (they have private security guards who hustle said undesirables away). It's a place where you can stroll, eat, or even dance to the music under the lights. The crowd it attracts is more upscale than in years past and, of course, it's a lot less crowded than the hectic Strip.

Imperial Palace Auto Collection. Imperial Palace Hotel, 3535 Las Vegas Blvd. S. ☎ **702/731-3311.** Admission $7 adults, $3 seniors and children under 12, free for children under 5 and AAA members. Daily 9:30am–11:30pm.

If you're not a "car person," don't assume you won't be interested in this premier collection of antique, classic, and special-interest vehicles. There's more here than just cars and trucks. Check out the graceful lines and handsome sculpture of one of the 43 Model J Dusenbergs (the largest collection in the world, valued at over $50 million). The craftsmanship and attention to detail make these cars, and others here, true works of art. There's also a great deal of history. Take a walk down President's Row where you can see JFK's 1962 "bubbletop" Lincoln Continental, Lyndon Johnson's 1964 Cadillac, Eisenhower's 1952 Chrysler Imperial 20-foot-long parade car, Truman's 1950 Lincoln Cosmopolitan with gold-plated interior, FDR's unrestored 1936 V-16 Cadillac, and Herbert Hoover's 1929 Cadillac.

Las Vegas Motor Speedway. 7000 Las Vegas Blvd. N. (directly across from Nellis Air Force base). ☎ **702/644-4443** for ticket information. Tickets $10–$75 (higher prices for major events). Take I-15 north to Speedway exit 54.

This 107,000-seat facility, the first new superspeedway to be built in the southwest in over 2 decades, opened with a 500K Indy Racing League event. A $100 million state-of-the-art motor sports entertainment complex, it includes a 1.5-mile super-speedway, a 2.5-mile FIA-approved road course, paved and dirt short-track ovals, and a 4,000-foot drag strip. Also on the property are facilities for Go-Kart, Legends Car, Sand Drag, and Motocross competition. The new speedway is accessible via shuttle buses to and from the Imperial Palace hotel, though some of the other major hotels have their own shuttles to the Speedway.

✪ Liberace Museum. 1775 E. Tropicana Ave. (at Spencer St.) ☎ **702/798-5595.** Admission $7 adults, $4.50 seniors over 60, $3.50 students, $2 children 6–12, children under 6 free. Mon–Sat 10am–5pm, Sun 1–5pm.

You can keep your Louvres and Vaticans and Smithsonians; *this* is a museum. Housed, like everything else in Vegas, in a strip mall, this is a shrine to the glory and excess that was the art project known as Liberace. You've got your costumes (bejeweled), your many cars (bejeweled), your many pianos (bejeweled), and many jewels (also bejeweled). It just shows what can be bought with lots of money and no taste. Unless you have a severely underdeveloped appreciation for camp or take your museum-going very seriously, you shouldn't miss it. The museum is 2½ miles east of the Strip on your right.

Luxor IMAX Theater/Secrets of the Luxor Pyramid. Luxor Las Vegas, 3900 Las Vegas Blvd. S. ☎ **702/262-4000.** Admission $7 for IMAX 2-D, $8.50 for 3-D; for "Secrets" Episode One $4, Episode Two $5. A combined ticket, including both episodes of "Secrets of the Luxor Pyramid" (described below), is $9. Sun–Thurs 10am–11pm, Fri–Sat 10am–11:30pm. Show times vary depending on the length of the film.

This is a state-of-the-art theater that projects films on a seven-story screen. There are two different films running, one in standard two dimensions, the other 3-D. The glasses for the latter are really cool headsets that include built-in speakers, bringing certain sounds right into your head. The movies change periodically but always include some extraordinary special effects. If you have a fear of heights, make sure to ask for a seat on one of the lower levels.

✪ **Magic and Movie Hall of Fame.** O'Shea's Casino, 3555 Las Vegas Blvd. S. (between Sands Ave. and Flamingo Rd.) ☎ **702/737-1343.** Admission $10 adults, $3 children under 12 accompanied by an adult. ($5 discount coupons available outside.) Tues–Sat 10am–6pm. Magic shows at 1 and 4:30pm.

Given its location in the cheesy and just a tad sleazy O'Shea's, one might be tempted to skip over this "Hall of Fame" as a cheap tourist trap. That would be a mistake. This well-produced and informative tribute to magicians, ventriloquists, and past movie stars has all the fun of old curiosity shows.

The tour begins with a chronological history of late 19th-century and 20th-century magicians. The whole thing is carnival creepy and reminds you of the days when magicians were mysterious and maybe just a little bit in touch with forces from the Great Beyond.

Surprisingly, there is also an extensive exhibit of the history of ventriloquism. Best of all, you can even try ventriloquism yourself with the help of a dummy, a mirror, and audio and written help. (It's not easy!) The "Movie" part is manifested in a large display of costumes from classic movies.

Race for Atlantis Ride IMAX 3-D Ride. 3500 Las Vegas Blvd. S. (in the Forum Shops at Caesars Palace). ☎ **800/634-6661.** Admission $9.50 adults, $6.75 children under 12. Sun–Thurs 10am–11pm, Fri–Sat 10am–midnight.

Following the trend in virtual reality theme park rides, Caesars Palace joined forces with IMAX to create the Race for Atlantis. If you've never been on a virtual reality ride, you will enjoy it, but the production values pale compared to the Star Trek Experience (but then again, that's also twice as expensive). Not for the weak of stomach.

The Secret Garden of Siegfried and Roy & ✪ Mirage Dolphin Habitat. Mirage Hotel, 3400 Las Vegas Blvd. S. ☎ **702/791-7111.** Admission $10, free for children under 10. Mon–Fri 11am–5:30pm, Sat–Sun 10am–5:30pm. (Dolphin exhibit only on Wed $5, when the Secret Garden is closed.) Hours subject to change.

Siegfried and Roy's famous white tigers have long had a free exhibit in the Mirage. They still do, but now they have an additional space, a gorgeous area behind the dolphin exhibit. Here, the white tigers are joined by white lions, Bengal tigers, an Asian elephant, a panther, and a snow leopard. (Many of these are bred by Siegfried &

Roy and are also in their nightly show.) It's really just a glorified zoo, featuring only the big-ticket animals; however, it is a very pretty place, with plenty of foliage and some bits of Indian- and Asian-themed architecture. Zoo purists will be horrified at the smallish spaces the animals occupy, but all are rotated between here and their more lavish digs at the illusionist team's home. What this does allow you to do is get very up close with a tiger, which is quite a thrill—those paws are massive indeed. Visitors are given little portable phonelike objects on which they can play a series of programs, listening to Roy and Mirage owner Steve Wynn discuss conservation or the attributes of each animal and deliver anecdotes.

The dolphin habitat is more satisfying. It was designed to provide a healthy and nurturing environment and to educate the public about marine mammals and their role in the ecosystem. The Mirage displays only dolphins already in captivity—no dolphins are taken from the wild. You can watch the dolphins frolic both above and below ground through viewing windows, in three different pools. (There is nothing quite like the kick you get from seeing a baby dolphin play.) The knowledgeable staff, who surely have the best job in Vegas, will answer questions. The staff also plays ball with the dolphins; they toss large beach balls into the pools, and the dolphins hit them out with their noses, leaping out of the water cackling with dolphin glee. You catch the ball, getting nicely wet, and toss it back to them. If you have never played ball with a dolphin, shove that happy child next to you out of the way and go for it.

Speedworld at Sahara. 2535 Las Vegas Blvd. S. (in the Sahara Hotel). ☎ **702/737-2111.** Indy-car simulator $8 (you must be at least 48 inches tall to ride), 3-D simulator $5. Mon–Thurs 10am–10pm, Fri–Sun 10am–midnight.

Consisting of two parts, the first is a virtual reality ride featuring a three quarter–sized replica of an Indianapolis race car. Hop aboard for an animated, simulated ride—either the Indy itself or a race around the streets of Las Vegas. It's a pretty remarkable experience. Next, a separate 3-D-motion theater sets you up, complete with goggles, to view a film that puts you right inside another race car, for yet another stomach-churning (more so than the virtual reality portion) ride. Speed junkies and race car buffs will be in heaven here.

STAR TREK: The Experience. Las Vegas Hilton, 3000 Paradise Rd. ☎ **702/732-5111.** www.startrekexp.com. Admission $13. Daily 11am–11pm.

It goes without saying that Trekkers (note use of correct term) will be delighted with this. On the other hand, normal, sensible fans, and those who couldn't care less about Star Trek, may find themselves saying, "I spent $12.95 and two hours in line for this?" Do expect to be beamed aboard the Enterprise (that's really kind of cool), and know that if you have a sensitive stomach, you can skip the actual motion simulator part, a wild, and sometimes headache-inducing, chase through space.

Stratosphere Thrill Rides. Stratosphere, 2000 Las Vegas Blvd. S. ☎ **702/ 380-7777.** Admission for either ride is $5, plus $5 to ascend the tower. (If you dine in the buffet room or Top of the World, there's no charge to go up to the tower.) Sun–Thurs 10am–midnight, Fri–Sat 10am–2am. Minimum height requirement for both rides is 48 inches.

Atop the 1,149-foot Stratosphere Tower are two marvelous thrill rides. The **Let It Ride High Roller** (the world's highest roller-coaster) was recently revamped to go at even faster speeds as it zooms around a hilly track that is seemingly suspended in midair. Even more fun is the **Big Shot,** a breathtaking free-fall ride that thrusts you 160 feet in the air along a 228-foot spire at the top of the tower, then plummets back down again. Sitting in an open car, you seem to be dangling in space over Las Vegas. We have one relative, a thrill-ride enthusiast, who said he never felt more scared than when he rode the Big Shot. After surviving, he promptly put his kids on it, who loved it.

2 Getting Married

This is one of the most popular things to do in Las Vegas. Why? It's very easy to get married here. Too easy. See that total stranger standing next to you? Grab him or her, head down to the **Clark County Marriage License Bureau** (200 S. 3rd at Briger Avenue; ☎ **702/ 455-3156;** open Monday to Sunday from 8am to midnight, 24 hours legal holidays) to get your license, find a wedding chapel (not hard since they line the north end of the Strip—Las Vegas Boulevard South), and tie the knot. Just like that. No blood test, no waiting period—heck, not even an awkward dating period.

You can pick a chapel just by driving down the Strip past the Stratosphere, but we've listed four of our favorites. You can also call **Las Vegas Weddings and Rooms** (☎ **800/488-MATE**), a one-stop shop for wedding services. They'll find a chapel or outdoor garden that suits your taste (not to mention such only-in-Vegas venues as the former mansions of Elvis Presley and Liberace), book you into a hotel for the honeymoon, arrange the ceremony, and provide every accessory you need. Theme weddings are a specialty. They even have a New Age minister on call who can perform a

Native American ceremony. And yes, you can get married by an Elvis impersonator.

✪ **Cupid's Wedding Chapel.** 827 Las Vegas Blvd. S. ☎ **800/543-2933** or 702/598-4444. Sun–Thurs 10am–10pm, Fri–Sat 10am–1am.

"The little chapel with the big heart." Well, it just might be. The manager explains that, unlike other chapels on the Strip, they schedule weddings an hour apart. This gives them time for the full production number; they pride themselves on offering "a traditional church wedding at a chapel price." "I am a diehard romantic," said the manager. "I want huggin', kissin', and I don't care if they faint—a wedding is a place for romance." You just know she cries at each and every service they perform.

The Little White Chapel. 1301 Las Vegas Blvd. S. ☎ **800/545-8111** or 702/382-5943. Open 24 hours.

This is arguably the most famous of the chapels on the Strip, maybe because they have the big sign saying Michael Jordan and Joan Collins were married there (not to each other), maybe because they were the first to do the drive-up window. It is indeed little and white. However, they feel like a factory line, processing wedding after wedding after wedding, 24 hours a day. Move 'em in and move 'em out. (No wonder they put in that drive-up window!) If you want something special, there are probably better choices, but for a true Vegas wedding experience, this is Kitsch Wedding Central.

San Francisco Sally's Victorian Chapel. 1304 Las Vegas Blvd. S. ☎ **800/658-8677** or 702/385-7777. Sun–Thurs 10am–4pm, Fri–Sat 10am–8pm.

An extremely tiny wedding chapel bursting at the seams with Victorian frills (fringed lamps, swags of lace curtains). They basically offer "an Olde Tyme Parlor Wedding." This is perfect if you want a very intimate wedding—like you, your intended, and someone to officiate. It literally can't hold more than six people. But if you love Victoriana, or you want to play dress up (they rent out costumes) at your wedding, this is the place. The women who run it refer to themselves as "a bunch of mother hens," are delightful, and will pamper you to within an inch of your life. (One couple drops in every year just to say hi.)

✪ **A Special Memory Wedding Chapel.** 800 S. 4th St. (at Gass Ave.) ☎ **800/9-MARRYU** or 702/384-2211. www.aspecialmemory.com. Sun–Thurs 8am–10pm, Fri–Sat 8am–midnight.

This is a terrific new wedding chapel, particularly when compared to the rather tired facades of the classics on the Strip. This is absolutely the place to go if you want a traditional, big production wedding; you won't feel in the least bit tacky or in any other way like you got married in Vegas. It's a New England church-style building, complete with steeple. The interior looks like a proper church (well, a plain one—don't think ornate gothic cathedral). Should all this just be too darn nice and proper for you, they also offer a drive-up window (where they do about 300 weddings a month!).

3 Especially for Kids

Like much of the rest of the world, you may be under the impression that Las Vegas has evolved from an adults-only fantasyland into a vacation destination suitable for the entire family. This is a myth. The gargantuan hotels that spent small fortunes on redecorating in an attempt to lure families with vast quantities of junk food and a lot of hype now vehemently deny that any such notion ever crossed their collective minds, and, no, they don't know how that roller coaster got into the parking lot.

To put things simply, Las Vegas makes money—lots and lots of money—by promoting gambling, drinking, and sex. These are all fine pursuits if you happen to be an adult, but if you haven't reached the magical age of 21, you really don't count in this town. In any case, the casinos and even the Strip itself are simply too stimulating, noisy, and smoky for young kids. Older progeny may have a tolerance for crowds and the incessant pinging of the slot machines, but they will be thoroughly annoyed with you when casino security chastises them if they so much as stop to tie their shoe laces anywhere near the gaming tables.

Nevertheless, you may have a perfectly legitimate reason for bringing your children to Las Vegas (like Grandma was busy, or you were just stopping through on your way from somewhere else), so here are some places to take the children both on and off the Strip.

Circus Circus (see p. 47) has ongoing circus acts throughout the day, a vast video-game and pinball arcade, and dozens of carnival games on its mezzanine level. Behind the hotel is Grand Slam Canyon, detailed below. **Excalibur** (see p. 30) also offers video and carnival games, plus thrill cinemas and free shows (jugglers, puppets, etc.). At **Caesars Palace,** the Magical Empire (for kids 12 and older only, see p. 101), Race for Atlantis IMAX ride (see p. 106), and OMNIMAX movies (see p. 102) are a thrill for everyone in the family. Star Trek: The Experience (see p. 107) deserves to draw families to the **Las Vegas Hilton,** but it may be a bit much for younger children. The ship battle in front of **Treasure Island** (see p. 39) is sure to please, as will the erupting volcano and the Secret Garden of Siegfried and Roy and dolphin habitat at the **Mirage** (see p. 106); while you're here, see the tigers and the sharks. Ditto the various attractions at **Luxor Las Vegas,** such as the Imax Theater (see p. 105).

Kids will enjoy **The Magic and Movie Hall of Fame** (see p. 106), but they'll want to leave before you do.

Appropriate shows for kids include Siegfried and Roy at the **Mirage** (see p. 106), Lance Burton at the **Monte Carlo** (see p. 27), EFX at the **MGM Grand** (see p. 25), and Cirque du Soleil's Mystère at **Treasure Island** (see p. 160). As a general rule, early shows are less racy than late-night shows.

Grand Slam Canyon Theme Park. 2880 Las Vegas Blvd. S. (behind Circus Circus Hotel). ☎ **702/794-3939.** Free admission; pay per ride. AE, DC, DISC, MC, V. Park hours vary; call ahead.

This isn't a half-bad place to spend a hot afternoon, especially now that Circus Circus, the casino/hotel that built this indoor amusement park, has undergone a face-lift. The glass dome that towers overhead lets in natural light, a solace to those of us who look peaked under the glow of the artificial kind. A double-loop roller coaster careens around the simulated Grand Canyon, and there's the requisite water flume, a laser tag area, and a modest number of other rides for kids of all ages. A dinosaur-bone excavation area will provide a good time for preschoolers and a place to rest for the supervising adults. Video games and an arcade are separate from the attractions, cutting down just a tad on the noise level. Jugglers and magicians provide impromptu entertainment. Our only caveat is don't leave kids here alone. They could easily get lost.

Las Vegas Natural History Museum. 900 Las Vegas Blvd. N. (at Washington). ☎ **702/384-3466.** Admission $5 adults; $2.50 children 4–12. Mon–Sun 9am–4pm.

Conveniently located across the street from the Lied Discovery Children's Museum (described below), this humble temple of taxidermy harkens back to elementary school field-trips circa 1965, when stuffed elk and brown bears forever protecting their kill were as close as most of us got to exotic animals. Worn around the edges but very sweet and relaxed, the museum is enlivened by a hands-on activity room and two life-sized dinosaurs that roar at one another intermittently. A small boy was observed leaping toward his dad upon watching this display, so you might want to warn any sensitive little ones that the big tyrannosaurs aren't going anywhere. Surprisingly, the gift shop here is particularly well stocked with neat items you won't mind too terribly buying for the kids.

Lied Discovery Children's Museum. 833 Las Vegas Blvd. N. (a half-block south of Washington, across the street from Cashman Field). ☎ **702/ 382-5437.** Admission $5 for adults, $4 for kids 12–17, $3 for kids 3–11. DISC, MC, V. Tues–Sat 10am–5pm, Sun noon–5pm.

A hands-on science museum designed for curious kids, the bright, airy, two-story Lied makes an ideal outing for toddlers and young children. With lots of interactive exhibits to examine, including a miniature grocery store, a bubble tube for encasing oneself inside a soap bubble, a radio station, and music and drawing areas, you'll soon forget your video poker losses. Clever, thought-inducing exhibits are everywhere. Learn how it feels to be a person with disabilities by playing basketball from a wheelchair. Feed a wooden "sandwich" to a cut-out of a snake, and to a human cut-out, and see how much nutrition each receives. See how much sunscreen their giant stuffed mascot needs to keep from burning. On weekend afternoons from 1pm until 3pm, free drop-in art classes are offered, giving you a bit of time to ramble around the gift store or read the fine print on the exhibit placards. The Lied also shares space with a city library branch, so after the kids run around you can calm them back down with a story or two.

MGM Grand Adventures. Behind the MGM Grand Hotel, 3799 Las Vegas Blvd. S. ☎ **702/891-3200.** Admission only (no rides): $2. Admission with unlimited rides: hotel guests $9, everyone else $11. Sky Screamer: 1 person $22.20, 2 people $17.50 each, 3 people $12.50 each. Open daily. Hours and cost vary seasonally.

This theme park, slapped together without a great deal of thought on a former parking lot, looks as if some Hollywood set designers dropped off a variety of hokey movie facades and then, unburdened, cheerfully rode off into the sunset. The attractions, such as a clothes-soaking log flume and kiddie bumper cars, are sparsely scattered among a great many food and T-shirt emporiums. It leaves one with the impression that fun has a lot to do with the contents of one's pocketbook and/or stomach. For some peculiar reason, the park sports three tiny boxing arenas where you and a friend can suit up like samurai and duke it out. This is also home of the Sky Screamer, a combination bungee jump/swing that will thrill kids old enough (and daring enough) to give it a try. (They must be at least 10 years old and 42 inches to ride the Screamer.) There is a separate charge for this ride on top of park admission, although you can pay $2 for park entrance alone, a better deal if you only wish to fly through the air. It's also fun just to sit on a bench and watch people on this contraption.

Scandia Family Fun Center. 2900 Sirius Ave. (at Rancho Dr. just south of Sahara). ☎ **702/364-0070.** Free admission, but there's a fee for each game or activity. Super Saver Pass $11 (includes 1 round of miniature golf, 2 rides, and 5 game tokens); Unlimited Wristband Package $16 (includes unlimited bumper boat and car rides, unlimited miniature golf, and 10 tokens for batting cages or arcade games). Sept to early June: Sun–Thurs 10am–11pm, Fri–Sat until midnight; mid-June to August: Sun–Thurs 10am–midnight, Fri–Sat until 1am.

This family amusement center just a few blocks off the Strip offers three 18-hole miniature golf courses ($5.50 per game, children under 6 free), a state-of-the-art video arcade with 225 machines, miniature car racing and bumper boats ($4 per ride; small children ride free with an adult), and automated softball- and baseball-pitching machines for batting practice ($1.25 for 25 pitches). A snack bar is on the premises.

Wet 'n' Wild. 2601 Las Vegas Blvd. S. (just south of Sahara Ave.) ☎ **702/ 871-7811.** www.wetnwild.com. Admission $24 adults, half-price seniors over 55, $18 children under 10, children under 3 free. Daily early May to Sept 30, 10am–6 or 8pm (sometimes later). Season and hours vary somewhat from year to year, so call ahead.

When temperatures soar, head for this 26-acre water park right in the heart of the Strip and cool off while jumping waves, careening down steep flumes, and running rapids. Among the highlights: **Royal Flush,** a thrill ride that washes you down a precipitous chute into a saucerlike bowl at 45 miles per hour, then flushes you into a bottomless pool; **Surf Lagoon,** a 500,000-gallon wave pool; **Banzai Banzai,** a roller-coasterlike water ride (aboard a plastic sled, you race down a 45°-angled 150-foot chute and skip porpoiselike across a 120-foot pool); **Der Stuka,** the world's fastest and highest water chute; **Raging Rapids,** a simulated white-water rafting adventure on a 500-foot-long river; **Lazy River,** a leisurely float trip; **Blue Niagara,** a dizzying descent inside intertwined looping tubes from a height of six stories; **Willy Willy,** a hydra-hurricane that propels riders on inner tubes around a 90-foot-diameter pool at 10 miles per hour; **Bomb Bay,** a bomblike casing 76 feet in the air that sends you on a speedy vertical flight straight down to a pool target; and the **Black Hole,** an exhilaratingly rapid space-themed flume descent in the dark enhanced by a bombardment of colorful fiber-optic star fields and spinning galaxy patterns en route to splashdown. There are additional flumes, a challenging children's water playground, and a sunbathing area with a cascading waterfall, as well as video and arcade games. Food concessions are located throughout the park, and you can purchase swimwear and accessories at the Beach Trends Shop. Also, be on the lookout for discount coupons. Many Las Vegas packages include a free admission (sometimes partial-day).

4 Playing Golf & Tennis

GOLF

There are dozens of local courses, including very challenging ones—the **Sheraton Desert Inn Country** has hosted many PGA tournaments. Beginner and intermediate golfers might prefer the other courses listed.

Angel Park Golf Club. 100 S. Rampart Blvd. (between Charleston Blvd. and Westcliff St). ☎ **888/446/5358** or 702/254-4653. $55 weekdays, $65 weekends, $5 twilight.

This 36-hole par-70/71 public course was designed by Arnold Palmer. Players call this a great escape from the casinos, and claim no matter how many times they play it, they never get tired of it. In addition to the 18-hole Palm and Mountain Courses, which are both very challenging, Angel Park offers a night-lit Cloud 9 course (12 holes for daylight play, 9 at night), where each hole is patterned after a famous par-3. **Yardage:** Palm Course 6,438 championship, 5,721 regular, 4,565 ladies; Mountain Course 6,783 championship, 6,272 regular, 5,143 ladies. **Facilities:** pro shop, night-lit driving range, 18-hole putting course, restaurant, snack bar, cocktail bar, beverage cart.

Black Mountain Golf & Country Club. 500 Greenway Rd. (in nearby Henderson). ☎ **702/565-7933.** Before 10am $52, before 1pm $30, after 1pm $20.

Two new greens have recently been added to this 18-hole, par-72 semiprivate course, which requires reservations 4 days in advance. It's considered a great old course, with lots of wildlife, including roadrunners. However, unpredictable winds may blow during your game. **Yardage:** 6,541 championship, 6,223 regular, 5,478 ladies. **Facilities:** pro shop, putting green, driving range, restaurant, snack bar, and cocktail lounge.

Craig Ranch Golf Club. 628 W. Craig Rd. (Losee Rd. and Martin Luther King Blvd.) ☎ **702/642-9700.** $16 walking, $24 in golf cart.

This is an 18-hole, par-70 public course. **Yardage:** 6,001 regular, 5,221 ladies. **Facilities:** driving range, pro shop, PGA teaching pro, putting green, and snack bar.

Desert Inn Golf Club. 3145 Las Vegas Blvd. S. ☎ **702/733-4290.** $215, $150 for guests.

The Desert Inn course gets the nod from champions. It's an 18-hole, par-72 resort course, the most famous and demanding in Las Vegas. *Golf Digest* calls it one of America's top resort courses and what Las Vegas golf is all about. The very high fees may make it out of your reach. The driving range is open to Desert Inn and Caesars guests only; anyone can play the course, but nonguests pay a higher fee. **Yardage:** 7,150 championship, 6,715 regular, 5,800 ladies. **Facilities:** driving range, putting green, pro shop, and restaurant. You can reserve 90 days in advance for Sunday to Thursday, 2 days in advance for Friday and Saturday.

Desert Rose Golf Club. 5483 Clubhouse Dr. (3 blocks west of Nellis Blvd., off Sahara Ave.) ☎ **702/431-4653.** Mon–Fri before 10am $51, after $38; Sat–Sun before noon $51, after $38.

This is an 18-hole, par-71 public course. **Yardage:** 6,511 championship, 6,135 regular, 5,458 ladies. **Facilities:** driving range, putting and chipping greens, PGA teaching pro, pro shop, restaurant, and cocktail lounge.

Las Vegas National Golf Club. 1911 Desert Inn Rd. (between Maryland Pkwy. and Eastern Ave.) ☎ **702/796-0016.**

This is an 18-hole, par-72 public course, and a classic layout. **Yardage:** 6,815 championship, 6,418 regular, 5,741 ladies. **Facilities:** pro shop, golf school, driving range, restaurant, and cocktail lounge.

TENNIS

Tennis buffs should choose one of the many hotels in town that have tennis courts.

Bally's (☎ **702/739-4598**) has eight night-lit hard courts. Fees per hour range from $10 to $15 for guests, $15 to $20 for nonguests. Facilities include a pro shop. Hours vary seasonally. Reservations are advised.

The **Flamingo Hilton** (☎ **702/733-3444**) has four outdoor hard courts (all lit for night play) and a pro shop. It is open to the public Monday to Friday from 7am to 8pm, Saturday and Sunday from 7am to 6pm. Rates are $20 per hour for nonguests, $12 for guests. Lessons are available. Reservations are required.

The **Riviera** (☎ 702/734-5110) has two outdoor hard courts (both lit for night play) that are open to the public, subject to availability; hotel guests have priority. It is open 24 hours. There is no charge for guests; nonguests pay $10 per hour. Reservations are required.

The **Desert Inn** (☎ 702/733-4557) has five outdoor hard courts (all lit for night play) and a pro shop. They are open to the public. Hours are daybreak to 10pm. Rates are $10 per person for a daily pass (you book for an hour but can stay longer if no one is waiting); they are free for guests. Reservations are necessary.

In addition to hotels, the **University of Nevada, Las Vegas (UNLV),** Harmon Avenue just east of Swenson Street (☎ 702/895-0844) has a dozen courts (all lit for night play) that are open weekdays from 6am to 9:45pm, on weekends from 8am to 9pm. Rates are $5 per person, per day on weekdays; $10 weekends. You should call before going to find out if a court is available.

5 An Excursion to Hoover Dam & Lake Mead

30 miles SE of Las Vegas

This is one of the most popular excursions from Las Vegas, visited by 2,000 to 3,000 people daily. Wear comfortable shoes; the tour involves quite a bit of walking. The best plan would be to tour the dam in the morning and enjoy some of the area's scenic beauty and recreation facilities in the afternoon.

ESSENTIALS

GETTING THERE   By Car   Go east on Flamingo or Tropicana to U.S. 515 south, which automatically turns into 93 south and takes you right to the dam. As you near it, you'll see a five-story parking structure tucked into the canyon wall on your left. Park here ($2 charge) and take the elevators or stairs to the walkway leading to the new Visitor Center.

If you would rather go on an **organized tour, Gray Line** (☎ 702/384-1234) offers several Hoover Dam packages, all of them including admission and a tour of the dam. The 4¹/₂-hour **Hoover Dam Shuttle Tour** departs daily at 7:45am, 9:45am, and 11:45am and includes pickup and drop off; the price is $29.50 for adults, $19.50 for children 10 to 16, $24.50 for seniors over 62, $15.50 for children under 10. Most elaborate is the **Grand Hoover Dam and Lake Mead Cruise Tour,** departing daily at 9:45am, which includes a 90-minute paddle-wheeler cruise on Lake Mead

Lake Mead & Vicinity

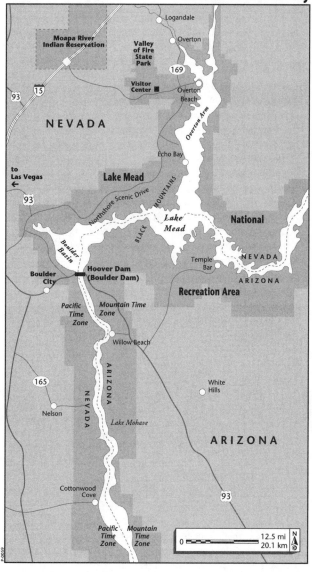

Logandale

Overton

Moapa River
Indian Reservation

Valley
of Fire
State
Park

169

Visitor
Center

Overton
Beach

NEVADA

Overton Arm

Echo Bay

to
Las Vegas
←

93

Lake Mead

Northshore Scenic Drive

BLACK MOUNTAINS

*Lake
Mead*

National

NEVADA

*Boulder
Basin*

ARIZONA

Boulder
City

**Hoover Dam
(Boulder Dam)**

Temple
Bar

Recreation Area

*Pacific
Time
Zone*

*Mountain Time
Zone*

ARIZONA

NEVADA

Willow Beach

165

White
Hills

Nelson

Lake Mohave

ARIZONA

Cottonwood
Cove

93

*Pacific
Time
Zone*

*Mountain
Time
Zone*

0   12.5 mi
       20.1 km

N

93

with a light lunch available for an extra cost, plus admission to Hoover Dam; adults $41, under 10 $35. You can inquire at your hotel sightseeing desk about other bus tours.

HOOVER DAM

In 1928, prodded by the seven states through which the river runs during the course of its 1,400-mile journey to the Gulf of California, Congress authorized construction of a dam at Boulder Canyon (later moved to Black Canyon). The Senate's declaration of intention was that "A mighty river, now a source of destruction, is to be curbed and put to work in the interests of society." Construction began in 1931. Because of its vast scope and the unprecedented problems posed in its realization, the project generated significant advances in many areas of machinery production, engineering, and construction. An army of more than 5,200 laborers was assembled, and work proceeded 24 hours a day. Completed in 1936, 2 years ahead of schedule and $15 million under budget (let's see James Cameron top that!), the dam stopped the annual floods and conserved water for irrigation, industrial, and domestic use. Equally important, it became one of the world's major electrical generating plants, providing low-cost, pollution-free hydroelectric power to a score of surrounding communities. Hoover Dam's $175 million cost has been repaid with interest by the sale of inexpensive power to a number of California cities and the states of Arizona and Nevada. The dam is a government project that paid for itself—a feat almost as awe-inspiring as its engineering.

The dam itself is a massive curved wall, 660 feet thick at the bottom and tapering to 45 feet where the road crosses it at the top. It towers 726.4 feet above bedrock (about the height of a 60-story skyscraper) and acts as a plug between the canyon walls to hold back up to 9.2 trillion gallons of water in Lake Mead—the reservoir created by its construction. All the architecture is on a grand scale, with beautiful art deco elements unusual in an engineering project. Note, for instance, the monumental 30-foot bronze sculpture, *Winged Figures of the Republic,* flanking a 142-foot flagpole at the Nevada entrance. According to its creator, Oskar Hansen, the sculpture symbolizes "the immutable calm of intellectual resolution, and the enormous power of trained physical strength, equally enthroned in placid triumph of scientific achievement."

The dam has become a major sightseeing attraction along with Lake Mead, America's largest artificial reservoir and a major Nevada recreation area.

Seven miles northwest of the dam on U.S. 93, you'll pass through **Boulder City,** which was built to house managerial and construction workers. Sweltering summer heat (many days it is 125°F) ruled out a campsite by the dam, whereas the higher elevation of Boulder City offered lower temperatures. The city emerged within a single year, turning a desert waste into a community of 6,000. By 1934 it was Nevada's third-largest town.

TOURING THE DAM

The very nice **Hoover Dam Visitor Center,** a vast three-level circular concrete structure with a rooftop overlook, opened in 1995. You'll enter the Reception Lobby, where you can buy tickets, peruse informational exhibits, photographs, and memorabilia, and view three 12-minute video presentations (respectively, about the importance of water to life, the events leading up to the construction of Hoover Dam, and the construction itself as well as the many benefits it confers). Exhibits on the Plaza Level include interactive displays on the environment, habitation, and development of the Southwest, the people who built the dam, and related topics. Yet another floor up, galleries on the Overlook Level demonstrate, via sculpted bronze panels, the benefits of Hoover Dam and Lake Mead to the states of Arizona, Nevada, and California. The Overlook Level additionally provides an unobstructed view of Lake Mead, the dam, the power plant, the Colorado River, and Black Canyon. (There are multiple photo opportunities throughout this trip.) You can visit an exhibit center across the street where a 10-minute presentation in a small theater focuses on a topographical map of the 1,400-mile Colorado River. It also has a cafeteria.

Thirty-minute tours of the dam depart from the Reception Lobby every 15 minutes or so daily, except Christmas. The Visitor Center opens at 8:30am, and the first tour departs soon after. The last tour leaves at 6pm, and the center closes at 6:30pm. Admission is $8 for adults, $7 for senior citizens, and $2 children 6 to 16, free for children under 6. More extensive, and expensive, hard-hat tours are offered every half hour between 9:30am and 3:30pm; it's not a bad idea to call in advance (☎ **702/294-3522**).

The tour begins with a 561-foot elevator descent into the dam's interior, where an access tunnel leads to the Nevada wing of the power plant. (You only cross to Arizona on the hard-hat tour.) In the three stops on the regular tour, you see the massive turbines that generate the electricity using the water flow, go outside on the down river side of the dam looking up at the towering structure (which is pretty awesome), and then go into one of the tunnels that contains a steel water diversion pipe that feeds the turbines. (It's one of the largest steel water pipes ever made—its interior could accommodate two lanes of automobile traffic.) Along the way, the park service guide gives the history of the dam project, usually with great fervor for the undertaking of the construction and the value of the project. Though the guides can be a tad overdramatic, you do get a sense of what a huge endeavor and achievement this was.

Some fun facts you might hear along the way: It took $6^1/2$ years to fill the lake. Though 96 workers were killed during the construction, contrary to popular myth, none were accidently buried as the concrete was poured (as it was poured only at a level of eight inches at a time). Look for a monument to them outside—"they died to make the desert bloom"—along with one for their doggy mascot who was also killed, although after the dam was completed. Compare their wages of 50¢ an hour to the wages of their Depression-era peers, who made 5¢ to 30¢.

LAKE MEAD NATIONAL RECREATION AREA

Under the auspices of the National Park Service, the 1.5-million-acre Lake Mead National Recreation Area was created in 1936 around Lake Mead (the reservoir lake resulted from the construction of Hoover Dam) and later Lake Mohave to the south (formed with the construction of Davis Dam). Before the lakes emerged, this desert region was brutally hot, dry, and rugged—unfit for human habitation. Today it is one of the nation's most popular playgrounds, attracting about nine million visitors annually. The two lakes comprise 290.7 square miles. At an elevation of 1,221.4 feet, Lake Mead itself extends some 110 miles upstream toward the Grand Canyon. Its 550-mile shoreline, backed by spectacular cliff and canyon scenery, forms a perfect setting for a wide variety of water sports and desert hiking.

INFORMATION   The **Alan Bible Visitor Center,** 4 miles northeast of Boulder City on U.S. 93 at Nev. 166 (☎ **702/293-8990**), can provide information on all area activities and services. You can pick up trail maps and brochures here, view informative films, and find out about scenic drives, accommodations, ranger-guided hikes, naturalist programs and lectures, bird watching, canoeing, camping, lakeside RV parks, and picnic facilities. The center also sells books and videotapes about the area. It's open daily 8:30am to 4:30pm. For information on accommodations, boat rentals, and fishing, call **Seven Crown Resorts** (☎ **800/752-9669**).

OUTDOOR ACTIVITIES

BOATING & FISHING   A store at **Lake Mead Resort and Marina** under the auspices of Seven Crown Resorts (☎ **800/752-9669** or 702/293-3484) rents fishing boats, ski boats, personal watercraft, and patio boats. It also carries groceries, clothing, marine supplies, sporting goods, water-skiing gear, fishing equipment, and bait and tackle. You can get a fishing license here ($45.50 a year or $17.50 for three days; $9 a year for children 12 to 15, under 12 free). The staff is knowledgeable and can apprise you of good fishing spots. Largemouth bass, striped bass, channel catfish, crappie, and bluegill are found in Lake Mead.

Other convenient Lake Mead marinas offering similar rentals and equipment are **Las Vegas Bay** (☎ **702/565-9111**), which is even closer to Las Vegas, and **Callville Bay** (☎ **702/565-8958**), which is the least crowded of the five on the Nevada Shore.

HIKING   The best season for hiking is November to March (it's too hot the rest of the year). Some ranger-guided hikes are offered via the **Alan Bible Visitor Center** (see above), which also stocks detailed trail maps. Three trails, ranging in length from three-fourths of a mile to 6 miles, originate at the visitor center.

LAKE CRUISES   A delightful way to enjoy Lake Mead is on a cruise aboard the *Desert Princess* (☎ **702/293-6180**), a Mississippi-style paddle wheeler. Cruises depart year-round from a terminal near Lake Mead Lodge and a dock right at Hoover Dam (inquire at the visitor center). It's a relaxing, scenic trip (enjoyed from an open promenade deck or one of two fully enclosed, climate-controlled decks) through Black Canyon and past colorful rock formations known as the "Arizona Paint Pots" en route to Hoover Dam, which is lit at night. Options include buffet breakfast cruises ($21 adults, $10 children under 12), narrated midday cruises ($16 adults, $6 children), cocktail/dinner cruises ($29 adults, $15 children), and sunset dinner/dance cruises with live music ($43 adults, children not allowed). Add $1 to all rates if you depart from Hoover Dam. Dinner is served in a pleasant, windowed, air-conditioned dining room. There's a full bar on board. Call for departure times.

7

About Casino Gambling

What? You didn't come to Las Vegas for the Liberace Museum? We are shocked. *Shocked.*

Yes, there are gambling opportunities in Vegas. We've noticed this. You will, too. The tip-off will be the slot machines in the airport as soon as you step off the plane. Or the slot machines in the convenience stores as soon as you drive across the state line. Let's not kid ourselves, gambling is what Vegas is about. The bright lights, the shows, the showgirls, the food—it's all there just to lure you in and make you open your wallet. (The free drinks certainly help ease the latter as well.)

You can disappoint them if you want, but what would be the point? *This is Las Vegas.* You don't have to be a high roller. You would not believe how much fun you can have with a nickel slot machine. You won't get rich, but neither will most of those guys playing the $5 dollar slots, either. Of course, that's not going to stop anyone from trying. Almost everyone plays in Vegas with the hopes of winning The Big One. That only a few ever do doesn't stop them from trying again and again and again. That's how the casinos make their money, by the way.

Remember that there is no system that is sure to help you win. We all have our own systems and our own ideas. Reading books and listening to others at the tables will help you pick up some tips, but if there were a surefire way to win, the casinos would have taken care of it (and we will leave you to imagine just what that might entail). Try to have the courage to walk away when your bankroll is up, not down. Remember, your children's college fund is just that, and not a gambling budget supplement.

The first part of this chapter tells you the basics of betting. Knowing how to play the games not only improves your odds but makes playing more enjoyable. In addition to the instructions below, you'll find dozens of books on how to gamble at all casino hotel gift shops, and many casinos offer free gaming lessons on the premises. The second part of this chapter describes all the major casinos in town. Remember that gambling is supposed to be entertainment; picking a gaming table where the other players are laughing, slapping each other on the back, and generally enjoying themselves tends to make for considerably more fun than a table where everyone is sitting around in stony silence, morosely staring at their cards. Unless you really need to concentrate, pick a table where everyone seems to be enjoying themselves, and you will too, even if you don't win. Maybe.

1 The Games

BACCARAT

The ancient game of baccarat, or *chemin de fer,* is played with eight decks of cards. Firm rules apply, and there is no skill involved other than deciding whether to bet on the bank or the player. Any beginner can play, but check the betting minimum before you sit down as this tends to be a high-stakes game. The cards are shuffled by the croupier and then placed in a box that is called the "shoe."

Players may wager on the "bank" or "player" at any time. Two cards are dealt from the shoe and given to the player who has the largest wager against the bank, and two cards are dealt to the croupier acting as banker. If the rule calls for a third card (see rules on chart shown here), the player or banker, or both, must take the third card. In the event of a tie, the hand is dealt over.

The object of the game is to come as close as possible to the number 9. To score the hands, the cards of each hand are totaled and the *last digit* is used. All cards have face value. For example: 10 plus 5 equals 15 (score is 5); 10 plus 4 plus 9 equals 23 (score is 3); 4 plus 3 plus 3 equals 10 (score is 0); and 4 plus 3 plus 2 equals 9 (score is 9). The closest hand to 9 wins.

Each player has a chance to deal the cards. The shoe passes to the player on the right each time the bank loses. If the player wishes, he or she may pass the shoe at any time.

Note: When you bet on the bank and the bank wins, you are charged a 5% commission. This must be paid at the start of a new game or when you leave the table.

BIG SIX

Big Six provides pleasant recreation and involves no study or effort. The wheel has 56 positions on it, 54 of them marked by bills from $1 to $20 denominations. The other two spots are jokers, and each pays 40 to 1 if the wheel stops in that position.

All other stops pay at face value. Those marked with $20 bills pay 20 to 1; the $5 bills pay 5 to 1; and so forth.

BACCARAT RULES
Player's Hand

Having

0-1-2-3-4-5	Must draw a third card.
6-7	Must stand.
8-9	Natural. Banker cannot draw.

Banker's Hand

Having	Draws	Does Not Draw
	When giving Player 3rd card of:	When giving Player 3rd card of:
3	1-2-3-4-5-6-7-9-10	8
4	2-3-4-5-6-7	1-8-9-10
5	4-5-6-7	1-2-3-8-9-10
6	6-7	1-2-3-4-5-8-9-10
7	Must stand.	
8-9	Natural. Player cannot draw.	

If the player takes no third card, the banker must stand on 6. No one draws against a natural 8 or 9.

BLACKJACK

The dealer starts the game by dealing each player two cards. In some casinos they're dealt to the player faceup, in others facedown, but the dealer always gets one card up and one card down. Everybody plays against the dealer. The object is to get a total that is higher than that of the dealer without exceeding 21. All face cards count as 10; all other number cards except aces count as their number value. An ace may be counted as 1 or 11, whichever you choose it to be.

Starting at his or her left, the dealer gives additional cards to the players who wish to draw (be "hit") or none to a player who wishes to "stand" or "hold." If your count is nearer to 21 than the dealer's, you win. If it's under the dealer's, you lose. Ties are a push and no-body wins. After all the players are satisfied with their counts, the dealer exposes his or her facedown card. If his two cards total 16 or less, the dealer must "hit" (draw an additional card) until reaching 17 or over. If the dealer's total goes over 21, he or she must pay all the players whose hands have not gone "bust." It is important to note here that the blackjack dealer has no choice as to whether he or she should stay or draw. A dealer's decisions are predetermined and known to all the players at the table.

HOW TO PLAY   Here are eight "rules" for blackjack.

1. Place the amount of chips that you want to bet on the betting space on your table.
2. Look at the first two cards the dealer starts you with. If your hand adds up to the total you prefer, place your cards *under your bet money,* indicating that you don't wish any additional cards. If you elect to draw an additional card, you tell the dealer to "hit" you by making a sweeping motion with your cards, or point to your open hand (watch your fellow players).
3. If your count goes over 21, you go "bust" and lose, even if the dealer also goes "bust" afterward. Unless hands are dealt faceup, *you then turn your hand faceup on the table.*
4. If you make 21 in your first two cards (any picture card or 10 with an ace), you've got blackjack. *You expose your winning hand immediately,* and you collect $1^1/2$ times your bet, unless the dealer has blackjack, too, in which case it's a push and nobody wins.
5. If you find a "pair" in your first two cards (say, two 8s or two aces) you may "split" the pair into two hands and treat each card as the first card dealt in two separate hands. *Turn the pair faceup on the table,* place the original bet on one of these cards, then place an equal amount on the other card. *Split aces are limited to a one-card draw on each.*
6. You may double your original bet and make a one-card draw after receiving your initial two cards. *Turn your hand faceup* and you'll receive one more card facedown.
7. Anytime the dealer deals himself or herself an ace for the "up" card, you may insure your hand against the possibility that the hole card is a 10 or face card, which would give him or her an automatic blackjack. To insure, you place an amount up to one-half of your bet on the "insurance" line. If the dealer does have a blackjack, you do not lose, even though he or she has your hand beat, and you keep your bet and your insurance money. If the dealer does not have a blackjack, he or she takes your insurance money and play continues in the normal fashion.
8. *Remember:* The dealer *must* stand on 17 or more and *must* hit a hand of 16 or less.

PROFESSIONAL TIPS   Advice of the experts in playing blackjack is as follows.

1. *Do not* ask for an extra card if you have a count of 17, 18, 19, 20, or 21 in your cards, no matter what the dealer has showing in his or her "up" card.
2. *Do not* ask for an extra card when you have 12, 13, 14, 15, 16, or more if the dealer has a 2, 3, 4, 5, or 6 showing in his or her "up" card.
3. *Do ask* for an extra card or more when you have a count of 12 through 16 in your hand if the dealer's "up" card is a 7, 8, 9, 10, or ace.

There's a lot more to blackjack-playing strategy than the above, of course. So consider this merely the bare bones of the game.

A final tip: Avoid insurance bets; they're sucker bait!

CRAPS

The most exciting casino action is always at the craps tables. Betting is frenetic, play fast-paced, and groups quickly bond yelling and screaming in response to the action.

THE TABLE   The craps table is divided into marked areas (Pass, Come, Field, Big 6, Big 8, and so on), where you place your chips to bet. The following are a few simple directions.

PASS LINE   A "Pass Line" bet pays even money. If the first roll of the dice adds up to 7 or 11, you win your bet; if the first roll adds up to 2, 3, or 12, you lose your bet. If any other number comes up, it's your "point." If you roll your point again, you win, but if a 7 comes up again before your point is rolled, you lose.

DON'T PASS LINE   Betting on the "Don't Pass" is the opposite of betting on the Pass Line. This time, you lose if a 7 or an 11 is thrown on the first roll, and you win if a 2 or a 3 is thrown on the first roll.

If the first roll is 12, however, it's a push (standoff), and nobody wins. If none of these numbers is thrown and you have a point instead, in order to win, a 7 will have to be thrown before the point comes up again. A "Don't Pass" bet also pays even money.

COME Betting on "Come" is the same as betting on the Pass Line, but you must bet *after* the first roll or on any following roll. Again, you'll win on 7 or 11 and lose on 2, 3, or 12. Any other number is your point, and you win if your point comes up again before a 7.

DON'T COME This is the opposite of a "Come" bet. Again, you wait until after the first roll to bet. A 7 or an 11 means you lose; a 2 or a 3 means you win; 12 is a push, and nobody wins. You win if 7 comes up before the point. (The point, you'll recall, was the first number rolled if it was none of the above.)

FIELD This is a bet for one roll only. The "Field" consists of seven numbers: 2, 3, 4, 9, 10, 11, and 12. If any of these numbers are thrown on the next roll, you win even money, except on 2 and 12, which pay 2 to 1 (at some casinos 3 to 1).

BIG 6 AND 8 A "Big 6 and 8" bet pays even money. You win if either a 6 or an 8 is rolled before a 7.

ANY 7 An "Any 7" bet pays the winner five for one. If a 7 is thrown on the first roll after you bet, you win.

"HARD WAY" BETS In the middle of a craps table are pictures of several possible dice combinations together with the odds the casino will pay you if you bet and win on any of those combinations being thrown. For example, if 8 is thrown by having a 4 appear on each die, and you bet on it, the bank will pay 10 for 1; if 4 is thrown by having a 2 appear on each die, and you bet on it, the bank will pay 8 for 1; if 3 is thrown, the bank pays 15 for 1. You win at the odds quoted if the *exact* combination of numbers you bet on comes up. But you lose either if a 7 is rolled or if the number you bet on was rolled any way other than the "Hard Way" shown on the table. In-the-know gamblers tend to avoid "Hard Way" bets as an easy way to lose their money. And note that the odds quoted are *not* 3 to 1, 4 to 1, or 8 to 1; here the key word is *for*—that is, 3 for 1 or 8 for 1.

ANY CRAPS Here you're lucky if the dice "crap out"—if they show 2, 3, or 12 on the first roll after you bet. If this happens, the bank pays for 8 for 1. Any other number is a loser.

PLACE BETS   You can make a "Place Bet" on any of the following numbers: 4, 5, 6, 8, 9, and 10. You're betting that the number you choose will be thrown before a 7 is thrown. If you win, the payoff is as follows: 4 or 10 pays at the rate of 9 to 5; 5 or 9 pays at the rate of 7 to 5; 6 or 8 pays at the rate of 7 to 6. "Place Bets" can be removed at any time before a roll.

SOME PROBABILITIES   Because each die has six sides numbered from 1 to 6, and craps is played with a pair of dice, the probability of throwing certain numbers has been studied carefully. Professionals have employed complex mathematical formulas in searching for the answers. And computers have data-processed curves of probability.

Suffice it to say that 7 (a crucial number in craps) will be thrown more frequently than any other number over the long run, for there are six possible combinations that make 7 when you break down the 1 to 6 possibilities on each separate die. As to the total possible number of combinations on the dice, there are 36.

Comparing the 36 possible combinations, numbers, or point combinations, run as follows:

> *2 and 12* may be thrown in *1 way* only.
>
> *3 and 11* may be thrown in *2 ways*.
>
> *4 and 10* may be thrown in *3 ways*.
>
> *5 and 9* may be thrown in *4 ways*.
>
> *6 and 8* may be thrown in *5 ways*.
>
> *7* may be thrown in *6 ways*.

So 7 has an advantage over all other combinations, which, over the long run, is in favor of the casino. You can't beat the law of averages.

KENO

This is one of the oldest games of chance. Originating in China, the game can be traced back to a time before Christ, when it operated as a national lottery. Legend has it that funds acquired from the game were used to finance construction of the Great Wall of China.

Keno was first introduced into the United States in the 1800s by Chinese railroad construction workers. Easy to play, and offering a chance to sit down and converse between bets, it is one of the most popular games in town—despite the fact that *the house percentage is greater than that of any other casino game!*

To play, you must first obtain a keno form, available at the counter in the keno lounge and in most Las Vegas coffee shops. In the latter, you'll usually find blank keno forms and thick black

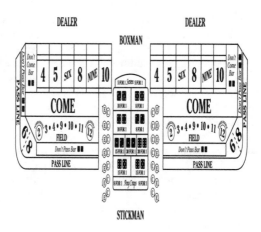

crayons on your table. Fill yours out, and a miniskirted keno runner will come and collect it. After the game is over, she'll return with your winning or losing ticket. If you've won, it's customary to offer a tip, depending on your winnings.

Looking at your keno ticket and the keno board, you'll see that it is divided horizontally into two rectangles. The upper half (in China the yin area) contains the numbers 1 through 40, the lower (yang) half contains the numbers 41 through 80. You can win a maximum of $50,000, even more on progressive games, though it's highly unlikely (the probability is less than a hundredth of a percent). Mark up to 15 out of the 80 numbers; bets range from about 70¢ on up. A one-number mark is known as a one-spot, a two-number selection is a two-spot, and so on. After you have selected the number of spots you wish to play, write the price of the ticket in the right hand corner where indicated. The more you bet, the more you can win if your numbers come up. Before the game starts, you have to give the completed form to a keno runner or hand it in at the keno lounge desk, and pay for your bet. You'll get back a duplicate form with the number of the game you're playing on it. Then the game begins. As numbers appear on the keno board, compare them to the numbers you've marked on your ticket. After 20 numbers have appeared on the board, if you've won, turn in your ticket immediately for a payoff before the next game begins. Otherwise, you will forfeit your winnings, a frustrating experience to say the least.

On a straight ticket that is marked with one or two spots, all of your numbers must appear on the board for you to win anything. With a few exceptions, if you mark from 3 to 7 spots, 3 numbers must appear on the board for you to win anything. Similarly, if you mark 8 to 12 spots, usually at least 5 numbers must come up for you to win the minimum amount. And if you mark 13 to 15 spots, usually at least 6 numbers must come up for a winning ticket. To win the maximum amount ($50,000), which requires that all of your numbers come up, you must select at least 8 spots. The more numbers on the board matching the numbers on your ticket, the more you win. If you want to keep playing the same numbers over and over, you can replay a ticket by handing in your duplicate to the keno runner; you don't have to keep rewriting it.

In addition to the straight bets described above, you can split your ticket, betting various amounts on two or more groups of numbers. To do so, circle the groups. The amount you bet is then divided by the number of groups. You could, if you so desire, play as many as 40 two-spots on a single ticket. Another possibility is to play three groups of four numbers each as eight spots (any two of the three groups of four numbers can be considered an eight-spot). It does get a little complex, since combination betting options are almost infinite. Helpful casino personnel in the keno lounge can help you with combination betting.

POKER

Poker is *the* game of the Old West. There's at least one sequence in every Western where the hero faces off against the villain over a poker hand. In Las Vegas poker is a tradition, although it isn't played at every casino.

There are lots of variations on the basic game, but one of the most popular is **Hold 'Em.** Five cards are dealt faceup in the center of the table and two are dealt to each player. The player uses the best five of seven, and the best hand wins. The house dealer takes care of the shuffling and the dealing and moves a marker around the table to alternate the start of the deal. The house rakes 1% to 10% (it depends on the casino) from each pot. Most casinos include the usual seven-card stud and a few have hi-lo split.

If you don't know how to play poker, don't attempt to learn at a table. Find a casino that teaches it in free gaming lessons.

Pai gow poker (a variation on poker) has become increasingly popular. The game is played with a traditional deck plus one joker. The joker is a wild card that can be used as an ace or to complete a straight, a flush, a straight flush, or a royal flush. Each player is dealt seven cards to arrange into two hands: a two-card hand and a five-card hand. As in standard poker, the highest two-card hand is two aces, and the highest five-card hand is a royal flush. The five-card hand *must* be higher than the two-card hand (if the two-card hand is a pair of sixes, for example, the five-card hand must be a pair of sevens or better). Any player's hand that is set incorrectly is an automatic lose. The object of the game is for both of the player's hands to rank higher than both of the banker's hands. Should one hand rank exactly the same as the banker's hand, this is a tie (called a "copy"), *and the banker wins all tie hands.* If the player wins one hand but loses the other, this is a "push," and no money changes hands. The house dealer or any player may be the banker. The bank is offered to each player, and each player may accept or pass. Winning hands are paid even money, less a 5% commission.

ROULETTE

Roulette is an extremely easy game to play, and it's really quite colorful and exciting to watch. The wheel spins and the little ball bounces around, finally dropping into one of the slots, numbered 1 to 36, plus 0 and 00. You can bet on a single number, a combination of numbers, or red or black, odd or even. If you're lucky, you can win as much as 35 to 1 (see the table). The method of placing single-number bets, column bets, and others is fairly obvious. The dealer will be happy to show you how to "straddle" two or more numbers and make many other interesting betting combinations. Each player is given different-colored chips so that it's easy to follow the numbers you're on.

A number of typical bets are indicated by means of letters on the roulette layout depicted here. The winning odds for each of these sample bets are listed. These bets can be made on any corresponding combinations of numbers.

SLOTS

You put the coin in the slot and pull the handle. What, you thought there was a trick to this?

ROULETTE BETS AND ODDS

Roulette Chart Key	Odds	Type of Bet
		Straight Bets
A	35 to 1	*Straight-up:* All numbers, plus 0 and 00.
B	2 to 1	*Column Bet:* Pays off on any number in that horizontal column.
C	2 to 1	*First Dozen:* Pays off on any number 1 through 12. Same for second and third dozen.
D	Even Money	
		Combination Bets
E	17 to 1	*Split:* Pays off on 11 or 12.
F	11 to 1	Pays off on 28, 29, or 30.
G	8 to 1	*Corner:* Pays off on 17, 18, 20, or 21.
H	6 to 1	Pays off on 0, 00, 1, 2, or 3.
I	5 to 1	Pays off on 22, 23, 24, 25, 26, or 27.

Actually, there is a bit more to it. But first, some background. Old-timers will tell you slots were invented to give wives something to do while their husbands gambled. Slots used to be stuck at the edges of the casino and could be counted on one hand, maybe two. But now they *are* the casino. The casinos make more from slots than from craps, blackjack, and roulette combined. There are 115,000 slot machines (not including video poker) in the county alone. Some of these are at the airport, steps from you as you deplane. It's just a matter of time before the planes flying into Vegas feature slots that pop up as soon as you cross the state line.

But in order to keep up with the increasing competition, the plain old machine, where reels just spun, has become nearly obsolete. Now all machines are computerized and have added buttons to push, so you can avoid carpal tunnel syndrome from yanking the handle all night. (The handles are still there on many of them.) The idea is still simple: Get three (sometimes four) cherries (clowns, sevens, dinosaurs, whatever) in a row, and you win something. Each machine has its own combination; some will pay you something with just one symbol showing; on most the more combinations there are, the more opportunities for loot. Some will even pay if you get three blanks. Study each machine to learn what it does.

The **payback** goes up considerably if you bet the limit (from two to as many as 45 coins). But while the payoff can be much bigger, the odds *against* winning also go up when you put in the limit. (So if you hit something on a machine and realize your $25 win would have been $500 had you only put in more money, take a deep breath, stop kicking yourself, and remember you might not actually have hit that winning combination so easily had you bet the limit.)

Progressive slots are groups of machines where the jackpot gets bigger every few moments (just as lottery jackpots build up). Bigger and better games keep showing up; for example, there's Anchor Gaming's much-imitated **Wheel of Gold,** wherein if you get the right symbol, you get to spin a roulette wheel, which guarantees you a win of a serious number of coins. **Totem Pole** is the Godzilla of slot machines, a behemoth that allows you to spin up to three reels at once (provided you put in the limit). And of course, there's our personal favorite, **Piggy Bankin'.** This has a LED display on which a silly tune plays and a pig cavorts (at erratic times, he trots across the screen, oinks, giggles when you lose, and imitates Elvis, among other playful actions). It's so much fun to watch you start putting in the coins just to get the pig to move, forget about the money. But

Slot Clubs

If you play slots or video poker, it definitely pays to join a slot club. These so-called clubs are designed to attract and keep customers in a given casino by providing incentives—meals, shows, discounts on rooms, gifts, tournament invitations, discounts at hotel shops, VIP treatment, and (more and more) cash rebates. Of course, your rewards are greater if you play just in one casino, but your mobility is limited.

When you join a slot club (inquire at the casino desk), you're given something that looks like a credit card, which you must insert into an ATM-like device whenever you play. (Don't forget to retrieve your card when you leave the machine, as we sometimes do—though that may work in your favor if someone comes along and plays the machine without removing it.) The device tracks your play and computes bonus points.

Which slot club should you join? Actually, you should join one at any casino where you play, since even the act of joining usually entitles you to some benefits. It's convenient to concentrate play where you're staying; if you play a great deal, a casino hotel's slot-club benefits may be a factor in your accommodations choice. Consider, though, particularly if you aren't a high roller, the slot clubs Downtown. You get more bang for your buck because you don't have to spend as much to start raking in the goodies.

One way to judge a slot club is by the quality of service when you enroll. Personnel should politely answer all your questions (for instance, is nickel play included? or is there a time limit for earning required points?) and be able to tell you exactly how many points you need for various bonuses.

Maximizing your slot-club profits and choosing the club that's best for you is a complex business. If you want to get into it in depth, order a copy of Jeffrey Compton's ***The Las Vegas Advisor Guide to Slot Clubs*** ($9.95 plus shipping), which examines just about every facet of the situation (☎ **800/244-2224**). Compton gives high ratings to the clubs at Caesars Palace, the Desert Inn, the Mirage, Treasure Island, the Flamingo Hilton, the Rio, the Sahara, Sam's Town, the Four Queens, the Golden Nugget, and Lady Luck.

meanwhile, money is building up in the piggy bank, an extra bonus you win if you hit the right symbol.

Other gimmick machines include **Clear Winner,** where you can satisfy your curiosity about the inner workings of a slot machine, and **Rockin' Reels,** which looks like a jukebox. And of course, there are always those **Big Giant Slot** machines, gimmicky devices found in almost every casino. They may not win as often as regular slots (though there is no definite word on it one way or the other), but not only are they just plain fun to spin, they often turn into audience participation gambling, as watchers gather to cheer you on to victory.

Are there surefire ways to win on a slot machine? No. But you can lose more slowly. The slots are on computer timers, and there are times when they are hitting and times when they are not. A bank of empty slots probably (but not certainly) means they aren't hitting. Go find a line where lots of people are sitting around with trays full of money. (Of course, yours will be the one that doesn't hit.) A good rule of thumb is that if your slot doesn't hit something in four or five pulls, leave it and go find another. It's not as though you won't have some choice in the matter. Also, each casino has some bank of slots that they advertise as more loose or with a bigger payback. Try these. It's what they want you to do, but what the heck.

SPORTS BOOKS

Most of the larger hotels in Las Vegas have sports book operations—they look a lot like commodities-futures trading boards. In some, almost as large as theaters, you can sit comfortably, occasionally in recliners and sometimes with your own video screen, and watch ball games, fights, and, at some casinos, horse races on huge TV screens. To add to your enjoyment, there's usually a deli/bar nearby that serves sandwiches, hot dogs, soft drinks, and beer. As a matter of fact, some of the best sandwiches in Las Vegas are served next to the sports books. Sports books take bets on virtually every sport.

VIDEO POKER

Rapidly coming up on slots in popularity, video poker works the same way as regular poker, except you play against the machine. You are dealt a hand, you pick which cards to keep and which to discard, and then you get your new hand. And, it is hoped, you collect your winnings. Somewhat more of a challenge and more active than slots because you have some control (or at least illusion of control) over your fate, they are easier to play than actual poker with a table full of folks who probably take it very seriously.

There are a number of varieties of this machine, with **Jacks are Better, Deuces Wild,** and so forth. Be sure to study your machine before you sit down. (The best returns are offered on the **Jacks are Wild** machines, when the payback for a pair of Jacks or better is 2 times your bet, and 3 times for three of a kind.) Some machines offer **Double Down:** After you have won, you get a chance to draw cards against the machine, with the higher card the winner. If you win, your money is doubled and you are offered a chance to go again. Your money can increase nicely during this time, and you can also lose it all very fast, which is most annoying. Technology is catching up with Video Poker, too. Now they even have touch screens, which offer a variety of different poker games, blackjack, and video slots—just touch your screen and choose your poison.

2 The Casinos

Casino choice is a personal thing. Some like to find their lucky place and stick with it, while others love to take advantage of the nearly endless choices Vegas offers. Everyone should casino-hop at least once to marvel (or get dizzy) at the decor/spectacle and the sheer excess of it all. But beyond decoration, there isn't too much difference. You've got your slot machines, gaming tables, big chandeliers.

Virtually all casinos make sure they have no clocks or windows— they do not want you to interrupt your losing streak by realizing how much time has passed. Of course, we've all heard the legend that Vegas casinos pump in fresh oxygen to keep the players from getting tired and wanting to pack it in. The veracity of this is hard to confirm, but we can only hope it's true, especially when we think of that time we looked up after a long stretch of gambling and discovered it was Thursday.

Don't be a snob, and don't be overly dazzled by the fancy casinos. Sometimes you can have a better time at one of the older places Downtown, where stakes are lower, pretensions are nonexistent, and the clientele are often friendlier.

What follows is description of most of the major casinos in Vegas, including a claustrophobia rating, whether or not they have a Big Giant Slot machine (it's a sucker bet, but we love them), and a completely arbitrary assessment based on whether or not we won there.

SOUTH STRIP

Excalibur. 3850 Las Vegas Blvd. S. ☎ **702/597-7777.**

As you might expect, the Excalibur casino is replete with suits of armor, stained-glass panels, knights, dragons, and velvet and satin heraldic banners, with gaming action taking place beneath vast iron and gold chandeliers fit for a medieval castle fortress. This all makes it fine for kitsch-seekers, but anyone hating crowds or sensitive to noise will hate it. The overall effect is less like a castle and more like a dungeon. A popular feature here is Circus Bucks, a progressive slot machine that builds from a jackpot base of $500,000; players can win on a $3 pull. A nonsmoking area is a plus. One of us won a lot of money here and refused to share it with the other, so our final judgment about the casino is, well, mixed.

Luxor Las Vegas. 3900 Las Vegas Blvd. S. ☎ **702/262-4000.**

More accessible than ever thanks to the addition of the air-conditioned people-mover from Excalibur, Luxor has been completely remodeled and, in our opinion, improved immeasurably. The additional space gives the casino a much more airy feel, which gives it a low claustrophobia level—in parts you can see all the way up the inside of the pyramid. There's a nonsmoking slot area. We already felt inclined to like this casino thanks to a good run at blackjack, and the redesign has made it even more inviting.

MGM Grand. 3799 Las Vegas Blvd. S. ☎ **702/891-7777.**

The world's largest casino—at 171,500 square feet, we've been to countries that were smaller!—is divided into four themed areas, in a futile attempt to make it seem smaller. Many of the Wizard of Oz decorations have been removed, but spend an hour in here and you might well feel like Dorothy after she got hit by the twister.

Monte Carlo. 3770 Las Vegas Blvd. S. ☎ **702/730-7777.**

All huge ceilings and white-light interiors: Obviously, they are trying to evoke gambling in Monaco. While the decor shows lots of attention, it perhaps had too much attention. Bulbs line the ceiling, and everywhere you look is some detail or other. It's busy on both your eyes and ears. So despite the effort put in, it's not a pleasant place to gamble.

✪ New York New York. 3790 Las Vegas Blvd. S. ☎ **702/740-6969.**

Another theme-run-wild place: tuxes on the backs of gaming chairs, change carts that look like yellow cabs, and so forth, all set in a miniature New York City. It's all fabulous fun, but despite a low claustrophobia level (thanks to an unusually high ceiling), it is a major case of sensory overload akin to the reaction elicited by a first-time look at the Strip. This may prove distracting. On the other hand, we won there, so we love it. And it is, if one can say this about anything in Vegas with a straight face, in spots quite beautiful. Serious gamblers understandably may sniff at it all and prefer to take their business to a more seemly casino, but everyone else should have about the most Vegasey time they can.

Orleans. 4500 W. Tropicana Ave. ☎ **702/365-7111.**

This is not a particularly special gambling space, though it has a low claustrophobia level. Cajun and Zydeco music are played over the sound system so you can two-step while you gamble, which can make losing somewhat less painful. It has a Wheel of Fortune machine that works like those other roulette wheel slots, but in this case, it actually plays the theme song from the TV show. It will even applaud for you if you win.

Tropicana. 3801 Las Vegas Blvd. S. ☎ **702/739-2222.**

The Trop casino is quite good-looking, and, yes, highly tropical, with gaming tables situated beneath a massive, stained-glass archway and art nouveau lighting fixtures. In summer it offers something totally unique: swim-up blackjack tables located in the hotel's stunning 5-acre tropical garden and pool area.

MID-STRIP

✪ **Bally's Las Vegas.** 3645 Las Vegas Blvd. S. ☎ **702/739-4111.**

Bally's casino is one of the cleanest and best-lit and definitely has that high-rent appeal. It's large (the size of a football field) with lots of colorful signage. The big ceiling makes for a low claustrophobia level. There's a Most Valuable Player Slot Club offering members cash rebates, room discounts, free meals, show tickets, and invitations to special events, among other perks. The casino hosts frequent slot tournaments, and free gaming lessons are offered. There is not, however, a Big Giant Slot machine. For shame.

Barbary Coast. 3595 Las Vegas Blvd. S. ☎ **702/737-7111.**

The Barbary Coast has a cheerful 1890s-style casino ornately decorated with $2 million worth of gorgeous stained-glass skylights and signs, as well as immense crystal-dangling globe chandeliers over the gaming tables. It's worth stopping in just to take a look around when you're in the central "four corners" area of the Strip. The casino has a free Fun Club for slot players; participants earn points toward cash and prizes.

✪ **Caesars Palace**. 3570 Las Vegas Blvd. S. ☎ **702/731-7110.**

Caesars casino is simultaneously the ultimate in gambling luxury and the ultimate in Vegas kitsch. Cocktail waitresses in togas parade about as you gamble under the watchful gaze of faux marble Roman statues. The very high ceiling makes for a very low claustrophobia level, especially thanks to the recent face-lift, which has lightened up the paint and made the whole casino much brighter. A notable facility in the latter is the state-of-the-art **Race and Sports Book,** with huge electronic display boards and giant video screens. (Caesars pioneered computer-generated wagering data that can be communicated in less than half a second and sophisticated satellite equipment that can pick up virtually any broadcast sporting event in the world.) It's a gorgeous and elegant place to gamble, but we've never won there, so we hate it.

Flamingo Hilton. 3555 Las Vegas Blvd. S. ☎ **702/733-3111.**

If you've seen the movie *Bugsy,* you won't recognize this as Mr. Siegel's baby. The Flamingo is in the middle of redoing its casino area, which is just as well, because right now it feels overly crowded, thanks to overall tight confines. It sprawls across a large space, meandering around corners, so it is very difficult to get out of. Actual daylight does stream in from windows and glass doorways on the Strip, however. There are slots here offering Cadillacs and Continentals as jackpots. One of our favorite slot machines is here, but we won't tell you which one to save it for ourselves. Sorry.

Gold Coast. 4000 W. Flamingo Rd. ☎ **702/367-7111.**

Adjacent to the Rio, this casino is not only well lit, but totally unique in Vegas: *It has windows!* It's a little thing, but it made us really excited.

Harrah's. 3475 Las Vegas Blvd. S. ☎ **702/369-5000.**

Confetti carpeting and fiber-optic fireworks overhead combine with murals and an overall Mardi Gras theme to make a festive environment. Does it help you win more? Who knows. But the different, better energy that has resulted from this recent, costly face-lift certainly couldn't hurt. Don't miss the "party pits," gaming-table areas where dealers are encouraged to wear funny hats, celebrate wins, and otherwise break the usual stern dealer facade. Singing, dancing, and the handing out of party favors have all been known to break out. Gambling is supposed to be fun, so enjoy it.

Imperial Palace. 3535 Las Vegas Blvd. S. ☎ **702/731-3311.**

The 75,000-square-foot casino here reflects the hotel's pagoda-roofed Asian exterior with a dragon-motif ceiling and giant wind-chime chandeliers. There is a nonsmoking slot machine area separate from the main casino (as opposed to just another part of the room, at best, in other casinos), and a Breathalyzer for voluntary alcohol limit checks on your way to the parking lot (useful since there are nine bars on the casino premises). One Big Giant Slot machine is red, white, and blue; try singing the National Anthem to it, and see if you win more money.

Maxim. 160 E. Flamingo Rd. ☎ **702/731-4300.**

This friendly, but dimly lit, facility (with some of the '70s frills) is the neighborhood bar of casinos. They have a racetrack game where you can place bets on little mechanical horses and jockeys—kind of a kid's toy for adults.

✪ The Mirage. 3400 Las Vegas Blvd. S. ☎ **702/791-7111.**

Gamble in a Polynesian village in one of the prettiest casinos in town. It has a meandering layout, and the low ceiling makes for a medium claustrophobia level, but neither of these things is overwhelming. This remains one of our favorite places to gamble. It's one of the most pleasant, and popular, casinos in town so it's more often than not crowded.

The Rio. 3700 W. Flamingo Rd. ☎ **702/252-7777.**

This Brazilian-themed resort's 85,000-square-foot casino is, despite the presence of plenty of glitter and neon, very dark. It has about the highest claustrophobia rating of the major casinos. Its sports book feels a little grimy. The waitresses wear scanty costumes (particularly in the back), probably in an effort to distract you and throw your game off. Do not let them. The part of the casino in the new Masquerade Village is considerably more pleasant (the very high ceilings help) though still crowded, plus the loud live show adds still more noise.

Treasure Island. 3300 Las Vegas Blvd. S. ☎ **702/894-7111.**

Treasure Island's huge casino is highly themed. If you have ever gone to Disneyland's Pirates of the Caribbean and thought, "Gee, if only this were a casino," this is the place for you. Kids seem to be everywhere, because they are dazzled by the pirate stuff. Many people complain they don't like the atmosphere here, possibly because that very theme backfires. Throughout the casino there is something called Slot 2000. Hit a button, and a video screen pops up showing a (female) casino worker, to whom you can talk. She will answer questions, send someone over with drinks, make reservations, and otherwise help make your time there better. If you win a jackpot, she will come and congratulate you. No, she can't see you, so don't try to flirt.

NORTH STRIP

Circus Circus. 2880 Las Vegas Blvd. S. ☎ **702/734-0410.**

This vast property has three full-size casinos that, combined, comprise one of the largest gaming operations in Nevada (more than 100,000 square feet). More importantly, they have an entire circus midway set up throughout, so you are literally gambling with trapeze stunts going on over your head. The other great gimmick is the slot machine carousel—yep, it turns while you spin the reels. Unfortunately, the casino is crowded and noisy, and there are lots of children passing through. That, plus some low ceilings (not in the Big Top, obviously), make for a very high claustrophobia rating, though the new more Commedia del'Arte clown motif (as opposed to the old garish circus motif) has upgraded its appearance.

✪ **Desert Inn.** 3145 Las Vegas Blvd. S. ☎ **702/733-4444.**

Possibly the most genuinely elegant casino in Vegas, it's also one of the smallest for a major hotel. They don't care—they are looking for one good James Bond figure, rather than the masses. Crystal chandeliers here replace the usual neon glitz, and gaming tables are comfortably spaced. The ambience is reminiscent of intimate European gaming houses and is downright quiet. Some might find this almost creepy. Others may find it a huge relief. Since there are fewer slot machines here than at most major casinos, there's less noise of ringing bells and clinking coins. Most table games have a $5 minimum. The very high ceiling gives it a nonexistent claustrophobia rating.

The Riviera. 2901 Las Vegas Blvd. S. ☎ **702/734-5110.**

The Riviera's 100,000-square-foot casino, one of the largest in the world, means that there are plenty of opportunities to get lost and cranky. A wall of windows lets daylight stream in (most unusual), and the gaming tables are situated beneath gleaming brass arches lit by recessed, pink neon tubing. This is one of the few places in town where you can play the ancient Chinese game of *sic bo* (a fast-paced dice game resembling craps).

The Sahara. 2535 Las Vegas Blvd. S. ☎ **702/737-2111.**

The Sahara is in the process of changing its casino's look and adding a large new area, so it might be worth checking out. This is one place where there seem to be more tables than slots and video poker machines, but that might change with the new addition. When we were last here, they had a whole row of Piggy Bankin' machines that were all paying off, so we were happy.

The Stardust. 3000 Las Vegas Blvd. S. ☎ **702/732-6111.**

Always mobbed, this popular casino features 90,000 square feet of lively gaming action, including a 250-seat race and sports book with a sophisticated satellite system and more than 50 TV monitors airing sporting events and horse racing results around the clock. We usually do well here, so even though it's a little loud we like it. Check out those $1 slots just inside the front door—they've been very good to us.

The Stratosphere. 2000 Las Vegas Blvd. S. ☎ **702/380-7777.**

Originally set up to evoke a world's fair, but ending up more like a circus, the Stratosphere redid the whole area in order to make it more appealing for the many adults who were staying away in droves. The newly redone facility aims for class but doesn't necessarily achieve it. It's not that it fails, it just no longer has any identity at all. They heavily advertise their high payback on certain slots and video poker: 98% payback on dollar slots and 100% payback on quarter video poker (if you bet the maximum on each). We can't say we noticed a difference, but other people around us were winning like crazy.

EAST OF THE STRIP

✪ **Hard Rock Hotel & Casino.** 4455 Paradise Rd. ☎ **702/693-5000.**

Where Gen X goes to gamble. The Hard Rock has certainly taken casino decor to a whole new level. The attention to detail and the resulting playfulness is admirable, if not incredible. Gaming tables have piano keyboards at one end; some slots have Fender guitar fret boards as arms; gaming chips have band names and/or pictures on them; slot machines are similarly rock-themed (check out the Jimi Hendrix machine!); and so it goes. The whole thing is set in the middle of a circular room, around the outskirts of which is various rock memorabilia in glass cases. Rock blares over the sound system, allowing boomers to boogie while they gamble. All this is genuinely amazing, but the noise level is above even that of a normal casino and we just hated it. It's worth looking at anyway.

✪ **Las Vegas Hilton.** 3000 Paradise Rd. ☎ **702/732-7111.**

The casino has two parts, thanks to the space-themed portion adjacent to the Star Trek Experience. In an area designed to look like a space port, you find space-themed slot machines, many of which have no handles—just pass your hand through a light beam to activate. Other gimmicks are throughout (though already some have been dropped since the recent opening), including urinals that give you an instant "urinalysis"—usually suggesting this is your lucky day to gamble. We do like a well-designed space in which to lose our money. Over in the original casino section, Austrian crystal chandeliers add a strong touch of class. It's actually on the medium size, but it does have an enormous sports book—at 30,500 square feet, the world's largest race and sports book facility.

DOWNTOWN

Binion's Horseshoe. 128 E. Fremont St. (between Casino Center Blvd. and 1st St.) ☎ **702/382-1600.**

Professionals who know say that "for the serious player, the Binions *are* this town." Benny Binion could neither read nor write, but boy, did he know how to run a casino. His venerable establishment has been eclipsed over the years, but it claims the highest betting limits in Las Vegas on all games (probably in the entire world, according to a spokesperson). It offers single-deck blackjack and $2 minimums, 10-times odds on craps, and high progressive jackpots. We especially like the older part of the casino here, which—with its flocked wallpaper, gorgeous lighting fixtures, and gold-tasseled burgundy velvet drapes—looks like a turn-of-the-century Old West bordello. Unfortunately, all this adds up to a very high claustrophobia level. Gaming facilities include a keno lounge, a race and sports book, a 500-seat bingo parlor, blackjack, craps, roulette, baccarat, mini-baccarat, pai gow poker, Let-It-Ride, Caribbean stud, Big Six, and slot and video poker machines. They have two Big Giant Slot machines, at least one of which has been very very good to us.

While you're visiting Binion's casino, be sure to see the display of $1 million (comprised of 100 $10,000 bills) encased in a gold horseshoe-shaped vault. If you'd like a photograph of yourself with all that moolah, you can get one taken free from 4pm to midnight daily.

California Hotel/Casino. 12 Ogden Ave. (at 1st St.) ☎ **702/385-1222.**

The California is a festive place filled with Hawaiian shirts and balloons. This friendly facility actually provides sofas and armchairs in the casino area—an unheard-of luxury in this town. This is the first place we found our favorite Piggy Bankin' machines.

Fitzgeralds. 301 Fremont St. (at 3rd St.) ☎ **702/388-2400.**

They recently redid their casino in greens and golds, and the over-all effect is not quite as tacky as you might expect. In fact, it's rather friendly, and with a medium to low claustrophobia level. The casino is actually two levels: From the upstairs part you can access a balcony from which you get an up-close view of the Fremont Street Experience. Their mascot, Mr. O'Lucky (a costumed leprechaun), roams the casino. You don't have to be nice to him. They have dollar Piggy Bankin' machines.

Four Queens. 202 Fremont St. (at Casino Center Blvd.) ☎ **702/385-4011.**

The Four Queens is New Orleans-themed, with turn-of-the-century-style globe chandeliers that make for good lighting and a low claustrophobia level. It's small but the dealers are helpful, which is one of the pluses of gambling in the more manageably sized casinos. The facility boasts the world's largest slot machine, more than 9 feet high and almost 20 feet long; six people can play it at one time! It's the Mother of all Big Giant Slot machines, and frankly, it intimidates even us. Here is also the world's largest blackjack table (it seats 12 players).

Golden Gate. 1 Fremont St. ☎ **702/382-3510.**

This is one of the oldest casinos Downtown, and though its age is showing, it's still fun to visit. As you might expect from the name, old San Francisco (think earthquake time) artifacts and decor abound. At one end of the narrow casino is the bar, where a piano player performs ragtime jazz that is better than the homogenized pap offered in most casino lounges. Unfortunately, the low ceiling, dark period wallpaper, and small dimensions give this a high claustrophobia level.

Golden Nugget. 129 E. Fremont St. (at Casino Center Blvd.) ☎ **702/385-7111.**

Frankly, this is not the standout that other casino properties owned by Steve Wynn are. It goes for luxury, of course, but so much is crammed into so little space that the only feeling that emerges is one of overcrowding. That's not to say we didn't like it, because we won a lot of money here. And compared to most other Downtown properties, this is the most like the Strip. It is much cleaner and fresher feeling, in an area filled with dingy, time-forgotten spaces.

✪ **Gold Spike.** 400 Ogden Ave. (at Las Vegas Blvd.) ☎ **702/384-8444.**

Okay, we just criticized dingy, time-forgotten spaces (see above) in Downtown, and the Gold Spike certainly lands in that category. So what? Here, everyone is equal, and everyone is having a good time, or at least they can sincerely join you in your misery. Best of all, they have penny slots! (Not very many, to be sure, and getting a seat at one can require patience.) Hey tightwads, take a buck and spend a few hours.

Lady Luck. 206 N. 3rd St. (at Ogden Ave.) ☎ **702/477-3000.**

Even though Lady Luck is an older casino with the anticipated drop in glamour, it's surprisingly cheerful and has a low to medium claustrophobia level. Decorations give it a festive quality, and cocktail waitresses pushing drink carts can mix you something right on the spot.

✪ **Main Street Station.** 200 N. Main St. (between Fremont St. and I-95). ☎ **702/387-1896.**

Part of a long-closed old hotel that has been recently renovated and reopened to great success, this is the best of the Downtown casinos, at least in terms of comfort and pleasant environment. Even the Golden Nugget, nice as it is, has more noise and distractions. The decor here is, again, classic Vegas/old-timey (Victorian-era) San Francisco, but with extra touches (check out the old-fashioned fans above the truly beautiful bar) that make it work much better than other attempts at the same. Strangely, it seems just about smoke-free, perhaps thanks in part to a very high ceiling. The claustrophobia level is zero.

8

Shopping

*U*nless you're looking for souvenir decks of cards, Styrofoam dice, and miniature slot machines, Las Vegas is not exactly a shopping mecca. It does, however, have several noteworthy malls that can amply supply the basics. And many hotels also offer comprehensive, and sometimes highly themed, shopping arcades, most notably Caesars Palace (details below). You might consider driving **Maryland Parkway,** which runs parallel to the Strip on the east and has just about one of everything: Target, Toys 'Я' Us, several major department stores, Tower Records, major drug stores (in case you forgot your shampoo and don't want to spend $8 on a new one in your hotel sundry shop), some alternative-culture stores (tattoo parlors and hip clothing stores), and so forth. It goes on for blocks.

1 The Malls

Boulevard Mall. 3528 S. Maryland Pkwy. (between Twain Ave. and Desert Inn Rd.) ☎ **702/732-8949.** Mon–Fri 10am–9pm, Sat 10am–8pm, Sun 11am–6pm.

The Boulevard is the largest mall in Las Vegas. Its 144-plus stores and restaurants are arranged in arcade fashion on a single floor occupying 1.2 million square feet. Geared to the average consumer (not the carriage trade), it has anchors like Sears, JCPenney, Macy's, Dillard's, and Marshalls. Other notables include The Disney Store, The Nature Company, a 23,000-square-foot Good Guys (electronics), GAP, GAP Kids, The Limited, Victoria's Secret, Colorado (for outdoor clothing and gear), Howard and Phil's Western Wear, and African and World Imports. There's a wide variety of shops offering moderately priced shoes and clothing for the entire family, books and gifts, jewelry, and home furnishings, plus more than a dozen fast-food eateries. In short, you can find just about anything you need here. There's free valet parking.

Fashion Show Mall. 3200 Las Vegas Blvd. S. (at the corner of Spring Mountain Rd.) ☎ **702/369-8382.** Mon–Fri 10am–9pm, Sat 10am–7pm, Sun noon–6pm.

This luxurious and centrally located mall, one of the city's largest, opened in 1981 to great hoopla. Designers Adolfo, Geoffrey Beene, Bill Blass, Bob Mackie, and Pauline Trigere were all on hand to display their fashion interpretations of the "Las Vegas look."

The mall comprises more than 130 shops, restaurants, and services. It is anchored by Neiman-Marcus, Saks Fifth Avenue, Macy's, Robinsons-May, and Dillard's. Other notable tenants: Abercrombie & Fitch, The Disney Store, The Walt Disney Gallery, The Discovery Channel Store, Lillie Rubin (upscale women's clothing), GAP, Benetton, Uomo, Banana Republic, Victoria's Secret, Caché, Williams-Sonoma Grand Cuisine, The Body Shop, Mondi (upscale women's clothing), Waldenbooks, Louis Vuitton, and Sharper Image. There are several card and book shops, a wide selection of apparel stores for the whole family (including large sizes and petites), nine jewelers, 21 shoe stores, and gift and specialty shops. There are dozens of eating places (see chapter 5 for specifics on **Chin's** and **DIVE!**). Valet parking is available, and you can even arrange to have your car hand washed while you shop.

Galleria at Sunset. 1300 W. Sunset Rd., at Stephanie St. just off I-515 in nearby Henderson. ☎ **702/434-0202.** Mon–Sat 10am–9pm, Sun 11am–6pm.

This upscale 1 million-square-foot shopping center, 9 miles southeast of Downtown Las Vegas, opened in 1996 with performing Disney characters on hand to welcome shoppers and a nighttime display of fireworks. The mall has a Southwestern motif, evidenced in the use of terra-cotta stone, interior landscaping, cascading fountains, and skylights; eight 20-foot hand-carved pillars flank the main entrance. Anchored by four department stores—Dillard's, JCPenney, Mervyn's California, and Robinsons-May—the Galleria's 110 emporia include branches of The Disney Store, GAP/GAP Kids/Baby GAP, The Limited and The Limited Too, Eddie Bauer, Miller's Outpost, Ann Taylor, bebe, Caché, Compagnie International, Lane Bryant, Lerner New York, Victoria's Secret, The Body Shop, B. Dalton, and Sam Goody. In addition to shoes and clothing for the entire family, you'll find electronics, eyewear, gifts, books, home furnishings, jewelry, and luggage here. Dining facilities include an extensive food court and two restaurants.

The Meadows. 4300 Meadows Lane (at the intersection of Valley View and U.S. 95). ☎ **702/878-4849.** Mon–Fri 10am–9pm, Sat–Sun 10am–7pm.

Another immense mall, the Meadows comprises 144 shops, services, and eateries, anchored by four department stores: Macy's, Dillard's,

Sears, and JCPenney. In addition, there are 15 shoe stores, a full array of apparel for the entire family (including maternity wear, petites, and large sizes), an extensive food court, and shops purveying toys, books, CDs and tapes, luggage, gifts, jewelry, home furnishings (The Bombay Company, among others), accessories, and so on. Fountains and trees enhance the Meadows' ultramodern, high-ceilinged interior, and a 1995 renovation added comfortable conversation/seating areas and made the mall lighter and brighter. It is divided into five courts, one centered on a turn-of-the-century carousel (a plus for kids). A natural history–themed court has a "desert fossil" floor, and an entertainment court is the setting for occasional live musical and dramatic performances. You can rent strollers at the Customer Service Center.

2 Factory Outlets

Las Vegas has two big factory outlets just a few miles past the southern end of the Strip. If you don't have a car, you can take a no. 301 CAT bus from anywhere on the Strip and change at Vacation Village to a no. 303.

Belz Factory Outlet World. 7400 Las Vegas Blvd. S. (at Warm Springs Rd.) ☎ **702/896-5599.** Mon–Sat 10am–9pm, Sun 10am–6pm.

Belz houses 145 air-conditioned outlets, including a few dozen clothing stores and shoe stores. It offers an immense range of merchandise at savings up to 75% off retail prices. Among other emporia, you'll find Adolfo II, Casual Corner, Levi's, Nike, Dress Barn, Oshkosh B'Gosh, Leggs/Hanes/Bali, Esprit, Aileen, Bugle Boy, Carters, Reebok, Spiegel, Guess Classics, Oneida, Springmaid, We're Entertainment (Disney and Warner Bros.), Bose (electronics), Danskin, Van Heusen, Burlington, Royal Doulton, Lennox (china), Waterford (crystal), and Geoffrey Beene here. There is also a carousel.

Factory Stores of America. 9155 Las Vegas Blvd. (at Serene St.) ☎ **702/897-9090.** Mon–Sat 10am–8pm, Sun 10am–6pm.

A 30-acre open-air mall with Spanish-style architecture, this is the only outlet center in the country with a casino bar/lounge on its premises. Its 41 stores include Corning/Revere, Izod, Mikasa, American Tourister, Van Heusen, B.U.M. Equipment, Spiegel, London Fog, VF (sportswear), Book Warehouse, Geoffrey Beene, and Adolfo II. Come here for clothing, housewares, shoes, china, and much, much more.

3 Hotel Shopping Arcades

Just about every Las Vegas hotel offers some shopping opportunities. The following have the most extensive arcades. *Note:* The Forum Shops at Caesars—as much a sightseeing attraction as a shopping arcade—are in the must-see category.

Bally's **Bally's Avenue Shoppes** number around 20 emporia offering pro team sports apparel, toys, clothing (men's, women's, and children's), logo items, gourmet chocolates, liquor, jewelry, nuts and dried fruit, flowers, handbags, and T-shirts. In addition, there are several gift shops, three restaurants, art galleries, and a pool-wear shop. There are blackjack tables and slot and video poker machines right in the mall, as well as a race and sports book. You can dispatch the kids to a video arcade here while you shop.

Caesars Palace Since 1978, Caesars has had an impressive arcade of shops called the **Appian Way.** Highlighted by an immense white Carrara-marble replica of Michelangelo's *David* standing more than 18 feet high, its shops include the aptly named Galerie Michelangelo (original and limited-edition artworks), jewelers (including branches of Ciro and Cartier), a logo merchandise shop, and several shops for upscale men's and women's clothing. All in all, a respectable grouping of hotel shops, and an expansion is in the works.

But in the hotel's tradition of constantly surpassing itself, in 1992 Caesars inaugurated the fabulous ❂ **Forum Shops,** an independently operated 250,000-square-foot Rodeo-Drive-meets-the-Roman-Empire affair complete with a 48-foot triumphal arch entranceway, a painted Mediterranean sky that changes as the day progresses from rosy-tinted dawn to twinkling evening stars, acres of marble, lofty scagliola Corinthian columns with gold capitals, and a welcoming goddess of fortune under a central dome. Its architecture and sculpture span a period from 300 B.C. to A.D. 1700. Storefront facades, some topped with statues of Roman senators, resemble a classical Italian streetscape, with archways, piazzas, ornate fountains, and a barrel-vaulted ceiling. The "center of town" is the magnificent domed Fountain of the Gods, where Jupiter rules from his mountaintop surrounded by Pegasus, Mars, Venus, Neptune, and Diana. And at the Festival Fountain, seemingly immovable "marble" animatronic statues of Bacchus (slightly in his cups), a lyre-playing Apollo, Plutus, and Venus come to life for a 7-minute revel with dancing waters and high-tech laser-light effects. The shows take place every hour on the hour. The whole thing is pretty incredible, but also very Vegas, particularly the Bacchus show, which is truly frightening and bizarre. Even if you don't like shopping, it's worth the stroll just to giggle.

More than 70 prestigious emporia here include Louis Vuitton, Plaza Escada, Bernini, Christian Dior, A/X Armani Exchange, bebe, Caché, Gucci, Ann Taylor, and Gianni Versace, along with many other clothing, shoe, and accessory shops. Other notables include: a Warner Brothers Studio Store (a sign at the exit reads thatius finitus folkus), The Disney Store, Kids Kastle (beautiful children's clothing and toys), Rose of Sharon (classy styles for large-size women), Sports Logo (buy a basketball signed by Michael Jordan for $695!), Field of Dreams (more autographed sports memorabilia), Museum Company (reproductions ranging from 16th-century hand-painted Turkish boxes to ancient Egyptian scarab necklaces), West of Santa Fe (Western wear and Native American jewelry and crafts), Antiquities (neon Shell gas signs, 1950s malt machines, Americana; sometimes "Elvis" is on hand), Endangered Species Store (ecology-themed merchandise), Brookstone (one-of-a-kind items from garden tools to sports paraphernalia), and Victoria's Secret. There's much more, including jewelry shops and art galleries.

And as if that weren't enough, in 1998 the Forum Shops added an extension. The centerpiece is a giant Roman Hall, featuring a 50,000-gallon circular aquarium and another fountain that also comes to life with a show of fire (don't stand too close—it gets really hot), dancing waters, and animatronic figures as the mythical continent of Atlantis rises and falls every 90 minutes. The production values are much higher than for the Bacchus extravaganza, but it takes itself more seriously so the giggle factor remains. The hall is also the entrance to the Race for Atlantis IMAX 3-D ride.

In this area, you will find a number of significant stores, including a DKNY, Emporio Armani, Niketown, Fendi, Polo/Ralph Lauren, Guess, Virgin Megastore, and FAO Schwartz. Do go see the latter, as it is fronted by a gigantic Trojan horse in which you can clamber while its head moves and smoke comes out its nostrils. We love it. Also in the shops is Wolfgang Puck's Chinois, a Cheesecake Factory, and a Caviartorium where you can sample all varieties of the high-priced fish eggs.

Circus Circus   There are about 15 shops between the casino and Grand Slam Canyon, offering a wide selection of gifts and sundries, logo items, toys and games, jewelry, liquor, resort apparel for the entire family, T-shirts, homemade fudge/candy/soft ice cream, and, fittingly, clown dolls and puppets. At Amazing Pictures you can have your photo taken as a pinup girl, muscle man, or whatever else your fantasy dictates. Adjacent to Grand Slam Canyon is a new shopping arcade themed after a European village, with cobblestone walkways and fake woods and so forth, and decorated with replicas of vintage circus posters. It's much nicer than what the tacky Circus Circus has had before. Among the stores are Marshall Russo, Headliners, The Sweet Tooth, and Carousel Classics.

Excalibur   The shops of "**The Realm**" for the most part reflect the hotel's medieval theme. Dragon's Lair, for example, features items ranging from pewter swords and shields to full suits of armor, and Merlin's Mystic Shop carries crystals, luck charms, and gargoyles. Other shops carry more conventional wares—gifts, candy, jewelry, women's clothing, and Excalibur logo items. A child pleaser is Kids of the Kingdom, which displays licensed character merchandise from Disney, Looney Tunes, Garfield, and Snoopy. Wild Bill's carries Western wear and Native American jewelry and crafts. And at Fantasy Faire you can have your photo taken in Renaissance attire.

Flamingo Hilton   The **Crystal Court** shopping promenade here accommodates men's and women's clothing/accessories stores, gift shops, and a variety of other emporia selling jewelry, beachwear, Southwestern crafts, fresh-baked goods, logo items, children's gifts, toys, and games.

Harrah's   Harrah's has finished a massive renovation that includes a new shopping center called **Carnivale Court.** It's entirely outdoors and features live, strolling entertainment plus a show at night with fireworks and circus-type acts. Among the store highlights is a Ghirardelli Chocolate store, a branch of the famous San Francisco-based chocolate company. Other stores include On Stage (a CD and video store) and Carnival Corner (gourmet foods and cigars).

Luxor Hotel/Casino   **Gaza Gallerie** is a new, 20,000-square-foot shopping arcade with eight full shops. Most of the stores emphasize clothing. Adjacent is the Cairo Bazaar, a trinket shop.

The MGM Grand   The hotel's **Star Lane Shops** include more than a dozen upscale emporia lining the corridors en route from the monorail entrance. The Knot Shop carries designer ties by Calvin Klein, Gianni Versace, and others. El Portal features luggage and handbags—Coach, Dior, Fendi, Polo Ralph Lauren, and other exclusive lines. Grand 50's carries *Route 66* jackets, Elvis T-shirts, photos of James Dean, and other mementos of the 1950s. MGM Grand

Sports sells signed athletic uniforms, baseballs autographed by Michael Jordan, and the like; it is the scene of occasional appearances by sports stars such as Floyd Patterson and Stan Musial. You can choose an oyster and have its pearl set in jewelry at The Pearl Factory. Other Star Lane Shops specialize in movie memorabilia, Betty Boop merchandise, *EFX* wares, children's clothing, decorative magnets, MGM Grand logo items and Las Vegas souvenirs, seashells and coral, candy, and sunglasses. Refreshments are available at a Häagen-Dazs ice cream counter and Yummy's Coffees and Desserts.

In other parts of the hotel, retail shops include a *Wizard of Oz* gift shop, Front Page (for newspapers, books, magazines, and sundries), a spa shop selling everything from beachwear to top-of-the-line European skin care products, a liquor store, a candy store, Kenneth J. Lane jewelry, and Marshall Rousso (men's and women's clothing). In addition, theme-park emporia sell Hollywood memorabilia, cameras and photographic supplies, MGM Grand and theme park logo products, toys, fine china and crystal, animation cels, collectibles (limited-edition dolls, plates, figurines), Hollywood-themed clothing and accessories, and Western wear. At Arts and Crafts you can watch artisans working in leather, glass, wood, pottery, and other materials, and at Photoplay Gallery you can have your picture taken as *Time* magazine's man or woman of the year.

Monte Carlo   An arcade of retail shops here includes Bon Vivant (resort wear for the whole family, dresswear for men), Crown Jewels (jewelry, leather bags, crystal, Fabergé eggs, gift items), florist, logo shop, jeweler, food market, dessert store, and Lance Burton magic paraphernalia shop.

Rio   The new 60,000-square-foot **Masquerade Village** is a nicely done addition to the Rio. It's done as a European village and is two stories, featuring a wide variety of shops including the nation's largest Nicole Miller, Speedo, and the N'awlins store, which includes "authentic" voodoo items, Mardi Gras masks, and so forth. It's attached to a cafe that sells beignets (from Cafe Du Monde mix) and chicory coffee.

The Riviera   The Riviera has a fairly extensive shopping arcade comprising art galleries, jewelers, a creative photographer, and shops specializing in women's shoes and handbags, clothing for the entire family, furs, gifts, logo items, toys, phones and electronic gadgets, and chocolates.

Sam's Town   Though Sam's Town does not contain a notably significant shopping arcade, it does house the huge **Western**

Emporium (almost department-store size) selling Western clothing for men and women, boots (an enormous selection), jeans, belts, silver and turquoise jewelry, Stetson hats, Native American crafts, gift items, and old-fashioned candy. You can have your picture taken here in period Western costume. Open daily at 9am; closing hours vary.

Stratosphere   Shopping is no afterthought here. The internationally themed second-floor **Tower Shops** promenade, which will soon house 40 stores, is entered via an escalator from the casino. Some shops are in "Paris," along the Rue Lafayette and Avenue de l'Opéra (there are replicas of the Eiffel Tower and Arc de Triomphe in this section). Others occupy Hong Kong and New York City streetscapes. Already-extant emporia include: The Money Company (money-motif items from T-shirts to golf balls), a T-shirt store, a magic shop, Key West (body lotions and more), Victoria's Secret, a magnet shop, Norma Kaplan (for glitzy/sexy women's footwear), an electronics boutique, a logo shop, and several gift shops. There are branches of Jitters (a coffee house) and Häagen-Dazs, and stores are supplemented by cart vendors.

Treasure Island   Treasure Island's shopping promenade—doubling as a portrait gallery of famed buccaneers (Blackbeard, Jean Lafitte, Calico Jack, Barbarosa)—has wooden ship figureheads and battling pirates suspended from its ceiling. Emporia here include the Treasure Island Store (your basic hotel gift/sundry shop, also offering much pirate-themed merchandise, plus a section devoted to Calvin Klein clothing), Loot 'n' Booty, Candy Reef, Captain Kid's (children's clothing), and Damsels in Dis'Dress (women's sportswear and accessories). The Mutiny Bay Shop, in the video-game arcade, carries logo items and stuffed animals. In the casino are the Buccaneer Bay Shoppe (logo merchandise) and the Treasure Chest (a jewelry store; spend those winnings right on the spot). And the Crow's Nest, en route to the Mirage monorail, carries Cirque du Soleil logo items. Cirque du Soleil and Mystère logo wares are also sold in a shop near the ticket office.

4 Vintage Clothing

The Attic. 1018 S. Main St. ☎ **702/388-4088.** Mon–Sat 10am–7pm, Sun 11am–5pm. MC, V.

Sharing a large space with **Cafe Neon**—a coffeehouse that also serves Greek-influenced cafe food so you can raise your blood sugar again after a long stretch of shopping—and a comedy club stage, and upstairs from an attempt at a weekly club (as of this writing, the Saturday night Underworld), The Attic (the current star of a Visa commercial) has plenty of clothing choices on many racks. During a recent visit, a man came in asking for a poodle skirt for his 8-year-old. They had one.

Buffalo Exchange. 4110 S. Maryland Parkway (at Flamingo, near Tower Records). ☎ **702/791-3960.** Mon–Sat 11am–7pm, Sun noon–6pm. MC, V.

This is actually part of a chain of such stores spread out across the western United States. If the chain part worries you, don't let it—this merchandise doesn't feel processed. Staffed by plenty of incredibly hip alt-culture kids (ask them what's happening in town during your visit), it is stuffed with dresses, shirts, pants, and so forth. Like any vintage shop, the contents are hit and miss; you can easily go in one day and come out with 12 fabulous new outfits, but you can just as easily go in and come up dry. It is probably the most reliable of the local vintage shops.

The Haight . 1647 E. Charleston Blvd. ☎ **702/387-7818.** Mon–Sat 11am–6pm, Sun noon–5pm. MC, V.

Upstairs from an antique store, this is in a small, old house. Not only is the stock in various rooms, they've turned the retro-tiled bathroom into the dressing room. They have a large selection of used Levis and otherwise specialize in '60s and '70s vintage clothing.

Our House. 1639 E. Charleston Blvd. ☎ **702/384-4748**. Mon–Sat 11am–5pm, Sun noon–5pm.

A tiny store filled with the most happening in new and vintage clothing (think club kid wear) and some new jewelry designs. Not a huge selection, but very kinda now, kinda wow. They are right next door to the Haight and the start of the Charleston antique row.

5 Reading Material: Used Books, Comics & a Notable Newsstand

USED BOOKS

Dead Poet Books. 3858 W. Sahara (corner of Valley View, near Albertson's). ☎ **702/227-4070.** Mon–Sat 10am–6pm, Sun noon–5pm. AE, DISC, MC, V.

Eliot? Byron? Tennyson? None of the above. Actually, the dead poet in question was a man from whose estate the owners bought their start-up stock. He had such good taste in books, they "fell in love with him" and wanted to name the store in his memory. Just one problem—they never did get his name. So they just called him "the dead poet." He wasn't a poet, but surely anyone with such fine taste in books must have been one in his soul. His legacy continues in this book-lover's haven.

A LAS VEGAS SPECIALTY STORE

Gambler's Book Shop. 630 S. 11th St. (just off Charleston Blvd.) ☎ **800/ 522-1777** or 702/382-7555. Mon–Sat 9am–5pm.

Here you can buy a book on any system ever devised to beat casino odds. Owner Edna Luckman carries more than 4,000 gambling-related titles, including many out-of-print books, computer software, and videotapes. She describes her store as a place where "gamblers, writers, researchers, statisticians, and computer specialists can meet and exchange information." On request, knowledgeable clerks provide on-the-spot expert advice on handicapping the ponies and other aspects of sports betting. The store's motto is "Knowledge is protection."

COMIC BOOKS

Alternative Reality Comics. 4800 S. Maryland Pkwy. ☎ **702/736-3673.** Mon–Sat 11am–7pm, Sun noon–6pm.

The place in Vegas for all your comic-book needs. They have a nearly comprehensive selection, with a heavy emphasis on the underground comics. But don't worry, the superheroes are here, too.

A NOTABLE NEWSSTAND

International Newsstand. 3900 Paradise Rd. (in Citibank Plaza). ☎ **702/ 796-9901.** Daily 8:30am–9pm. AE, MC, V.

Homesick for local news? No matter where you are from, come here. It's crammed full of seemingly every city newspaper in the land, plus a large selection of foreign-city papers. They surely don't have everything, but it seems like they do. Okay, the actual count is every major U.S. city, plus 10 other countries. One impressed shopper said this would put many a formerly worthy newsstand in any cosmopolitan city to shame. There is also a wide array of magazines, both foreign and domestic, though they get less space than at other newsstands thanks to the newspapers.

6 Antiques

Antiques in Vegas? You mean really old slot machines, or the people playing the really old slot machines?

Actually, Vegas has quite a few antique stores—nearly two dozen, of consistent quality and price, nearly all located within a few blocks of each other. We have one friend, someone who takes interior design *very* seriously, who comes straight to Vegas for most of her best finds (you should see her antique chandelier collection!).

To get there, start in the middle of the 1600 block of E. Charleston Blvd. and keep driving east. The little stores, nearly all in old houses dating from the '30s, line each side of the street. Or you can stop in at **Silver Horse Antiques** (1651 E. Charleston Blvd.) and pick up a map to almost all the locations, with phone numbers and hours of operation.

For everything under one roof, try **Sampler Shops Antique Mall,** 6115 W. Tropicana Ave. (open Mon–Sat noon–6pm, Sun noon–5pm). Over 200 small antique shops sell their wares in this mall, which offers a diversity of antiques ranging from exquisite Indian bird cages to Star Wars memorabilia (let's not call those sorts of items "antiques" but rather "nostalgia").

Las Vegas After Dark

*Y*ou will not lack for things to do at night in Vegas. It is a town that truly comes alive only at night. Don't believe us? Just look at the difference between the Strip during the day, when it's kind of dingy and nothing special, and at night, when the lights hit and the place glows in all its glory. Night is when it's happening in this 24-hour town. In fact, most bars and clubs don't even get going until close to midnight. That's because it's only around then that all the many restaurant workers and people connected with the shows get off the clock and can go out and play themselves. It's extraordinary. Just sit down in a bar at 11pm; it's empty. You might well conclude it's dead. Return in 2 hours and find it completely full and jumping.

But you also won't lack for things to do before 11pm. There are shows all over town, ranging from traditional magic to cutting-edge acts like *Mystère*. The showgirls remain, topless and otherwise; Las Vegas revues are what happened to vaudeville, by the way, as chorus girls do their thing in between jugglers, comics, magicians, singers, and specialty acts of dubious category. Even the topless ones are tame; all that changes is that already scantily clad showgirls are even more so.

Every hotel has at least one lounge, usually offering live music. The days of fabulous Vegas lounge entertainment, when sometimes the acts were of better quality than the headliners (and headliners like Sinatra would join the lounge acts onstage between their own sets), are gone. Most of what remains are homogeneous and bland, and serve best as a brief respite or background noise. On the other hand, finding the most awful lounge act in town can be rewarding on its own. (To this end, seek out **Cook E. Jarr and the Crumbs,** a rapidly aging and tasteless crew universally revered as the worst lounge act in Vegas. They were last spotted at the Continental Hotel.)

Vegas still does attract the best in headliner entertainment in its showrooms and arenas. Bette Midler did an HBO special from the MGM Grand in early 1997, and U2 started its PopArt tour at UNLV's stadium. Liza Minnelli, Harry Belafonte, Penn and Teller,

Melissa Manchester, Wayne Newton, Chaka Khan, Johnny Mathis, Barbara Mandrell, Englebert Humperdinck, and Wynnona have all played Vegas recently. (And up until just a few years ago, the legendary Sinatra still did regular stints here.) It is still a badge of honor for comedians to play Vegas, and there is almost always someone of marquee value playing one showroom or the other.

Of course, if you prefer alternative or real rock music, your choices are more limited. More rock bands are coming through town, attracted to either the Hard Rock Hotel's venue or the Huntridge Theater, so that means you can actually see folks like Marilyn Manson and Beck in Vegas. But otherwise, the alternative club scene in town is severely limited. Check out the listings below for bars and coffeehouses, several of which offer live alternative or blues music.

If you want to know what is playing during your stay, consult local free alternative papers the *Scope* (biweekly, with great club and bar descriptions in their listings) and *City Life* (weekly, with no descriptions but comprehensive listings of what's playing where all over town). Both can be picked up at restaurants, bars, record and music stores, and hep retail stores.

Admission to shows runs the gamut, from about $19 for *An Evening at La Cage* (a female impersonator show at the Riviera) to $80 and more for top headliners or *Siegfried and Roy*. Prices usually include two drinks or, in rare instances, dinner.

To find out who will be performing during your stay, and for up-to-date listings of shows (prices change, shows close), you can call the various hotels featuring headliner entertainment, using toll-free numbers. Or call the **Las Vegas Convention and Visitors Authority** (☎ 702/892-0711) and ask them to send you a free copy of *Showguide* or *What's On in Las Vegas* (one or both of which will probably be in your hotel room).

In addition to the below listed, consider the **Fremont Street Experience,** described in chapter 6.

1 What's Playing Where

Below is a list of the major production shows playing at our press time in Las Vegas. In the following section, we've reviewed some of the major ones.

- **Bally's:** ✪ *Jubilee!* (Las Vegas–style review)
- **Excalibur:** *An Evening in Vienna* and *King Arthur's Tournament* (medieval-themed revue)

- **Flamingo Hilton:** *Forever Plaid* (off-Broadway revue featuring '60s music) and *The Great Radio City Spectacular* (Las Vegas–style revue featuring the Radio City Music Hall Rockettes)
- **Harrah's:** *Spellbound* (magic revue)
- **Imperial Palace:** *Legends in Concert* (musical impersonators)
- **Jackie Gaughan's Plaza:** *The Xtreme Scene* (sexy Las Vegas–style revue)
- **MGM Grand:** ✪ *EFX* (special-effects revue featuring David Cassidy)
- **The Mirage:** ✪ *Siegfried and Roy* (magical extravaganza)
- **Monte Carlo:** ✪ *Lance Burton: Master Magician* (magic show and revue)
- **Rio Suite Hotel:** *Danny Gans* (impressions)
- **Riviera Hotel:** *An Evening at La Cage* (female impersonators), *Crazy Girls* (sexy Las Vegas–style revue), and *Splash* (aquatic revue)
- **Stardust:** *Enter the Night* (Las Vegas–style revue)
- **Stratosphere Tower:** *American Superstars* (an impression-filled production show), *Viva Las Vegas* (Las Vegas–style revue)
- **Treasure Island:** ✪ Cirque du Soleil's *Mystère* (unique circus performance)
- **Tropicana:** *Folies Bergère* (Las Vegas–style revue)

2 The Major Production Shows

Since this portable guide is more limited in scope than our regular *Frommer's Las Vegas* guide, we've only included reviews of the better or more important shows.

American Superstars. Stratosphere. 2000 Las Vegas Blvd. S. ☎ **800/99-TOWER** or 702/380-7777.

One of the increasing number of celebrity impersonator shows (cheaper than getting the real headliners), "American Superstars" is one of the few where said impersonators actually sing live. Five performers do their thing; celebs impersonated vary depending on the evening. A typical Friday night featured Gloria Estefan, Charlie Daniels, Madonna, Michael Jackson, and Diana Ross and the Supremes. (And recently, they added the Spice Girls—the catty among us will notice the impersonators have better figures than the real Girls.) The performers won't be putting the originals out of work anytime soon, but they aren't bad. Actually, they are closer in voice than in looks to the celeb in question (half the black performers were played by white actors), which is an unusual switch for

Vegas impersonators. The "Charlie Daniels" actually proved to be a fine fiddler in his own right and was the hands-down crowd favorite. The live band actually had a look-alike of their own: Kato Kaelin on drums (it's good that he's getting work). The youngish crowd (by Vegas standards) included a healthy smattering of children, and seemed to find no faults with the production. The action is also shown on two large, and completely unnecessary, video screens flanking the stage, so you don't have to miss a moment.

- **Showroom Policies:** Nonsmoking with maître d' seating.
- **Price:** Admission $25.25 includes tax.
- **Show Times:** Fri–Wed at 7 and 10pm. Dark Thurs.
- **Reservations:** Up to 3 days in advance.

✪ **Cirque du Soleil's Mystère.** Treasure Island, 3300 Las Vegas Blvd. S. ☎ **800/392-1999** or 702/894-7722.

The in-house ads for *Mystère* (say miss-*tair*) say "Words don't do it justice," and for once, that's not just hype. The show is so visual that trying to describe it is a losing proposition. And simply calling it a circus is like calling the Hope Diamond a gem, or the Taj Mahal a building. It's accurate, but something seems a little left out of the description.

Cirque du Soleil began in Montréal as a unique circus experience, not only shunning the traditional animal acts in favor of gorgeous feats of human strength and agility, but also adding elements of the surreal and the absurd. The result seems like a collaboration between Salvador Dali and Luis Buñuel, with a few touches by Magritte and choreography by Twyla Tharp. Mirage Resorts has built them their own theater, an incredible space with an enormous dome and super hydraulics that allow for the Cirque performers to fly in space. Or so it seems.

While part of the fun of the early Cirque was seeing what amazing stuff they could do on a shoestring, seeing what they can do with virtually unlimited funds is spectacular. Unlike, arguably, other artistic ventures, Cirque took full advantage of their new largesse, and their art only rose with their budget. The show features one simply unbelievable act after another (seemingly boneless contortionists and acrobats, breathtakingly beautiful aerial maneuvers), interspersed with Dadaist, commedia dell'arte clowns, and everyone clad in costumes like nothing you've ever seen before. All this and a giant snail. The show is dreamlike, suspenseful, funny, erotic, mesmerizing, and just lovely. At times, you might even find yourself moved to tears. However, for some children, it might be a bit too sophisticated

---

ii   Family-Friendly Shows

Appropriate shows for kids, all described in this chapter, include the following:

- Siegfried and Roy at the Mirage *(see p. 168)*
- Lance Burton at the Monte Carlo *(see p. 166)*
- *EFX* at the MGM Grand *(see p. 162)*
- Cirque du Soleil's *Mystère* at Treasure Island *(see p. 160)*

As a general rule, early shows are less racy than late-night shows.

---

and arty. Even if you've seen Cirque before, it's worth coming to check it out, thanks to the large production values. It's a world-class show, no matter where it's playing. That this is playing in Vegas is astonishing.

- **Showroom Policies:** Nonsmoking with preassigned seating.
- **Price:** $70 adults, $35 for children under 11 (drinks and tax extra).
- **Show Times:** Wed–Sun at 7:30 and 10:30pm. Dark Mon–Tues.
- **Reservations:** You can reserve by phone via credit card up to 7 days in advance (do reserve early since it often sells out).

✪ **Danny Gans: The Man of Many Voices.** Rio Suites, 3700 W. Flamingo Rd. ☎ **800/PLAY-RIO** or 702/252-7777.

Danny Gans has taken over the newly refurbished Copacabana Showroom for an indefinite run. If he's still on when you visit, don't miss him. Gans, who has starred on Broadway, is an impressionist extraordinaire. Natalie Cole, who heard him perform her father's famous song, "Unforgettable," exclaimed, "No one has ever done a better impression of my dad." His show is also unforgettable. In addition to startlingly realistic impressions of dozens of singers (everyone from Sinatra to Springsteen), he does movie scenes (such as Fonda and Hepburn in *On Golden Pond*), Bill Clinton, weird duets (Michael Bolton and Dr. Ruth, or Stevie Wonder singing to Shirley MacLaine "I Just Called to Say I Was You"), and, of course, a first-rate Elvis. A mind-boggling highlight is Gans's rendition of "The Twelve Days of Christmas" in 12 different voices, which necessitates rapidly switching back and forth from such diverse impressions as Paul Lynde, Clint Eastwood, Peter Falk, and Woody Allen, among others. This show gets a standing ovation every night.

- **Showroom Policies:** Nonsmoking with maître d' seating.
- **Price:** $60 (including two drinks, tax, and gratuities).
- **Show Times:** Wed–Sun at 7:30pm. Dark Mon–Tues.
- **Reservations:** Tickets can be ordered up to 30 days in advance.

☼ **EFX.** MGM Grand, 3799 Las Vegas Blvd. S. ☎ **800/929-1111** or 702/891-7777.

Essentially the first major show of the post–Cirque du Soleil era, *EFX's* $40 million makeover (thanks to new star David Cassidy) has used its money wisely, updating the classic Vegas revue into essentially a live action version of the modern over-the-top Strip hotels. It's not so much cheese anymore, as expensive and occasionally jaw-dropping cheese. Which is not to say it's bad—quite the opposite. The nominal story line, about a man who has lost his imagination, allows the very likable Cassidy, playing on his regular guy image, to assume the personas of King Arthur, P. T. Barnum, Houdini, and H. G. Wells, in order to deliver set pieces of better than usual dancing, magic, singing, acrobatics, and illusion. And, of course, special effects ("EFX" is the movie industry term for same). The sets are lavish beyond belief; the costumes and some of the acting show the Cirque influence (faintly Grand Guignol); and the choreography is considerably more imaginative and fresh than that of any other such show in town. The songs are somewhat bland but sung almost totally live, and some prove surprisingly hummable. And the effects (flying saucers and cast members, fire-breathing dragons, 3-D time travel, lots of explosions) show where the money is. Cranks may occasionally spot wires, and sometimes said effects are a little painful on the eyes and ears (and they overdo it on the fog machine). The ticket price isn't cheap, so it might be worth taking the less-expensive seats in the mezzanine, as the view is just as good from there.

- **Showroom Policies:** Nonsmoking with preassigned seating.
- **Price:** $49.50–$70.
- **Show Times:** Tues–Sat at 7:30 and 10:30pm. Dark Sun–Mon.
- **Reservations:** You can reserve by phone any time in advance.

Enter the Night. The Stardust, 3000 Las Vegas Blvd. S. ☎ **800/824-6033** or 702/732-6111.

It's kind of cute how the Stardust has tried to stage a full-size topless revue on a small- to medium-size stage. Okay, maybe not *cute*, but the production does seem to be busting at its seams, and it never quite reconciles its aspirations with its reality. There is no plot or point to this; the theme is "enter the night" (of course) and about the passion and mystery that will then ensue, but the songs and actions are vague as to how this is supposed to come about. Instead, what you get is one of those "Why is that girl parading around in her underwear?" sort of shows. It's a question that can be quite relevant, depending on your seats, since a circular catwalk extends into the audience; some seats are perched right on the rail edge of this, virtually squashing the occupant's face into a showgirl's midriff. In fact, some of those topless breasts could put out an eye. (Besides, it spoils the illusion when you are close enough to see all that pancake makeup.) Your seat placement is worth noting for this reason, if you don't want to be that up close and personal with a virtually naked total stranger. Others might pay extra.

Anyway, it's a revue, featuring songs about listening to your heart, dancing (the Space Age Viking dance number was a camp highlight), and one blonde (presumably Aki, "Showgirl for the 21st Century") in a flesh-colored G-string performing nearly nude *en pointe* ballet. All this is delivered with a Mickey Mouse Club enthusiasm, which is a bit disconcerting when half the performers are partially naked. There is also nearly naked ice skating, which was actually better than you might think; the skaters are very good and make use of the world's tiniest patch of ice in dramatic and resourceful ways. They were also a huge crowd pleaser, as was the delightful Argentinean gaucho act.

- **Showroom Policies:** Nonsmoking with preassigned seating.
- **Price:** Most seats $30, booths $35 to $45 (includes two drinks, tax, and gratuity).
- **Show Times:** Tues, Wed, Thurs, Sat at 7:30 and 10:30pm; Sun–Mon at 8pm only. Dark Fri.
- **Reservations:** You can reserve up to a month in advance by phone.

An Evening at La Cage. Riviera Hotel and Casino, 2901 Las Vegas Blvd. S. ☎ **800/634-6753** or 702/734-9301.

No, not inspired by the French movie nor the recent American remake, nor even the Broadway musical. Actually, it's more the stage show from *Priscilla, Queen of the Desert*. Female impersonators dress up as various entertainers (with varying degrees of success) to lip synch to said performers' greatest hits (with varying degrees of success). Celebs lampooned can include Cher, Bette Midler, Judy Garland, Whitney Houston, Dionne Warwick and, intriguingly, Michael Jackson. A Joan Rivers impersonator, looking not unlike the original but sounding (even with the aid of, oddly, a constant echo) not at all like her, is the hostess, delivering scatological phrases and stale jokes. They do make the most of a tiny stage with some pretty stunning lighting, though the choreography is bland. Still, it's a crowd pleaser—one couple was back for their fourth (all comped) visit.

- **Showroom Policies:** Nonsmoking with maître d' seating.
- **Price:** $26.66–$35 (includes two drinks; gratuity extra).
- **Show Times:** Wed–Mon at 7:30 and 9:30pm, with an extra show at 11:15pm Wed and Sat. Dark Tues.
- **Reservations:** Tickets can be purchased at the box office only, in advance if you wish.

The Great Radio City Spectacular. Flamingo Hilton, 3555 Las Vegas Blvd.S. ☎ **800/221-7299** or 702/733-3333.

This is the wholesome showgirls show. If you aren't familiar with the venerable Rockettes tradition, the short black-and-white film on their history that opens the production will get you up to date. It also sets the stage for the big entrance by the ladies, arguably the world's best-known chorus line. A headliner accompanies them—this star changes frequently. As of this writing, it was Paige O'Hara, the voice of Belle from Disney's *Beauty and the Beast.* Regardless of who it is, the star's musical numbers are interspersed with a variety of dance productions by the Rockettes that serve as a veritable history of dance, ranging from tap to '40s swing, waltzes, March of the Wooden Soldiers, and the like. Of course, the signature Rockettes' high kicking line is worked into at least half the numbers. That's their greatest hit—if O'Hara remains with the show, you can count on seeing her do hers, from the aforementioned *Beauty and the Beast.* The variety acts are standard Vegas: A juggler who keeps up a disturbing, David Helfgott–like banter under his breath and a magician who tries too hard. The stand-out here was the trained dogs act, which reduced even cynical viewers to goo. These are all pound-rescued mutts with plenty of star quality, and they work the crowd like pros.

- **Showroom Policies:** Nonsmoking with maître d' seating.
- **Price:** Dinner show based on main-course price ($48 and up includes tax and gratuity). Cocktail show $40 (includes two drinks, tax, and gratuity).
- **Show Times:** Nightly dinner show at 7:45pm, cocktail show at 10:30pm.
- **Reservations:** You can reserve by phone 2 weeks in advance.

Imagine: A Theatrical Odyssey. Luxor, 3900 Las Vegas Blvd. S. ☎ **800/ 288-1000** or 702/262-4000.

Probably the most stunning showroom in Las Vegas, entirely Egyptian-themed, and though the insides of pyramids surely didn't look like this, it's mighty impressive anyway. Unfortunately, what is presented only occasionally lives up to the standards of the setting. Expect another mixed-bag Vegas revue; a jungle-themed tiki torch opening number leads to some high drama magic, then more music and dancing, some Chinese jugglers, and an underwater-themed production number, plus a look into the future, which seems to consist of Day-Glo costumes and twinkle lights, with a Sixties-mod James Bond soundtrack. Far better were the Cirque du Soleil–inspired bungee jump acrobatic act over the audience and the spectacular concluding Chinese aerialists.

- **Showroom Policies:** nonsmoking with preassigned seating.
- **Price:** $40 (includes tax).
- **Show Times:** Wed–Mon 7:30 and 10:30pm.
- **Reservations:** By phone up to 7 days in advance.

✪ **Jubilee!** Bally's, 3645 Las Vegas Blvd. S. ☎ **800/237-7469** or 702/ 739-4567.

A classic Vegas spectacular, crammed with singing, dancing, magic, acrobats, elaborate costumes and sets, and of course, bare breasts. It's a basic review, with production numbers featuring homogenized versions of standards (Gershwin, Cole Porter, some Fred Astaire numbers) sometimes sung live, sometimes lip-synched, and always accompanied by lavishly costumed and frequently topless showgirls. Humorous set pieces about Samson and Delilah and the sinking of the *Titanic* (!) show off some pretty awesome sets (and they were doing the Titanic long before a certain movie), while the finale features aerodynamically impossible feathered and bejeweled costumes and headpieces designed by Bob Mackie. So what if the dancers are occasionally out of step and the action sometimes veers into the dubious (a Vegas-style revue about a disaster that took more than 1,000 lives?) or even the inexplicable (a finale praising beautiful and barebreasted girls suddenly stops for three lines of "Somewhere Over the Rainbow")? With plenty of rhinestones and nipples on display, this is archetypal Vegas entertainment and the best of those presently offered.

- **Showroom Policies:** Nonsmoking with preassigned seating.
- **Price:** $49.50 and up (tax included; drinks extra).

12 Inaccuracies in the Movie *Showgirls* by the Showgirls in Jubilee!

1. Nomi Malone wouldn't be in a Las Vegas production because she can't sing (or act).

2. Showgirls do not live in trailers.

3. Showgirls aren't discovered in strip bars.

4. Showgirls do not pimp themselves at conventions or trade shows.

5. Hotel owners do not throw lavish cast parties.

6. A lead dancer does not become a celebrity.

7. No one learns a show in a day.

8. Pushing someone down the stairs doesn't get you a lead role, it gets you fired.

9. Ice is used backstage to treat injuries, not to erect nipples.

10. Leaving rehearsal to go to Spago to drink champagne is generally frowned upon.

11. Showgirls are not coke-sniffing, champagne-drinking lesbians.

12. Anyway, showgirls do not drink champagne backstage—we prefer Jack Daniel's!

- **Show Times:** Sun–Wed at 8pm, Thurs and Sat at 8 and 11pm. Dark Fri.
- **Reservations:** You can reserve up to 6 weeks in advance.

○ **Lance Burton: Master Magician.** Monte Carlo, 3770 Las Vegas Blvd. S. ☎ **800/311-8999** or 702/730-7000.

Magic acts are a dime a dozen in Vegas of late. Along with impersonator acts, they seem to have largely replaced the topless showgirls of yore. Most seem more than a little influenced by the immeasurable success of Siegfried and Roy. So when someone pops up who is original—not to mention charming and, yes, actually good at his job—it comes as a relief.

Monte Carlo dumped a lot of money into building the lush Victorian music hall–style Lance Burton Theater for the star, and it was worth it. Handsome and folksy (he hails from Lexington, Kentucky), Burton is talented and engaging, for the most part shunning the big-ticket special effects that seem to have swamped most other shows in town. Instead, he offers an extremely appealing production that starts small, with "close-up" magic. These rather lovely tricks, he tells us, are what won him a number of prestigious magic competitions. They are truly extraordinary (we swear that he tossed a bird up in the air, and the darn thing turned into confetti in front of our eyes. Really.) Burton doesn't have patter, per se, but his dry, laconic, low-key delivery is plenty amusing and in contrast to other performers in town who seem as if they have been spending way too much time at Starbucks. He does eventually move to bigger illusions, but his manner follows him—he knows the stuff is good, but he also knows the whole thing is a bit silly, so why not have fun with it? Accompanying him are some perky showgirls, who border on the wholesome, and talented comic juggler Michael Goudeau. The latter is a likable goofball who instantly wins you over (or should) when he juggles three beanbag chairs. All this and extremely comfortable movie theater–style plush seats with cup holders. And for a most reasonable price.

- **Showroom Policies:** Nonsmoking with preassigned seating.
- **Price:** $35 and $40 (includes tax; drinks extra).
- **Show Times:** Tues–Sat at 7:30 and 10:30pm. Dark Sun–Mon.
- **Reservations:** Tickets can be purchased 60 days in advance.

Legends in Concert. Imperial Palace, 3535 Las Vegas Blvd. S. ☎ **702/ 794-3261.**

A crowd pleaser, which is probably why it's been running since May 1983. Arguably the best of the Vegas impersonator shows (though it's hard to quantify such things), "Legends" does feature performers live, rather than lip-synching. Acts vary from night to night (in a showroom that could use a face-lift) on a nice large stage with modern hydraulics but twinkle lighting that is stuck in a *Flip Wilson Show* time warp. The personal touches here include scantily clad (but well-choreographed) male and female dancers, and an utterly useless green laser. When we went, the performers included Neil Diamond (whose "America" was accompanied by red-, white, and blue–clad showgirls covered in flags of all nations), an actual piano-playing Elton John, the Blues Brothers (a reasonable John Belushi, but a not even close Dan Ackroyd), and the inevitable Diana Ross, Four Tops, and young thin Elvis (who performs hits from the fat old Elvis years). The latter, by the way, was preceded by a reverent multimedia presentation (the stage also has video screens that show not only the live action but clips by the real celebs). Best of all, Wayne Newton was there. Yes, the *real* one.

During the Blues Brothers bit, the band showed a rare display of spontaneity. When one audience member called out a request for "country," they actually broke into the theme from *Rawhide*. Maybe it was a planned moment, but we were impressed that it didn't seem that way.

- **Showroom Policies:** Nonsmoking, with maître d' seating.
- **Price:** $29.50 (includes two drinks or one Polynesian cocktail such as a mai tai or zombie; tax and gratuity extra).
- **Show Times:** Mon–Sat at 7:30 and 10:30pm. Dark Sun.
- **Reservations:** You can make reservations by phone up to 2 weeks in advance.

MADhattan. New York New York Hotel & Casino, 3790 Las Vegas Blvd. S. ☎ **800/693-6763** or 702/740-6815.

Something like Showtime at the Apollo meets Stomp meets "Bring in 'Da Noise, Bring in 'Da Funk." A variety of "street scene"–type performers appear (you can just hear the producers asking for acts that were "gritty" and "urban" but not threateningly so), from a postmodern percussionist to girl groups to "Noise/Funk"–style tap dancing. While this line-up does bring more people of color to the stage than is regularly found in Vegas, older audiences may be turned off by the noise and lack of a storyline, while younger audiences might well notice they can get similar but better entertainment in Chicago and New York, for a lot cheaper, and, ironically, may opt instead for something more traditionally Vegas.

- **Showroom Policies:** Nonsmoking with preassigned seating.
- **Price:** $40 (tax extra)
- **Show Times:** Tues–Sat 7:30 and 10:00pm.
- **Reservations:** By phone up to 7 days in advance.

✪ **Siegfried & Roy.** The Mirage, 3400 Las Vegas Blvd. S. ☎ **800/627-6667** or 702/792-7777.

A Vegas institution for more than 2 decades, illusionists Siegfried and Roy started as an opening act, became headliners at the Frontier, and finally were given their own $30 million show and $25 million theater in the Mirage. They (and their extensive exotic animal menagerie) have amply repaid this enormous investment by selling out every show since. No wonder the Mirage has them booked "until the end of time."

But while the spectacle is undeniable (and the money right on the stage), the result is overproduced. From the get-go, there is so much light, sound, smoke, and fire; so many dancing girls, fire-breathing

Wayne Newton's Top-10 Favorite Lounge Songs

Wayne Newton is the consummate entertainer. He has performed more than 25,000 concerts in Las Vegas alone, and in front of more than 25 million people worldwide. Wayne has received more standing ovations than any other entertainer in history. Along with his singing credits, his acting credits are soaring—one of his more recent credits is Vegas Vacation. Make sure you catch him playing at the MGM Grand. No trip to Vegas is complete without seeing the "King of Las Vegas"... WAYNE NEWTON!

1. "You're Nobody, Til Somebody Loves You"(*You don't have a body unless somebody loves you!*)
2. "Up a Lazy River" (*or "Up Your Lazy River!"*)
3. "Don't Go Changin' (Just the Way You Are)" (*The clothes will last another week!*)
4. "Having My Baby" (*Oh God!!*)
5. "The Windmills of My Mind" (*A mind is a terrible thing to waste!*)
6. "The Wind Beneath My Wings" (*Soft and Dry usually helps!*)
7. "Copacabana"
8. "When the Saints Go Marching In"
9. "I Am, I Said" (*HUH?!*)
10. "The Theme from the Love Boat" (*or "Would A Dinghy Do?"*)

dragons, robots, and other often completely superfluous effects; not to mention an original (and forgettable) Michael Jackson song, that they overwhelm the point of the whole thing. Or maybe they've *become* the point of the whole thing. The magic, which was the Austrian duo's original act, after all, seems to have gotten lost. Sometimes literally. The tricks are at a minimum, allowing the flash pots, lasers, and whatnot to fill out the nearly 2-hour show. More often than not, when a trick was actually being performed, our attention was elsewhere, gawking at an effect, a showgirl, or something. Only the gasps from the audience members who actually happened to be looking in the right place let us know we missed something really neat.

Tellingly, the best part of the show is when all that stuff is switched off, and Siegfried and Roy take the stage to perform smaller magic and chat with the audience. The charm that helped get them so far shines through, and spontaneity is allowed to sneak in. The white tigers are certainly magnificent, but they don't do much other than get cuddled (charmingly) by Roy and badly lip-synch to pretaped roars. The duo is clearly doing something right, judging from the heartfelt standing ovations they receive night after night. But more than one couple was heard to say it was not the best show they had seen, and also to express a feeling that it was overpriced. At these ticket costs (essentially $90 *per person!*) almost anything is. Go if you can't live without seeing a true, modern Vegas legend, but you can find better entertainment values in town.

- **Showroom Policies:** Nonsmoking with preassigned seating.
- **Price:** $89 (includes 2 drinks, souvenir brochure, tax, and gratuity).
- **Show Times:** Performances are Fri–Tues at 7:30 and 11pm, except during occasional dark periods.
- **Reservations:** Tickets can be purchased 3 days in advance.

3 Piano Bars

In addition to the establishments listed below, consider the ultra-elegant **Palace Court Terrace Lounge,** adjoining the Palace Court restaurant at Caesars (see chapter 5), or **Gatsby's** at the MGM Grand (see chapter 5), which also has a sophisticated and stunning adjoining piano bar. And **Cafe Nicolle** (see chapter 5) has a small but agreeable genuine piano bar.

Alexis Park Resort: Pisces Bistro. 375 E. Harmon Ave. ☎ **702/796-3300.** No cover or minimum.

The very upscale Alexis Park offers live entertainment in a beautiful room under a 30-foot domed ceiling; planters of greenery cascade from tiered balconies. When the weather permits, it's lovely to sit at umbrella tables on a terra-cotta patio overlooking the pool. Live music is featured Tuesday to Saturday nights from 8pm until about midnight; a versatile pianist and vocalist perform everything from show tunes to oldies to Top 40. Light fare is available.

The Bar at Times Square. 3790 Las Vegas Blvd. S. (in New York, New York). ☎ **702/740-6969.** No cover or minimum.

If you are looking for a quiet piano bar, this is not the place for you. Here, in the middle of the Central Park part of the New York New York casino, every night two pianos are going strong, and the young hipster, cigar-smoking crowd overflows out the doors. The bar always seems to be packed with a singing, swaying, drinking throng full of camaraderie and good cheer—or, at least, booze. Hugely fun, provided you can get a foot in the door. And yes, every night, right outside, the ball on top drops at midnight, for a little auld lang syne.

The Carriage House: Kiefer's. 105 E. Harmon Ave. ☎ **702/739-8000.** No cover or minimum.

This rooftop restaurant has a plushly furnished adjoining piano bar/ lounge. Windowed walls offer great views of the Las Vegas neon sky- line, making this a romantic setting for cocktails and hors d'oeuvres. There's piano music Thursday to Saturday from 7 to 11pm.

Nicky Blair's. 3925 Paradise Rd. (between Flamingo and Twain). ☎ **702/ 792-9900.** No cover or minimum.

A Los Angeles legend, Nicky Blair closed the doors of his venerable L.A. establishment to open a new version here. Pity the Rat Pack is gone; this would be their hangout in the '90s. A U-shaped bar dominates an elegantly dark space, with hardwood floors and banquettes up against one wall. There are plenty of bartenders and waitresses on hand to serve the middle-aged, upscale (and largely local) clientele. The tables seem well spaced, so a romantic tête-à-tête should be possible. You can order the full menu from the restaurant. The piano goes from 7pm until closing, which is midnight Monday to Thursday, 2am Friday and Saturday.

4 Other Bars

In addition to the venues listed below, consider hanging out at **Country Star,** the **Hard Rock Cafe,** and **Planet Hollywood,** all de- scribed in chapter 5. You might also check out the incredible night- time view at the bar atop the **Stratosphere Hotel**—nothing beats it. There's also the **Viva Las Vegas Lounge** at the Hard Rock Hotel, through which every rock-connected person in Vegas will eventually pass.

Holy Cow. 2432 Las Vegas Blvd. S. (at Sahara Ave.) ☎ **702/732-COWS.**

Okay, so maybe you go to serious bars for serious drinking, but any- place with a giant bovine on the roof and an extensive cow theme on the inside can't be all bad. Cows are everywhere—cow paintings, cow-motif lighting fixtures, a "sidewalk of fame" of cow hoof prints outside, even slot machines called (irresistibly) "Moolah"—so if you are a heifer-a-phobe, stay away. The microbrew pub upstairs offers a free tour, or you can taste its four hand-crafted microbrews: pale ale, wheat beer, brown ale, and a monthly changing brewmaster's special, which sometimes contains the word *blueberry* in it. Pub grub is also offered, which they assure us requires only one stomach to consume.

✪ Main Street Station: Triple 7 Brew Pub. 200 Main St. ☎ 702/ 387-1896.

Yet another of the many things the new(ish) Main Street Station hotel has done right. Stepping into its microbrew pub feels like stepping out of Vegas. Well, maybe except for the dueling piano entertainment. Part modern warehouse look (exposed pipes, microbrew fixtures visible through exposed glass at the back, very high ceiling), but with a hammered tin ceiling that continues the hotel's Victorian decor, this is a look more appropriate to North Beach in San Francisco. Dare we say it? The result produces an environment that is a bit on the yuppified side, but that escapes being pretentious. And frankly, it's a much-needed modern touch for the Downtown area. They have their own brewmaster and a number of microbrews ready to try, and if you feel like a quick bite, there is also an oyster and sushi bar, plus fancy burgers and pizzas. It can get noisy during the aforementioned piano duel act, but otherwise casino noise stays out. And Downtown being all too heavy on the old Las Vegas side (which is fine for a time but not *all* the time), this is good for a suitable breather.

✪ Peppermill's Fireside Lounge. 2985 Las Vegas Blvd. S. ☎ 702/ 735-7635.

Walk through the classic Peppermill's coffee shop (not a bad place to eat, by the way) on the Strip, and you land in its dark, plush, cozy lounge. A fabulously dated view of hip, it has low, circular banquette seats, fake floral foliage, low neon, and electric candles. But best of all is the water and fire pit as the centerpiece—a piece of kitsch thought long vanished from the earth, which attracts nostalgia buffs like moths to flames. It all adds up to a cozy, womblike place. Perfect for crashing down a bit after some time spent on the hectic Strip. The enormous, exotic froufrou tropical drinks (including the signature basketball-sized margaritas) will ensure that you sink into that level of comfortable stupor.

Pink E's. 3695 W. Flamingo. ☎ 702/252-4666.

Sick of the attitude at Club Rio? (And well you should be.) Escape directly across the street to Pink E's, where the theme is pink. You were expecting maybe sea-foam? Anyway, at least one regular described this as "the only place to go if you are over 25 and have a brain." And like pink. Because everything here is: the many pool tables, the Ping-Pong tables, the booths, the lighting, the lava lamp on the bar, and even the people. In its own way, it's as gimmick-ridden as the Beach dance club, but surely no one would put out a pink pool table in all seriousness? Yeah, it's a ludicrous heresy, but don't you want to play on one? Anyway, Pink E's offers retro diner food and a DJ on weekends. The dress code basically translates to "no gangsta wannabe wear." Go, but wear all black just to be ornery.

Sand Dollar Blues Lounge. 3355 Spring Mountain at Polaris. ☎ **702/ 871-6651.**

The kind of funky, no decor (think posters and beer signs), atmosphere-intensive, slightly grimy, friendly bar you either wish your town had or wish it had something other than. Just up the road from Treasure Island, this is a greatantidote to artificial Vegas. Attracting a solid mix of locals and tourists (employees claim the former includes everything from bikers to chamber of commerce members), the Sand Dollar features live blues (both electric and acoustic, with a little Cajun and Zydeco thrown in) every night.

The Sky Lounge (at the Polo Towers). 3745 Las Vegas Blvd. S. ☎ **702/ 261-1000.**

It may not quite be the view offered by the Stratosphere Hotel's bar, but it's pretty darn good and easier to get to. You see too much of the Holiday Inn Boardwalk directly across the street and not quite enough of the MGM Grand to the left, but otherwise there are no complaints. The decor is too modern (heavy on '80s black and purple), but overall the place is quiet (especially during the day) and civil. A jazz vocal/piano performs at night (when the views are naturally best). Worth a trip for an escape from the mob, though you won't be the only tourist fighting for window seats.

Tom & Jerry's. 4550 S. Maryland (and Harmon). ☎ **702/736-8550.**

The dull exterior belies what is inside: a lively bar with three different rooms, each with its own entirely different feel and atmosphere. Decidedly catering to the UNLV crowd (it's right across the street, after all), it prides itself on being ethnically diverse and holding no pretensions. "Drink cheap, be loose, have fun" is the owner's motto, and the result is a bar more enjoyable than the words "college bar" might make you think. The bar has incredible drink specials, a dance room features cover bands, and the final room is full of pool tables.

5 Dance Clubs

🟢 **The Beach.** 365 S. Convention Center Dr. (at Paradise Rd.). ☎ **702/731-1425.** Cover $10 and up Fri/Sat and special events.

If you are a fan of loud, crowded, 24-hour party bars filled with tons of good-looking fun seekers, then bow in this direction, for you have found Mecca. This huge, tropical-themed nightclub is, according to just about anyone you ask, the "hottest" club in the city. It's a two-story affair with five separate bars downstairs and another three up. Just in case walking the 20 feet to the closest one is too much of an effort, they also have bikini-clad women serving beer out of steel tubs full of ice (they also roam the floor with shot belts). The drinks are on the pricey side ($3.75 for an 8-ounce domestic beer). Also downstairs is the large two-story dance floor, which dominates the center of the room and is built around a full-service bar at one end. The crowd is aggressively young and pretty, more men than women (70/30 split), and about 60% tourist, which is probably why the place can get away with charging a $10 cover. Party people look no farther. There's free valet parking, and if you've driven here and become intoxicated, they'll drive you back home at no charge.

Club Rio. Rio Suite Hotel, 3700 W. Flamingo Rd. ☎ **702/252-7777.** As advertised: Cover $10 for men, local women free, out-of-state women $5—but frequently when we went by on a weekend night, the cover was $20 for everyone.

This is the hottest night spot in Vegas (along with the Beach) as of this writing, but apparently it's been made so by people who don't mind long lines, restrictive dress codes, attitudinal door people, hefty cover charges, and bland dance music. Waits can be interminable and admittance denied thanks to the wrong footwear or shirt. Once inside, you find a large, circular room, with the spacious dance floor taking up much of the space. Giant video screens line the upper parts of the walls, showing anything from shots of the action down below to catwalk footage. Comfy circular booths fill out the next couple of concentric circles; these seem mostly reserved, and when empty they leave the impression that the place isn't very full—so why the wait? Music on a recent visit included a Madonna medley and the perennial "Celebration," not the most au courant of tunes. The total effect is of a grown-up, not terribly drunken frat and sorority mixer.

🟢 **Drink.** 200 E. Harmon Ave. (at Koval Lane). ☎ **702/796-5519.** Cover $5–$10 ($15–$25 when major artists are performing); women are admitted free Tues nights. No minimum.

Where Gen X Vegas hangs out. Decor is hip, which in this case means an odd mix of industrial warehouse, peeling plaster, and brick country cottage exterior; somehow, it works. Soundproofing is impressive; you can literally pass from the hard rock room to the dance room with only a second's worth of the two overlapping into each other. A recent saunter in the hard rock room heard a mix of retro and more current rock. (A song by The Cult segued into "Magic Carpet Ride," which went into "Spill the Wine," which went into some anonymous '90s faux metal/hard rock song.) The different sounds mean different appeals for different rooms, thus something for everyone. Despite a young, fashion-conscious crowd, it's friendlier than you would imagine, with virtually no attitude, surprisingly enough. (If you go there after Club Rio, the difference in attitude is almost palpable.) Of the nightly dance clubs, this is the one to go to, unless a hip quotient frightens you. Open Monday to Thursday till 3am, Friday and Saturday till 5am. Closed Sunday. Self-parking is free, valet parking $3.

RA. 3900 Las Vegas Blvd. S. (in the Luxor). ☎ **702/262-4000.** Cover $10 for up to 4 people.

The futuristic Egyptian-themed Ra is the new hot spot in Vegas. The vibe is that Vegas "We're a show, and an attraction," but is still not overly pretentious and the staff are friendly, which is a rare thing for a hot club. It might be worth it to go just to gawk at the heavy gilt decor. Current dance music (mostly techno) is on the soundtrack. The later you go, the more likely the mid- to upper-twenties clientele will be entirely local.

Studio 54. 3799 Las Vegas Blvd. S. (in MGM Hotel). ☎ **702/891-1111.** Cover: Men $10 Sun–Thurs, $20 Fri–Sat; women free.

The legendary Studio 54 has been resurrected here in Las Vegas, but with all the bad elements and none of the good ones. Forget Truman, Halston, and Liza doing illegal (or at least) immoral things in the bathroom stalls; that part of Studio 54 remains but a fond memory. However, the snooty, exclusive door attitude has been retained. Hooray. Oddly, this doesn't lead to a high class clientele; of all the new clubs, this is the most touristy and trashy. If the real Studio 54 were this boring, no one would remember it today.

Utopia. 3765 Las Vegas Blvd., S. (in the Epicenter). ☎ **702/736-3105.** Cover varies.

According to *Scope* Magazine, Utopia is "less a discotheque and more a revolution"—which is an apt description, considering that in Las Vegas, underground once-a-week nightclubs usually disappear in a matter of weeks. The music is progressive house, tribal, trance, techno, and rave. The atmosphere is industrial, foggy, and heavy with lasers and other dazzling visuals. A cool and outrageous crowd fills three rooms with fun, peace, and love, in a heart-pounding, techno way. It's for the tragically hip, but isn't it good to know they are out there in Vegas?

6 Strip Clubs

No, not entertainment establishments on Las Vegas Boulevard South. This would be the *other* kind of "strip." Yes, people come to town for the gambling and the wedding chapels, but the lure of Vegas doesn't stop there.

Cheetah's. 2112 Western Ave. ☎ **702/384-0074.** MC, V (but cash preferred—they have an ATM machine). Cover $10. Topless.

This is the strip club used in the movie *Showgirls,* but thanks to the magic of Hollywood and later renovations by the club, only the main stage will look vaguely familiar to those few looking for Nomi Malone. The management believes, "If you treat people right they will keep coming back," so the atmosphere is friendlier than at other clubs. They "encourage couples—people who want to party come here. We get a 21 to 40 aged party kind of crowd," the manager told us. And indeed there is a sporty, frat bar feel to the place. $10 table dance, $20 couch dance. Open 24 hours.

Club Paradise. 4416 Paradise Rd. ☎ **702/734-7990.** $10 cover, 2-drink minimum (drinks $4.50 and up). MC, V. Unescorted women allowed. Topless.

Possibly the nicest of the strip clubs (the outside looks a lot like the Golden Nugget), Club Paradise seems rather like a hot nightclub where most of the women happen to be topless. The glitzy stage looks like something from a miniature showroom, and the place is relatively bright by strip club standards. Not too surprisingly, they get a very white-collar crowd here. The result is not terribly sleazy, which may please some and turn off others. The club says it is "women-friendly," and indeed there were a few couples, including one woman who was receiving a lap dance herself—and didn't seem too uncomfortable. Lap dances $20. Open Monday to Sunday from 6pm to 6am.

Glitter Gulch. 20 Fremont St. ☎ **702/385-4774.** No cover, 2-drink minimum (drinks $5.75). Topless.

Two Strippers Give 9 Strip-Bar Etiquette Tips

Brittany and Kitty each have several years' experience working in strip bars, so they know what they're talking about. And they both really are sweet girls, honest.

1. Bathe.
2. Don't lie and say you never go into these places.
3. Don't take off your wedding ring—we can still see the mark it leaves.
4. Don't ask if we take credit cards. Bring cash!
5. Don't fall asleep—just because we are open 24 hours, we aren't a hotel.
6. Don't wear wool pants—they scratch.
7. Don't ask for our phone number.
8. Don't lick us. We're not Popsicles.
9. Don't forget: We *aren't* dumb strippers. We are a lot smarter than you think.

Right there in the middle of the Fremont Street Experience, Glitter Gulch is either an eyesore or the last bastion of Old Las Vegas, depending on your point of view. The inside is modern enough: black light and bubble fountains, arranged around a runway strip. As you enter, you are assigned your own (overly clothed) waitress who escorts you to your table. They also offer limo service to the hotels. There is even a line of souvenir clothing. Given such services and its convenient location, this is the perfect place for the merely curious—you can easily pop in, check things out, goggle and ogle, and then hit the road, personal dignity intact. Table dances cost $20. Open Sunday to Thursday from noon to 4am, Friday to Saturday from noon to 6am.

Olympic Gardens. 1531 Las Vegas S. Blvd. ☎ **702/385-8987.** Cover $15 (includes 2 drinks). AE, DISC, MC, V (they have an ATM machine). Unescorted women allowed. Topless.

Possibly the largest of the strip clubs, this almost feels like a family operation, thanks to the middle-aged women handling the door. They also have a boutique selling lingerie and naughty outfits. Table dances $20, more in VIP room. Open Monday to Sunday from 2pm to 6am.

Index

See also separate Accommodations, Restaurant, and Buffet indexes, below.

Page numbers in italics refer to maps.

GENERAL INDEX

Accommodations, 21–59. *See also*
  Accommodations index
    best bets, 21–24
    reservations services, 22
Activities, 114–16, 121
Airlines, 9–10, 12
Airport, 10–11, 13, 17
Alexis Park Resort, 24, 48, 81, 170
Algiers Hotel, 46–47
American Superstars, 159–60
Amusement parks, 108, 110–13
Angel Park Golf Club, 114
Antiques, 155–56
Arcades, shopping, 3, 149–53
Atlantis IMAX 3-D Ride, *103,*
  106, 110
Attractions, 101–14
Auto Collection, *103,* 104–5
Auto racing, 105

Baccarat, 123–24
Bally's Las Vegas, 33–34
    buffets, 61, 96–97
    casino, 138
    Jubilee!, 158, 165–66
    shopping arcade, 149
    tennis, 115
Banks, 17
Barbary Coast Hotel & Casino, 40,
  138
Bars, 171–73
    piano, 170–71
    topless, 176–77
Bellagio, 34
Best Western Mardi Gras Inn,
  52–53
Big Six, 123–24
Binion's Horseshoe Casino, 6–7,
  94–95, 143
Black Mountain Golf & Country
  Club, 114
Blackjack, 124–26

Blue Castle Pharmacy, 80
Boat cruises, 116, 118, 121
Boating, 121
Bookstores, 154–55
Boulder City, 119–20
Boulevard Mall, 146
Buffets and Sunday brunches, 3,
  60, 86, 95–100. *See also* Buffet
  Index
    best, 61
Burton, Lance, 111, 159, 161,
  166–67
Buses, 10–11

Cabs, 17
Caesars Magical Empire, 3, 101–2,
  103, 110
Caesars OMNIMAX Theatre, 102,
  103, 104, 110
Caesars Palace, 22, 35–36. *See also*
  Forum Shops at Caesars Palace
    attractions, 101–2, 104, 106,
      110
    buffet, 97
    casino, 24, 139
    for children, 110–11
    dinner show, 3, 101–2, 110
    restaurants, 69–76
    shopping, 149–50
Calendar of events, 6–8
California Hotel/Casino & RV
  Park, 56–57, 143
Camping. *See* RV parking
Car racing, 105
Car rentals, 11, 16
Car travel, 16–17, 19
    to Hoover Dam, 116
    to Las Vegas, 11
Casino hotels, 2, 21–59. *See also*
  specific hotels
    casinos, 24, 136–45
    shopping arcades, 3, 149–53
    shows, 158–70
Cassidy, David, 159, 161–62

Celebrity impersonators, 159–62, 167–68
Center Strip Inn, 41
Children, 9
    accommodations, 24, 29
    restaurants, 86
    shows, 111, 161
    sights and activities, 110–14
Children's Museum, *103*, 112
Circus Circus Hotel/Casino, 47
    attractions, 110–11
    casino, 141
    for children, 24, 29, 110–11
    shopping arcade, 150–51
Cirque du Soleil, 3, 111, 159–61
Convention Center, 14, 18
    accommodations near, 48–54
    buffets near, 99
    casinos near, 142–43
    convention dates for 1999, 8
    restaurants near, 81–90
Courtyard Marriott, 48, 50
Craig Ranch Golf Club, 114–15
Craps, 126–28
Cruises, 116, 118, 121
Currency exchange, 18

Dance clubs, 174–76
Danny Gans: The Man of Many Voices, 159, 161–62
Desert Inn Country Club Resort and Casino, 21–22, 42–44
    casino, 141
    golf, 114–15
    restaurants, 76
    tennis, 116
Dining. *See* Restaurants; *and* Restaurant Index
Dinner shows, 3, 61, 101–2, 110
Disabled travelers, 9
Doctors, 18–19
Dolphin Habitat, Mirage, *103*, 106–7, 111
Downtown. *See* Glitter Gulch
Drag performers, 159, 163–64

EFX, 159, 161–62
El Cortez Hotel & Casino, 57
Emerald Springs Holiday Inn, 53
Emergencies, 18–19

Enter the Night, 159, 162–63
Entertainment. *See also* Headliners; Music; Shows
    current schedule, 158
Evening at La Cage, 159, 163–64
Excalibur, 30–31
    casino, 137
    for children, 29, 110
    Evening in Vienna, 158
    shopping arcade, 151

Factory outlets, 148
Fashion Show Mall, 78–79, 146–47
Female impersonators, 159, 163–64
Festivals, 6–8
Fishing, Lake Mead, 121
Fitzgeralds Casino Holiday Inn, 55–56, 93–94, 144
Flamingo Hilton, 23, 36–37
    buffet, 98
    casino, 139
    Forever Plaid, 159
    Great Radio City Spectacular, 159, 164
    shopping arcade, 151
    tennis, 115
Football, 8
Forum Shops at Caesars Palace, 3, 149–50
    restaurants, 71–76
Four Queens, 56, 144
Fremont Street, 8, 14, 16. *See also* Glitter Gulch
Fremont Street Experience, 3, 16, *103*, 104, 158

Galleria at Sunset, 147
Gambler's Book Shop, 155
Gambling, 122–45
    casinos, 24, 136–45
    games, 123–36
    laws, 19
Gay men and lesbians, 9
Glitter Gulch, 3, 13–14, 16. *See also* Fremont Street
    accommodations, 54–59
    buffets, 99–100
    casinos, 143–45
    restaurants, 92–95

Gold Coast casino, 139
Gold Spike, 2, 144–45
Golden Gate casino, 144
Golden Nugget, 24, 54–55
   buffet, 99
   casino, 144
   restaurants, 95
Golf, 7, 114–15
Grand Slam Canyon Theme Park,
   103, 110–11
Great Radio City Spectacular, 159,
   164

Hard Rock Cafe, 86–87, 171
Hard Rock Hotel & Casino, 23, 50
   bars, 171
   casino, 142
Harrah's Las Vegas, 37
   casino, 139
   shopping arcade, 151
   Spellbound, 159
Headliners, 157–58
Hiking, 121
Holiday Inn Casino Boardwalk,
   31–32
Hoover Dam, 101, 116, 118–20
Hospitals, 18–19

Imagine: A Theatrical Odyssey, 165
IMAX Theater, Luxor, *103*, 105–6
IMAX 3-D Ride, Race for Atlantis
   Ride, 106, 110
Imperial Palace Auto Collection,
   103, 104–5
Imperial Palace Hotel, 41
   attractions, 104–5
   casino, 139–40
   Legends in Concert, 159,
      167–68
Information sources, 4, 13

Jackie Gaughan's Plaza Hotel/
   Casino, 57–58, 159
Jubilee!, 158, 165–66

Keno, 128–30

La Quinta Inn, 51–52
Lady Luck Casino Hotel, 58, 99, 145
Lagasse, Emeril, 60, 63–64
Lake Mead National Recreation
   Area, 120–21

Lance Burton: Master Magician,
   159, 161, 166–67
Las Vegas Convention Center. *See*
   Convention Center
Las Vegas Hilton, 21, 51
   attractions, 51, 107–8
   buffet, 99
   casino, 142–43
   for children, 111
   restaurants, 81
Las Vegas Motor Speedway, *103*,
   105
Las Vegas Natural History
   Museum, *103*, 111–12
Las Vegas-style reviews, 158–59,
   162–66
Legends in Concert, 159,
   167–68
Liberace Museum, 3, *103*, 105
Lied Discovery Children's
   Museum, *103*, 112
Liquor laws, 19
Lounge music, 157, 171–73
Luxor IMAX Theater, *103*,
   105
Luxor Las Vegas, 32–33
   attractions, 105–6, 111
   buffet, 96
   casino, 137
   for children, 29, 111
   dance club, 175
   Imagine: A Theatrical Odyssey,
      165
   shopping arcade, 151
Luxor Pyramid, Secrets of the,
   103, 105–6

McCarran International Airport,
   10–11, 13, 17
MADhattan, 168
Magic and Movie Hall of Fame,
   103, 106, 111
Magic shows, 111, 159, 161,
   166–67
Main Street Station, 58–59
   bars, 172
   buffet, 61, 99–100
   casino, 24, 145
Malls, shopping, 146–48
Married, getting, 108–10
Masquerade Village, 152
Maxim casino, 140

Mead, Lake, 116, 118–21
    boating and fishing, 121
    cruises, 116, 118, 121
Meadows, The (mall), 147–48
MGM Grand Adventures, *103*,
    112–13
MGM Grand Hotel, Casino, &
    Theme Park, 25–27
    attractions, 112–13
    casino, 137
    for children, 29, 112–13
    dance club, 175
    EFX, 159, 161, 162
    restaurants, 23, 63–66, 68–69
    shopping arcade, 151–52
Miller, Mark, 60, 62–63
Mirage, 23, 38–39. *See also*
    Treasure Island at the Mirage
    attractions, 106–7, 111
    buffet, 61, 97–98
    casino, 24, 140
    for children, 111
    restaurants, 74–75
    Siegfried and Roy (show), 111,
        159, 161, 168–70
    Siegfried and Roy, Secret
        Garden of, 106–7, 111
    volcano at, 38, 101, 104, 111
Mirage Day Spa, 39
Mirage Dolphin Habitat, *103*,
    106–7, 111
Mohave, Lake, 120
Money, 18
    cash and credit, 17
Monte Carlo Resort & Casino,
    27–28
    casino, 137
    Lance Burton: Master Magician,
        159, 161, 166–67
    restaurants, 69
    shopping arcade, 152
Moroccan restaurants, 84–85
Motel 6, 53–54
Movie Hall of Fame, Magic and,
    103, 106, 111
Movies set in Las Vegas, 2
Museums, 105, 111–12
Music
    alternative and rock, 158
    headliners, 157–58
    lounge, 157, 171–73

    music, 157, 171–73
    piano bars, 170–71
Musical impersonators, 159–62,
    167–68. *See also* Female
    impersonators
Mystère (Treasure Island), 3, 111,
    159–61

Natural History Museum, *103*,
    111–12
New York New York Hotel &
    Casino, 23, 28–30
    casino, 24, 137–38
    MADhattan, 168
    piano bar, 170–71
    restaurants, 68
Newsstand, 19, 155
Newton, Wayne, top 10 favorite
    lounge songs, 169
Nightlife, 157–77. *See also* Bars;
    Dance clubs; Headliners; Music;
    Shows
    current schedule, 158

OMNIMAX Theatre, Caesars,
    102, *103*, 104, 110
Orleans, 33, 138
O'Shea's Casino, 106, 111
Outlet malls, 148

Package tours, 12
Pai gow poker, 131
Parking, 19
Piano bars, 170–71
Pirate battle, at Treasure Island, 70,
    101, 111
Planet Hollywood, 75, 86, 171
Poker, 130–31
    video, 135–36
    World Series of Poker, 6–7
Police, 19
Post office, 19–20
Production shows. *See* Shows
Puck, Wolfgang, 60, 62, 68–69,
    71, 73

Race for Atlantis Ride IMAX 3-D
    Ride, 106, 110
Radio City Music Hall Rockettes,
    159, 164
Reservations services, for
    accommodations, 22

Residence Inn by Marriott, 52
Restaurants, 60–100. *See also*
   Restaurant Index
   best bets, 60–62
   dinner shows, 3, 61, 101–2,
      110
   Moroccan, 84–85
Rio Suite Hotel, 39
   buffet, 98
   casino, 140
   dance club, 174
   Danny Gans, 159, 161–62
   restaurants, 72
   shopping arcade, 152
Riviera Hotel & Casino, 44
   casino, 141
   Crazy Girls, 159
   Evening at La Cage, 159,
      163–64
   shopping arcade, 152
   Splash, 159
   tennis, 116
Rockettes, Radio City Music Hall,
   159, 164
Rodeos, 7
Roulette, 131, 132
RV parking, 31, 47, 53, 56–57,
   120

Safety, 20
Sahara Hotel & Casino, 44–45,
   107, 141–42
Sam Boyd's, 100
Sam's Town, 152–53
Scandia Family Fun Center, *103,*
   113
Secret Garden of Siegfried and
   Roy, 106–7, 111
Secrets of the Luxor Pyramid, *103,*
   105–6
Ship battle, at Treasure Island, 70,
   101, 111
Shopping, 146–56
Showboat Hotel, 6
Showgirls. *See* Vegas-style reviews
Showgirls (film), 2, 45, 74, 166,
   176
Shows, 158–70. *See also specific
   shows*
   admission prices, 158
   for children, 111, 161
   current schedule, 158–59

Siegfried and Roy
   Secret Garden of, 106–7, 111
   show, at the Mirage, 111, 159,
      161, 168–70
Sky Parade, 104
Slot clubs, 134
Slots, 131, 133, 135
   penny, 2, 144–45
   progressive, 133
Special events, 6–8
Speedway, Las Vegas Motor, *103,*
   105
Speedworld at Sahara, 103, 107
Sports books, 135, 139
Stardust Resort & Casino, 45
   casino, 142
   Enter the Night, 159, 162–63
Star Lane Shops, 151–52
Star Trek: The Experience, 51,
   103, 107–8, 111
Stratosphere Las Vegas, 24, 45–46
   American Superstars, 159–60
   attractions, 108
   bar atop, 171, 173
   casino, 142
   restaurants, 76–80
   shopping arcade, 153
   Viva Las Vegas, 159
Stratosphere Thrill Rides, *103,*
   108
Strip, the, 13–14
   accommodations
      Mid-Strip, 33–42
      North Strip, 42–48
      South Strip, 24–33
   buffets
      Mid-Strip, 96–98
      South Strip, 96
   casinos, 2
      Mid-Strip, 138–41
      North Strip, 141–42
      South Strip, 137–38
   east of. *See* Convention Center
   restaurants
      Mid-Strip, 69–76
      North Strip, 76–80
      South Strip, 63–69
   walking, 1–2
Strip clubs, 176–77
Super 8 Motel, 54
Swimming, 23, 113–14